Meaning and Change

Meaning and Change

EXPLORATIONS IN
THE CULTURAL SOCIOLOGY
OF MODERN SOCIETIES

ROLAND ROBERTSON

New York • New York University Press • 1978

Library of Congress Catalog Card Number: 77–90143
ISBN 0-8147-7374-5

Printed in Great Britain

TO MY MOTHER

Preface

In writing the chapters which follow I have benefited from conversations with a number of colleagues and friends. I am particularly grateful to Rainer Baum for comments on earlier versions of chapters three, four and five. Benjamin Nelson has been of great help in numerous conversations and writings. I am grateful to others, including Burkart Holzner, Ed Swanson, Geoffrey Guest, Barbara Renchkovsky, John Marx and Laurie Taylor.

I am deeply indebted to Jim Feather of Basil Blackwell for encouragement, efficiency and, not least, patience. Jenny Robertson has been her usual helpful self, which is to say a very great deal.

Some portions of this book have appeared in other forms in books or journals.

Quite a large number of secretaries have been of assistance, most notably those of the Department of Sociology, University of Pittsburgh.

Pittsburgh, Pennsylvania, June, 1977

Contents

Acknowledgments

Chapter two is a considerably modified and extended version of Roland Robertson, 'The Sociocultural Implications of Sociology: A Reconnaissance', in T. J. Nossiter, A. H. Hanson and Stein Rokkan (eds.), *Imagination and Precision in the Social Sciences: Essays in Memory of Peter Nettl*, Faber and Faber, London, 1972. The author is grateful to Faber and Faber for permission to republish parts of that essay.

Chapter seven is a heavily edited version of Roland Robertson, 'The Sociology of Religion: Problems and Desiderata', *Religion: A Journal of Religion and Religions*, I, 2 (1971). Thanks are due to Routledge and Kegan Paul for permission to use this article.

Chapter eight is a slightly revised version of an article written in collaboration with Colin Campbell and entitled 'Religion in Britain: The Need for New Research Strategies', *Social Compass*, XIX, 2 (1972). The editor of *Social Compass* is hereby thanked for permission to republish in amended form, as is Colin Campbell.

Chapter nine is an amended version of 'Sociologists and Secularization', *Sociology*, 5 (1971). The author is grateful to the editor and to the British Sociological Association for permission to republish.

PART ONE

Theory, Meaning and Change

Chapter One

Introduction

In recent years there have been a number of significant and much discussed attempts by social theorists to generalize about a perceived crisis in two major aspects of modern societies. The first of these is pivoted upon the problematic nature of the relationship between received culture and the operation of social institutions; while the second has to do with modes of individual existence. In the first case the problem is seen as residing in the decline in the authoritativeness and legitimacy of received culture, in the second case the problem inheres in questions concerning styles of relating to society and modern life in general. We can thus speak in two phrases of there being great concern, on the one hand, with cultural authority and, on the other hand, with personal identity. Even more briefly we can speak of there being a perceived problem of *meaning*. The problematic nature of meaning has been presumably rendered thus through certain changes in the fairly recent history of the relevant societies. Such are the considerations which have led to the title of this book.

It is not controversial to maintain nowadays that this general category of concerns was at the very core of the interests and writing of the so-called classical sociologists. Indeed, it is almost certainly in large part because of the perception of these concerns in relation to modern societies that there has been such a massive shift of interest towards the classical sociologists in recent years. In other words, the work of Durkheim, Simmel, Weber and Marx – and other less conspicuous figures – presses in on us because of their direct relevance to our understanding of the societies in which we live. They become, in effect, contemporary theorists and researchers. It is perhaps only in those terms that we will be able fully to understand their work, and to stand a chance of eventually placing them unambiguously as part of the past of social science. There may, indeed, be good reasons for thinking of the classical sociologists as of the past in terms of *pure* sociological theory, which was the main thrust of Parsons' *The Structure of Social Action*. But as empirically oriented theorists they have not yet been widely treated in parallel manner. This lack derives in large part from the fact that there has been a strong tendency to assess the empirical contributions of the classicists from a methodological angle, rather than from the perspective of the plausibility, perspicacity and veracity of their insights and generalizations. We would claim that the classical sociologists (and many of the philosophers who influenced them) are of particular importance to us in these puzzling times not merely because of their remarkable intelligence, dedication and historical knowledge, but also because their work constitutes some of our most important data concerning the early phases of the sociocultural and psychic circumstances in which we now live. In other words, they lived at the brink of our world.

Thus the 'contemporization' of the founding fathers is a most important feature of the modern diagnosis and prognosis of contemporary civilizations, societies and life-circumstances. Slowly, with much irritated resistance from some quarters, we are acquiring the tendency to speak of Durkheim, Simmel, Weber, Marx and others as our contemporaries, not simply as parts of the history of social science and as part of our cultural tradition.

Interestingly, the probable consequence of such developments will, in quite a short space of time, lead to a decline in the auratic significance of these men. They will not, in other words, be so acutely exposed as great, to-be-revered intellectuals of the past who weigh down upon us by virtue of their constituting a segment of an authoritative cultural tradition. Thus we seem to be changing our attitudes towards the classics via circumstances which they themselves drew attention to, namely the increasing fragility of the controlling effects of cultural tradition, a perception which they shared with philosophers and psychologists (notably Freud) of their own time.

Perhaps we may regard the very recent proliferation of statements on 'the problems of our time' as symptomatic of that state of affairs; in the sense that perhaps only in recent years have sociologists and other analysts of the human condition gained the courage to write on the diagnostic or prognostic scales exhibited by the classicists. Perhaps we now feel simultaneously more in debt to *and* more willing to emulate the endeavors of the founding fathers. That can, of course, only be part of the explanation for the re-emergence of something like a classical style in modern sociology, but it is, we suspect, a very significant part.

One of the main substantive consequences of focusing the work of the classical sociologists on the time and the societies in which modern social scientists live is – as we try to show in at least three of the chapters which follow – to sharpen the sense of their being concerned with the future of the individual and with the nature of processes of individuation. Most students of sociology know well that Durkheim and Simmel spoke very directly to this theme, while its salience in the work of Marx and Weber is becoming more evident as more research and translation is accomplished. On the other hand, since sociology grew in the post-classical period on the basis of a basically sociologistic stance this aspect of classical sociology has received little sustained attention. Individual-society relationships were until very recently largely considered to be the domain of social psychology, which can hardly be said to have pursued the issue in anything remotely like the terms of the second half of the nineteenth century and the first twenty years of the present century. Social psychology has not addressed such matters as the nature of individualisms or relationships between individuals and societies *qua* societies. Nor has it focused on cultural conceptions of the *raison d'être* of the individual. Each of these were, as a matter of degree, concerns of classical sociology, concerns which in significant part hinged in the case of the German sociologists upon their interest in *life*, and not simply in societal or social phenomena. The present nature and the future of 'the individual' has, however, become a very important focus in modern societies – although because of its sociologism sociology has lagged in coming to terms with that generalized focus.

The same kind of observation must apply to the modern concern with culture, although the neglect of the relevance of the classical sociologists is less in this case. The lesser severity of that neglect derives mainly from the fact that the cultural foci of Weber and Durkheim have been kept very much alive by sociologists of religion. For these two men culture was first and foremost a matter of religion or at least a secularized form thereof. Simmel's penetrating writings on culture have played virtually no part in modern sociology (a circumstance which we seek to rectify at various points in this book). The preservation of the cultural focus by students of religion has almost certainly been one of the reasons for the more general neglect of the cultural dimension in Durkheim, Weber and, to a lesser extent, Simmel. For the indifference of the average sociologist to religion has been one of the main features of the discipline since the 1920s. Perhaps there is no stronger indictment that could be made intellectually against modern sociology than its tragic neglect of the religious dimension and its secular 'followthroughs'. On the other hand, the average sociologist of religion has seemed to wallow in his sequestered status. The upshot is that matters which, as it were, fall between religious and non-religious aspects of sociocultural and individual life have been grossly neglected. Having uttered these strong remarks it must be quickly said that there are, of course, some people who have resisted both general indifference (and indeed outright hostility) and sociology-of-religion parochialism.[1]* Nevertheless it is not surprising that sociology was so ill-equipped to respond analytically to the concerns with culture and consciousness of the 1960s and 1970s. It is only the realization that these themes relate intimately to matters of legitimacy, authority and the very modes of operation of modern societies that has jarred some 'mainstream sociologists' into belated activity on these fronts.

The realization that the 'soft variables' may well not be separable from the 'hard variables' has many implications; for example, the growing realization that the subject of modernization cannot be adequately tackled without at the same time dealing with cultural tradition and problems of invariance and continuity – that, to put it another way, modernization is coded in terms of starting points and determinate trajectories of change. But we should not exaggerate the degree to which the lessons have been learned. Cultural sociologists are still charged with being too 'humanistic', too 'philosophical' or whatever. And, staying on the gloomy side for a moment longer, it should be noted that there are very discernible signs of resistance to cultural and religious matters even among those who claim to be the leaders of the back-to-the-European-classics movement. This is particularly evident among some West Europeans, who sometimes seem to think that the new-found interest in the classics in America is simply a matter of rectifying past omissions; whereas it is almost certainly the case that much of the American revival of classical sociology is centered precisely upon the motifs which we stated at the beginning of this introduction.

Undoubtedly a reason for the past and to an extent continuing neglect of particular classical themes is that in America and Britain students of sociology have not been acquainted with the kind of philosophy which lay at the back of much of the classical sociologists' endeavors. Thus a vast number of modern sociologists have been exposed only to those forms of philosophy that allegedly have relevance to sociology *as a science*; which hardly assists in realizing the details of the impact of, *inter alia*, Rousseau, Kant and Hegel on the classical sociologists. In a sense, the resistance to speculative philosophy – as well as to history – is part and

* Notes for this chapter begin on p. 8.

parcel of the resistance to cultural matters. We shall see later in this book that resistance to culture is indeed a major characteristic of modern societies, but that is no reason for sociology to echo that phenomenon unreflectingly. Without reflection on culture sociology thereby becomes a symptom of that which it seeks to analyze. That unfortunately may well be, as Simmel might have put it, an inherent tragedy of doing sociology; but to say that something is tragic does *not* mean that we should therefore yield to the tragedy. In that sense sociology should perhaps never be thought of as a pure discipline but always as being grounded in extra-sociological commitments which prevent it from over-yielding to its subject matter.

For want of a better term 'cultural sociology' best describes the direction in which we are pointing. Cultural sociology is certainly not a school or a particular theoretic tendency. Rather it is a style of analysis – a standpoint which insists on the salience of concern with life as well as with society, concern with the role of ideas and symbols and the transmission of historicity, and a number of other matters which are best exposed by way of detailed case-studies, this book being very much a sequence of monographic stabs at problem-areas in modern societies and modern sociology. It should really go without saying that in light of the foregoing the essays which follow frequently take us far back in time in order to obtain analytic leverage on modern trends.

It is possible to classify some of the more recent attempts to deal analytically with cultural authority and individuation in terms of their acceptance or rejection of the decline in cultural authority and the increase in individuation. Thus we find Rieff saying in effect that both are seemingly irresistible trends which societies and individuals have to live with;[2] Habermas saying that both are irresistible and to be welcomed, as long as the individuation can be capitalized upon so that reflective communication between individuals (communicative rationality) may take-over from where traditional culture (substantive rationality) left-off;[3] and, from a psychoanalytic standpoint, Ernest Becker also accepting the two processes, but with the proviso that new forms of individualistic, or 'heroic', individualism are needed.[4] On the other hand, we find Bellah disturbed about these developments and thus advocating the intellectual reconstruction of culture and the undoing of some major aspects of the individuation process;[5] Bell arguing for the restoration of a transcendent cultural tradition and regretting the allegedly thrill-oriented nature of modern individualism;[6] and Berger concerning himself with the possibilities of re-integrating individuals in relation to both social and cultural domains.[7] In these various scenarios we also find that religion appears to quite a significant degree. Rieff and Habermas seem to accept the extensive-secularization thesis, while Bellah and Bell emphatically reject it. Becker looks for new forms of individualistic religion, while Berger hovers between accepting the secularization thesis and very much regretting that circumstance. These (and other) provocative contributions to the social-scientific analysis of modern societies will be considered either implicitly or explicitly in a number of the essays which follow, the method which we have just used for classifying them also informing our deliberations.[8]

In the second chapter we note some particular aspects of the practice and relevance of sociology in the modern period, with particular attention to the relationship between sociology as culture and the wider cultural setting. This was written in particular response to the so-called crisis of the late 1960s. The next four chapters focus in one way or another on differentiations within the matrix *culture-society-individual*, the first of the set (chapter three) being specifically concerned with Max Weber and the relevance of his work on religion to modern sociology in the large. The fact that there is a separate chapter on Weber (as well as the fact that his work is the pivot of the chapter on inner-worldly mysticism) should be tempered by the recognition that the works of Simmel, Durkheim and Marx also get attention – in that order of conspicuousness. (In chapters four, five and six a special effort is made to recast the sociological interpretation of Simmel; by emphasizing his Kantianism, his interest in culture, and – not least – his relevance to large-scale, societal matters.) The second, much shorter, part of the book (chapters seven, eight and nine) is more methodological, programmatic and religion-centered than the first part, focusing on some very specific matters in the study of religion. However, chapter eight has a much wider relevance to the study of culture and meaning than its title implies, while the final chapter also has relevance to the general discussion of cultural change – even though its specific focus is the secularization process.

NOTES

1. Very selectively, mention should be made of the work of Talcott Parsons, Clifford Geertz, Benjamin Nelson, Guy E. Swanson, Robert Bellah and Peter Berger. The present author has attempted to keep

the 'cultural flag' flying in a number of different substantive areas. See in particular: Roland Robertson, *The Sociological Interpretation of Religion*, Oxford and New York, 1970; J. P. Nettl and Roland Robertson, *International Systems and the Modernization of Societies*, London and New York, 1968; Roland Robertson and Laurie Taylor, *Deviance, Crime and Socio-Legal Control*, London, 1973.

2. In particular: Philip Rieff, *The Triumph of the Therapeutic*, New York, 1966.
3. In particular: Jürgen Habermas, *Legitimation Crisis* (trans. T. McCarthy), Boston, 1975.
4. In particular: Ernest Becker, *The Denial of Death*, New York, 1973; and *Escape from Evil*, New York, 1975.
5. In particular: Robert N. Bellah, *Beyond Belief*, New York, 1970; and *The Broken Covenant*, New York, 1975.
6. In particular: Daniel Bell, *The Cultural Contradictions of Capitalism*, New York, 1976.
7. In particular: Peter L. Berger et al., *The Homeless Mind*, New York, 1973.
8. Too recent for discussion in this book is the perspicacious Alvin W. Gouldner, *The Dialectic of Ideology and Technology*, New York, 1976. One of the most intriguing developments in modern thought is the interest in cultural matters among many Marxist and neo-Marxist scholars. Cf. Marshall Sahlins, *Culture and Practical Reason*, Chicago, 1976.

Chapter Two

Sociology and Sociocultural Change

Inside each one of us, in varying proportions there exists part of yesterday's man; it is yesterday's man who inevitably predominates in us, since the present amounts to little as compared with the long past, in the course of which we were formed and from which we result. But we do not sense this man from the past, since he is so much a part of us; he is the unconscious part of ourselves. Consequently, we do not take him into account, any more than we take account of his legitimate requirements. On the contrary, we are very much aware of the most recent acquisitions of civilization since, being recent, they have not yet had time to settle into our unconscious.

Emile Durkheim

Nature's shackles on the ego, sprung by the mind, have turned into an enchainment by mind itself. Although the necessity and superior might which history exerts upon individual personality may appear in the guise of freedom, since this history is of the human mind, in truth history – as something given, as a reality, a suprapersonal power – represents no less an oppression of the ego by an external agency.

Georg Simmel

We are concerned in this chapter with sociological purpose and action.[1]* Traditionally, sociologists have conceived of their discipline in one-dimensional terms – the *substance* of their arguments, findings, propositions and theories has been related to the *logic* of their procedures and methodologies. In the modern period two other dimensions have not received attention until very recently: the relationship between sociology and general cultural characteristics of the societies in which it is located; and the relationship between sociology and trajectories of social change. In brief, we address the sociocultural significance of sociology; not only because such a theme is itself of sociological interest,

* Notes for this chapter begin on p. 41.

but also, and more particularly, because it bears very much on the practice of sociology.

Once the question of sociological identity has been raised in this way, the individual sociologist has but two, broadly conceived, choice-alternatives: either to embrace his self-consciousness, or to insulate himself from it. The first alternative clearly leads to a further choice-point: what should the content of that consciousness be? Much of what follows in this opening chapter is devoted to considering this question. We will suggest at various points that the insulative posture is becoming increasingly difficult to sustain – not so much through logical weaknesses of the arguments that can be advanced in its favor, but through sociocultural and psychological circumstances. The distinction between the *logic* of argument and inquiry and the *circumstances* of argument and inquiry is relevant to what follows – but not in the sense that the distinction is virtuously upheld. The distinction is analytically necessary; but, we argue, the two are so compellingly indissoluble in empirical and ontological terms that it is high time that we fully embraced this compulsion. A long line of philosophers and analysts of sociocultural life have in one way or another argued for this. Marxian epistemology clearly falls in this category, as does the work of those in the modern period – outstandingly Polanyi (certainly no Marxist) – who have either directly or indirectly maintained the artificiality (in a significant sense, the impossibility) of separating the philosophy of science from the sociology and psychology of science.[2] There is evidently an emergent agreement (which needs precise crystallization) that sociology has little to gain from reverential deference in the direction of 'hardline' philosophy of science, much of which is based at best on an idealized and often clearly fallacious reconstruction of the logical procedures of physicists.[3] This attitude has, of course, been promulgated continuously by action-oriented, descriptivistic and intuitivistic sociologists. What *is* new is the attenuation of positivism and scientism among the more analytically-minded members of the sociological community.

The sociological community became increasingly self-conscious in the modern period, initially in the U.S.A., through the mere assertion of professional protectiveness and expansiveness. More recently, however, self-consciousness has taken a new turn. Much has been written about sociological 'self-images', while sociology has been made especially conspicuous through its prominence in crises in institutions of higher education and reactions to that prominence – perhaps exampled most dramatically by the French government's attempt in the late 1960s to limit the teaching of the discipline and the Vatican's censorial statements about sociology. Neil Smelser has called sociology the new 'psychoanalysis – without the mystique',[4] while Andreski speaks of sociology as being sorcery-like.[5] It would be easy to produce many similar statements. This chapter in part explores the implications which these have for sociological practice. In principle, however, the latter theme could be, indeed needs to be, tackled quite independently of such considerations.

The mode of discussion which we adhere to most closely is indicated well in Bellah's analysis of the evolution of religious symbol systems. Bellah points out that his own analysis is 'a symptom of the modern religious situation as well as an analysis of it'; and he locates this observation in the view that in the modern period life has become 'an infinite possibility thing'.[6] Men can now, he argues, to a large extent *choose* their forms of symbolization. Or, as Germani puts it, action is being interpreted increasingly as *elective*, as opposed to prescriptive.[7] Such statements clearly have important implications for sociology itself; although it is doubtful whether in the late 1970s many subscribe to the degree of open-endedness of modern life indicated by the *1960s* views of Bellah, Germani and many others.

Auguste Comte's ideas about the cognitive and ethical superiority of sociology have rarely been viewed favorably. Nevertheless, the major point of this essay is to consider what are basically Comtean themes. There were in fact two major dimensions of Comte's program.[8] The one which has been taken least seriously was that which he elaborated in the later years of his life, namely his conception of sociology as a 'religion of humanity'. (We have the impression, however, that during the 1960s social scientists became more fond of discussing this aspect of Comte's work.)[9] It is Comte's presentation of the institutional structure of such a 'religion' in terms of the structure of the Catholic Church which has been the focus of most ridicule; partly, of course, since in adumbrating his well-known 'law of the three stages' Comte had emphatically insisted upon the evolutionary demise of religious thought-styles and their replacement by scientific modes of thought, at the apex of which was placed sociology. It is this latter theme which comprised the second and most salient dimension of Comte's thoughts on the significance of sociology; that is, the evolutionary cultural ascendancy of science, to be crowned by the most complex science, sociology.

It is not our purpose either to evaluate or explicate the *minutiae* of Comte's writings. We have started with Comte mainly because we suspect that it is the negative response which his work has generally elicited which has functioned as a block against investigation of the problem of the cultural significance of sociological styles of thought. It is, however, of much more than passing interest to note that the ideas of Comte's major intellectual predecessor, Saint-Simon, have come to be more readily accepted.[10] It is in respect of solutions to technical, administrative and programmatic issues that many now argue, either implicitly or explicitly, for the exceptional importance of social science. That stance seemed to have been on the wane following the events of the later 1960s, but there is little doubt that the resurgence of 'applied sociology' in the mid-1970s indicates its resurgence. As is widely known, at the end of the 1950s and in the early 1960s a group of sociologists and social observers proposed that modern industrial societies had been to all intents and purposes divested of ideological cleavages and that the major problems of industrial societies henceforth were to be essentially administrative ones – problems to be tackled in terms of the norms of social science.[11] The over-riding problem was how to implement and sustain 'the good society'. The last fifteen years or so have in fact witnessed a remarkable growth in the degree to which social scientists have become involved in central and local government and in advisory positions generally. Given the greater efforts put into the professionalization of sociology in America and given also the tradition of pragmatic optimism of American culture it is not surprising that it is in the U.S.A. that this tendency is most manifest.[12] Sociologists, political scientists, psychologists and economists have become key factors in major administrative, evaluative and policy-forming sectors of American society. There have been intimate links between the end-of-ideology movement and many of the sociologists and political scientists working closely in, for or in reference to American governmental agencies – most generally in terms of intellectual continuity, but also in terms of personnel.[13]

The pathetic elements of the end-of-ideology thesis as we consider it in retrospect and with hindsight are very obvious.[14] Racial crises in America and elsewhere and a resurgence of militant politics, notably but not exclusively among the young, have risen to a crescendo since the original flowering of the end-of-ideology viewpoint. In a way which is more ironic than anything else we can also see that there were traces of suicidal prophecy in the end-of-ideology thesis. For it is clear that much of what is central, and indeed innovative, about the ideological formulations of recent years consists in an ideological response to the existing and projected realities of the bureaucratized and rationally administered society. Thus the end-of-ideology prognosis has in fact been, at least in part, responsible for its own partial negation.[15]

Notwithstanding the prestige of and demand for sociological expertise at the present time, it is also true that sociology is still 'on trial'. The tendency for modern governments and other agencies to draw increasingly upon the intellectual resources of sociologists should not be regarded too readily as a sign that the sociologist is genuinely regarded by his clients as a kind of 'know-all' or a fount of modern wisdom. For there are many indications that the sociologist may be utilized by various agencies as a symbol of taking a problem seriously and/or a scapegoat to be invoked should the occasion arise. Thus we should be sensitized to the applicability of the distinction between the cases in which the sociologist is used *ritually* as a fount of wisdom and those in which he is used *substantively* so. There is, however, a more serious respect in which sociology is on trial. The great visibility of sociology in the crises in institutions of higher learning in the late 1960s made the general community of sociologists, as opposed to the relatively small élite who were involved in practical affairs, highly vulnerable and placed it in a defensive position – although, there was, of course, societal variation in this respect. The split within the sociological community which developed as a consequence is still evident; and possibly deepening.

The last few years have thus seen some rather dramatic changes within the sociological community. Only a few years ago there was a widespread feeling that sociology had come of age and that the tasks which had to be performed were fairly obvious; and, concomitantly, there set in a surge of interest in methodological and technological issues. Now in the context of the often-bewildering strains which have afflicted most industrial societies,[16] more and more sociologists have become concerned about the nature and purposes of their discipline. And so they should. For it is clear that the social sciences (but particularly sociology) have become a crucial site of cultural tension in a number of modern societies. The late-1960s drift in intellectual preference away from the natural and physical sciences among school, college and university students involved a challenge to many of contemporary sociology's most salient, professionally prescribed, attributes. The 'analytical rationality' of much of sociology was precisely that which was more generally under challenge by many of the discipline's undergraduate and graduate students.[17] Many, but by no means all, sociologists began to look critically at their analytic styles and substantive pre-occupations in the light of changes of possible major significance.[18]

There are profound dangers in talking of sociology as if it were a self-contained discipline. It is, of course, a highly amorphous, discontinuous, and blurred science – it is not a normal science. However, it is this writer's conviction that there *is* a core sociological perspective (which is a normative judgement about the sociological task) and that there are core sociological problems (which is a proposition about the themes that analysts of sociocultural life have traditionally addressed and a claim as to continuity between sociology past and present). One of the problems in 'being a sociologist' is that sociology not only shares with more normal sciences the problem of attending to new information in the sense of sheer quantity, but it also has greater problems of relevance assessment and faces the phenomenon of sociology in disguise, by which we mean the fact that much of what is obviously relevant is frequently generated in other intellectual and in 'everyday' contexts. From the points of view of both the generalist and the specialist, sociology is clearly a highly pluralistic discipline, but more so in a competitive – indeed a conflictful – than in a division-of-labour sense.

Bearing such difficulties in talking about sociology as a whole very firmly in mind, it is still possible to delineate and pinpoint the more thrustful tendencies within the sociological field at any given point in time. Our concern at this stage is to attempt such an exercise, be it all very briefly; although it should be strongly emphasized that the developments which have been chosen relate closely, and deliberately so, to our major immediate concern; that is, the sociocultural significance of sociology.

Planning, Prediction and Control

This development is closely bound-up with the increase in involvement of social scientists in governmental affairs which we have already mentioned. But aside from the mere growth in number of 'The New Mandarins'[19] we should also note that the whole question of the relationship between social-scientific analysis and the course of social change has been given more attention in recent years. (Much less has been done in reference to cultural change; but the situation is changing rapidly.)[20] Many sociologists have again raised the theme concerning the implications which can be drawn from within sociology itself for the shape of the good society – something which clearly goes well beyond the 'politically-given' approach of the 'administrative mandarins'.[21] Closely related to this development we may note also the growing importance of varieties of evaluative and applied research – stances which frequently involve the sociologist in simultaneously analyzing and evaluating the performance of the collectivities upon which he or she focuses.[22] Generally, developments such as these are predicated in one way or another upon sociology becoming 'locked-into' societal change. Sociology becomes both a mode of analysis of and a critical component in the course of change in human societies.

It is noteworthy that interests in *large-scale* planning have occurred in social science in spite of what appeared to be only a few years ago an 'establishment' kind of social philosophy proscribing such activities, associated in particular with the name of Popper.[23] Popper labelled attempts at large-scale planning and prediction as forms of holistic historicism – combining 'Plato's will to arrest change' with 'Marx's doctrine of its inevitability'. His arguments have apparently not had much long-run impact; although an ironic aspect of the situation is that acceptance of Popperism in respect of planning-and-prediction has been particularly conspicuous among Marx-inspired students. However, what the Popperians in their ultra-rationalism failed to understand is that in secular modern societies man and woman cannot apparently make do without eschatological and theodical notions.[24] Conceptions of the future – both individual and societal – as well as ideas making sense of inequality, misfortune, and the like are seemingly vital features of the human condition. To be sure rationalization, in the Weberian sense, does occur on secular lines in such spheres – of which the recent concern with assisting people to face-up to the realities of death is a good example. However, that is indeed an exemplification of planning at the individual or family level. Planning – as well as predicting and forecasting – at the formal-collectivity and societal levels also have their eschatological and theodical functions. They convey images of 'realistic hope' and provide rationales for many forms of injustice and suffering.

Thus even though many social-scientists of the various planning, predicting and forecasting schools may eschew interest in cultural matters *per se* they do nevertheless by their own activity clearly assist in the construction of a future-oriented culture – a culture which is in principle as analyzable in terms of its dimensions of meaning, as is any religious belief system or ideology; while in any case they have to make assumptions, however naive, about the course of cultural change in order to explicate their predictions and prescriptive plans. In this connection it should be added that some social scientists, particularly those working in the field of what might be called phenomenal anticipations, do clearly entertain a very crucial cultural variable – namely the future-oriented reality constructions of the individuals and groups in the populations with which they deal.[25]

One of the major points of significance about the growth of interest in planning, predicting and forecasting as far as the present context is concerned is that it can (and should) be related sociologically to such phenomena as interest in science fiction and developments in the field of theology.[26] Sometimes, in fact, predictors, such as Herman Kahn, have been called 'new theologians'. We may view these kinds of endeavors as providing functionally necessary images of a future which is no longer accessible in terms of traditional religious conceptions or tension-management mechanisms. (The rapid growth in interest in the occult and astrology is an important modern adaptation to the uncertainty of the future – as in a different respect is the re-emergence of mysticism, in both religious and secular forms.) But we should also realize that apart from the purely extrapolative kind of endeavor or the one which inquires into images of the future held by respondents to survey inquiries, many of the predictions, speculations and conjectures about the future[27] are no less than competing scenarios – in the sense that social scientists have it largely in their power within certain quasi-factual limits to persuade others (and each other) that certain things are just short of being inevitable. And those who work in reference to political agencies clearly on occasions have an interest in painting bleak images of the future precisely in order that the 'prophecy' should be a suicidal one – i.e., the prediction is made deliberately in the hope that its statement will bring about its refutation. Good examples are provided by the extremes of demographic and ecological pessimism.

This prediction-planning phenomenon is an excellent case in which there is a crying need for thorough 'sociological transcendence'. By this we mean that so central to societal reality construction is the work of social scientists operating in this field that we need comprehensive explorations of the phenomenology of their endeavors. Their work is *so* 'locked into' societal change, so close to the very course of social and cultural change itself, that it is rapidly becoming a part of the reality which sociologists typically study. If one of sociology's main tasks is to comprehend – and ideally account for – the beliefs and values by and in terms of which societies operate, then it has to move to a level of discussion in which all those who image the future – those who predict and plan, those who sketch fictional possibilities, those who anticipate – are treated as engaging in a fundamentally similar process.[28]

Moreover, we need to know much more about the degree to which people live under the weight of the perceived future and the adjustments made to that burden where it is perceived as being excessively heavy. In this connection the recent concern in popular books with the problems of death and dying is an obvious example of an area demanding 'sociological transcendence'. On the other hand, there may be a limit to the extent to which people can tolerate the future – reflected in those science fiction novels which are addressed to the problems of populations possessing unconditional immortality.

We also need to know more about that orientation to the future which crystallized among revolutionary students in the late 1960s – partly under the intellectual tutelage of Marxist thinkers, notably Rosa Luxemburg and Mao Tse-tung. This orientation basically consists in the idea that a society, or any sociocultural system, can only be understood experientially and analytically (the two are closely fused in this scenario) through militantly engaging with its most fundamental characteristics. Future possibilities and probabilities can, so the argument goes, only be grasped at the moment of full 'revelation' of the system. (In fact this posture is based on the viable insight that oppositions are always to a significant extent 'cognitive victims' of that which they oppose.)[29] The stranglehold of the oppositional target can only be prised open – and then never completely – by pressing it so hard that in the very process of its collapse a future emerges which is dictated not solely by the denigrated system but by the process of overcoming it.[30] From an analytic-sociological point of view the most relevant consideration in this respect is that the way in which society is analyzed, or analytically criticized, is crucial to the kinds of probabilities and possibilities which the sociologist will discover. This is a view which has probably been pressed most strongly by German critical theory, but that fact does not mean that that particular perspective is thereby rendered as the most commendable.

Inner Layers of Sociocultural Life

A second general development worthy of note is on the face of it very different and covers a wide variety of more or less independently pursued sociological activities. It can best be described as a generalized concern with the deeper layers of social relationships and social experience. Whereas sociology originally studied what to us now seem to have been the more manifest and intuitively visible aspects of social interaction and social structure, many of its modern practitioners seem to be concerned with going more and more deeply into the very core of social life – a 'questioning' of the very fabric of the assumptions upon which social life is based. Such explorations range from the detailed analysis of the ways in which individuals present themselves in social life to a probing of the underpinnings of conventionally accepted everyday realities. Insofar as sociology has traditionally been a 'debunking' science there is nothing new about this, especially in the light of the fact that sociologists have for a long time insisted upon the importance of distilling and explicating the latent as opposed to the manifest, being as conscious of objective function as of subjective meaning and so on. But in the main sociologists have until recently confined these exercises to what one might call the 'outer layers' of sociocultural life – that is, to such areas as the social and cultural bases of economic, political and religious belief and practice. As it is, we know that sociology has been regarded with much suspicion solely on these grounds.

Nineteenth-century sociology tended to rely – although there were a few exceptions – on the idea of there being some extra-sociocultural force underlying the operation of social life, such as the cunning of reason, the hidden hand, the dialectic, and so on. Durkheimian sociologism heralded the first major break into a conception of sociocultural reality as *the* reality (under Comtean inspiration). It was not until the middle of the twentieth century that sociologists became widely interested in 'the problem of reality'. Polanyi has tentatively linked a phase-movement in physical science (numericism and geometricism; mechanicism; emphasis upon systems of mathematical invariance) to artistic change (Byzantine mosaicism; Impressionism; Surrealism).[31] These individual phases are, as Polanyi himself cogently states, visions of ultimate reality. Without fully attending here to the problem of whether analysis of sociocultural life has proceeded in a similar way, it can be safely said that sociology has developed significantly in the direction of 'mathematical surrealism' in the modern period.[32] The mathematical side of this is exhibited best in abstract sociology in general. (The mere application of mathematics to data is, in the present context, irrelevant.) The 'surrealist' aspect is to be witnessed in the questioning of 'the reality of reality' (about which we shall say more shortly). To date there has been relatively little effort displayed in linking these developments; but in the field of ethnomethodology[33] we may glimpse a significant degree of recognition of the importance of the linkage – while the revival of interest in the philosophy of Whitehead, notably among theologians,[34] provides an obviously relevant basis for exploration of the linkage, concerned as he so deeply was with the phenomena of reality and scientific analysis. Simmel's work is also of considerable relevance to this theme.

Exploration of these deeper layers of the social condition to which we have referred has the effect of rendering precarious not only the existence of the everyday world taken-for-granted, in the sense that sociology makes many facets of sociocultural life seem fragile, but also in the even more profound sense of making the individual's own social existence seem fragile. In brief, whereas sociology has traditionally functioned as questioning the general fabric of structures and grounds of belief – in Berger's phrase, *plausibility structures*[35] – in human societies (i.e., the 'field' in which the individual operates), it entered a phase in the late 1960s of many of its practitioners laying bare even more 'secret' and taken-for-granted realities of everyday existence; such as reality construction, language, and non-verbal communication – in increasing order of 'interference with the world'.

The phrase 'interference with the world' demands elaboration. The basic idea involved here is the degree of penetration of taken-for-grantedness. It is almost certainly the case that close and comprehensive inspection on a comparative basis would show that what is taken-for-granted varies significantly from one cultural context to another. Another dimension of variation concerns the disposition of the society to turn the exposure of taken-for-grantedness (including hiddenness) into an inner-directed therapy and/or an other-directed instrument of social-relational manipulation.

Some of the inner layers of social life have been tapped in a particularly vivid way by recent sociologists of knowledge.[36] Recent developments in the sociology of knowledge are crucial to the present discussion for two major reasons. First, a sociological concern with fundamentals of reality construction by social individuals and groups – the pivotal theme of modern sociology of knowledge – takes as its basic focus extremely elemental cognitive and perceptual assumptions.[37] It is probably more 'challenging' to the social order than purely psychological inquiries into cognition and perception, in that it connects with interpersonal beliefs and modes of communication and the constitution of reality. And, ideally, it is not content with illuminating what Berger calls the 'fictive' realities by and in terms of which social systems operate. As Holzner argues, a sociological approach to the construction of reality acknowledges above all that such construction 'occurs in a social context'. We must therefore 'transcend the phenomenology of it until we reach a sociology of reality construction'.[38] That is, we should attend analytically and explanatorily to the dynamics of reality construction. It can be readily seen that this type of sociology of knowledge is far more 'threatening' to the social order than the classical sociology of knowledge which dealt with ideologies, grand systems of belief and *weltanschauungen*, precisely because of its focus on more elemental and basic modes of cognition; i.e., those which are more continuous and vital to all individuals or groups. It is both more personal *and* more general. Furthermore its epistemological implications are more profound. By emphasizing the precariousness of reality, by pointing-up the plurality of subjective realities, and hierarchies of reality conceptions, it introduces a relativistic and indeed a solipsistic problem of a much greater kind than that posed by most classical sociologists of knowledge.[39]

In pointing to the notion of precariousness it is, however, important to emphasize two things – which apply particularly to Berger-and-Luckmann sociology of knowledge. First, it can be argued that the diagnosis of precariousness *per se* relates not so much to first-order, phenomenal features of everyday social life but rather to a sociological, second-order and analytical level. That is, precariousness is diagnosed on the basis of comprehending from an analytic distance the nature of 'everyday matter-of-factness'. It seems a kind of 'miracle' that something which is open to analytic perusal can survive and persist. But this is a *sociological* judgement and not a statement as such about the subjective, phenomenal character of social life; which leads us to a second point: the diagnosis of precariousness – in effect, the prising open of the sociocultural order – probably does indirectly have the consequence of making the social world seem phenomenally precarious, that is precarious at the everyday-living level. But we have to be sensitized to the likelihood that the form of this phenomenal precariousness differs from society to society. There may be a parallel here with the relationship between psychoanalysis as scientific diagnosis and psychoanalysis as phenomenal life-style.[40] In its latter form people self-consciously live in terms of the principles of psychoanalysis – their lives are governed by the interpretive norms of psychoanalysis. At the social level we are familiar enough with popularized presentations of game theory, transaction theory and exchange theory.[41] Again, there is a crucial difference between saying 'these are the principles which govern social behavior' and 'this is the way in which I operate socially'.

The second major reason for the importance of the new focus in the sociology of knowledge is the light which it casts on *sociological* culture. Classical sociology of knowledge itself turned very much on the epistemological relationships between sociology and the wider society; in fact it became obsessed by them in its post-Mannheim phase. But we can see rather easily that the newer focus on reality construction has added to this a formidable ontological problem. Seen in the perspective of the theme of the social construction of reality, sociology is 'merely' a specialized mode of reality construction. The very statement of this proposition bears profoundly upon a problem which beset Mannheim's sociology of knowledge. As has been noted on many occasions, Mannheim trapped himself by making propositions about the social determination of knowledge – the principles of which when applied to the propositions themselves, and logically they had to be so applied, violated those same propositions. The sociological perspective was used as a springboard for making statements about the social determination of knowledge; and yet the comprehensive application of such statements obviously included the sociological perspective itself.[42]

Sociology as Social Eidos

All human societies have always had some form of social eidos – the stock of ideas which relate to social institutions and activities.[43] Social science is in this sense but one type of social eidos. Historically, religion has been the major form of social eidos; and the analytic side of religion – namely, theology ('the queen of the sciences') – can clearly be regarded as functionally similar to some behavioral sciences, notably sociology and psychology. In the modern period theology has been increasingly secularized in the sense that it has come to lean on secular philosophies and sociologies.[44] Death-of-God Theology, The Theology of Hope, and Process Theology are excellent examples. But theology of course still concerns itself with basically metaphysical questions. To this extent it can in some respects clash with social and behavioral science; *and* ask very basic questions of the latter.

One of the most conspicuous cases in which a tension between theology and sociology appears is in the work of Peter Berger. It may be instructive to look at the problem in the terms which Berger has posited.[45] Two of Berger's major concerns have been to establish an appropriate relationship between sociology and theology and to inquire into the limitations of sociological consciousness. Although some aspects of these themes are only tangentially related to the present discussion, the claims which Berger makes for his particular theological and religious perspectives, and the disadvantages of the sociological consciousness which he depicts by way of comparison, assist in throwing the problems with which we are directly concerned into sharp relief. In any case, the sociology of religion, especially in its wider range of reference, is particularly facilitative in gaining sensitization to the general nature of the sociocultural significance of sociology.

In his essays which are most clearly oriented towards theological, religious and philosophical issues, Berger sees sociology as performing an essentially unmasking function. Sociology exposes the social dimension of belief. On the other hand, Berger explicitly contends, along grounds very close to the orthodox functionalist position, that the 'fictions' of sociocultural life are fundamental to the operation of human society: 'For most of us, as we grow up and learn to live in society, its forms take on the appearance of structures as self-evident and as solid as those of the natural cosmos. Very likely society could not exist otherwise. Nor is it likely that socialization could take place if this were not the case.'[46] For Berger the everyday realities, the self-evident structures, in terms of which 'normal' people live, are functionally necessary. He speaks very much of social fictions and social fictitiousness, and yet maintains very firmly that 'to take fictions as reality can become a moral alibi. It then becomes possible to avoid responsibility for one's actions. To live in unperceived fictions is morally dangerous because it leads to inauthenticity.'[47] (It is in these terms that Berger once expressed the view that social science is a 'profane auxiliary to Christian faith'.)[48]

Berger's self-confessed conservatism[49] comes through very clearly in these remarks. His view of socialization is of the fairly conventional sociological kind — that is, socialization consists in induction into the normative thoughtways of a given sociocultural order. Such a view suggests that sociocultural systems depend upon constant generational re-confirmation of their traditional norms and values — that uninstitutionalized deviance constitutes a failure of the socialization process. Nothing seems more destined to make sociology redundant than an insistence upon this way of looking at socialization processes. Our conceptions of socialization might much more usefully and realistically be re-shaped by acknowledging the electiveness (as opposed to the prescriptiveness) which is clearly evident in many modern societies. Viewed in this light socialization becomes a process of learning how to elect, and not how to follow automatically traditional or rational-legal prescriptions (or indeed charismatic ones). In modern circumstances of great individuation it seems entirely unrealistic to speak positively of individuals assimilating large chunks of traditional values in a relatively unreflective manner.

Berger's position may be compared to that of Dahrendorf who has posed the question of the ontological status of what he calls 'sociological man'.[50] Like Berger, Dahrendorf sees sociological analysis as viable only in terms of regarding individuals as acting and responding in the phenomenal world in terms of social roles. But whereas for Berger role-playing is a fundamental characteristic of the phenomenal world, Dahrendorf argues that it is only for the analytic purposes of sociology that we should regard the phenomenal world as consisting in individuals-in-role. Dahrendorf maintains that sociologists erect a fictional man, sociological man, who is seen in terms analogous to the way in which economists erected an analytic-fictional type of economic man. Beyond, or behind, this analytic fiction lies a 'real' man – to whose well-being, Dahrendorf contends, sociology should be morally committed. Thus, whereas Berger proposes that social individuals have in the main to live a fictional, inauthentic existence, Dahrendorf is saying that the sociologist in order to be genuinely scientific has to speak as if social individuals live in terms of the fictions associated with role playing. The complexities of this particular theme cannot be resolved here. Much of the problem has to do with the nature of the societal context to which the sociologist makes reference; for it is no accident of the differential development of sociology and social psychology that role analysis has been developed mainly in the U.S.A. Whereas Dahrendorf's essay on this problem created much controversy in Germany, American reception of the idea of seeing society as made-up of roles, and man as essentially a role-playing being, has apparently been unproblematic. Thus we have to recognize fully the possibility that although the language and conceptual apparatus of sociology has been widely transnationalized, the relationship between concept and analytic mode, on the one hand, and phenomenal referent, on the other, differs from society to society. We can say that whereas in American sociology the role concept has been phenomenally emergent, in Germany it has been analytically imposed. Such an observation clearly assumes considerable significance in the context of conceiving of sociology as a mode of reality construction – and the examples could be multiplied. A more central point, however, is that both Berger and Dahrendorf, in their different ways, seem to get caught in a three-part dilemma: sociology, society and philosophical-ideological preference constitute, respectively, three competing attachments.[51]

Berger's attitude towards society is, as he himself puts it, not 'ultimately serious'. To be ultimately serious about society, he argues, 'means *ipso facto* to be caught within it'.[52] We have already glimpsed, however, that one's analysis of society hinges crucially on the image of society which one erects in the first place. Berger having depicted society as essentially based on myths and fictions cannot afford, given his own moral and religious commitments, to embrace 'ordinary' social life with any enthusiasm. In these terms sociology emerges for Berger as having profound limitations. According to him, sociology takes the world seriously and therefore suffers from worldly encapsulation. Only a stance which does not see the humor of social life, its fragility, in a sense its absurdity, can gain sufficient transcendence to see the world for what it is – or, to put it the other way round, only a transcendence of social life can yield the perception that the world is basically humorous, fragile and absurd. It should be noted that in Berger's work there has been a shift from a concern with existentialist themes – manifested in the emphasis upon humor, absurdity, and particularly the search for authenticity – to an emphasis upon the significance of the supernaturally transcendent. In recent works Berger has tried to relativize sociology, as he puts it; since according to him sociology has done enough relativizing.[53] Indeed, he says, it is perhaps the very relativizing proclivity of sociology which has enabled us to see the simplicty of relativizing sociology itself. Thus from proclaiming that sociology, or rather social science generally, is a major supplement to Christian faith, Berger has moved to a position in which he claims that sociology is essentially dismal and pessimistic, and that its immanentism, its lack of transcendence, is an inadequate perspective on the significance of human life.

But no more than Mannheim could escape relativization by relationalization, can Berger escape relativization by his style of transcendentalizing. For the very arguments which he generates in support of the supernatural presence are sociological – they are based on *sociocultural* 'signals' of supernatural transcendence.

Historically the links between religion and sociology have been emphatically clear. Comte, Marx, Weber and Durkheim – all of them – related sociology to religion in their distinctive ways. In Weber's famous piece on science as a vocation the question of the relation between a scientific commitment and the fundamental problems of personal meaning is perhaps most piquantly stated.[54] The importance of Durkheim's thesis about religion being the means by which primitives thought about society needs no elaboration. In the modern period it is precisely the broader issues of meaning which are beginning again to engage the attention of students of religion; and it has become increasingly obvious, as we have seen, that social science is a major part of the meaning pattern of modern society. The sociology of religion – in its broadest frame of reference – is thus inherently concerned with *two* major sources of meaning. Indeed, as we have argued elsewhere, pursuit of this sub-discipline involves a confrontation between these two general bases of cultural meaning, the sociological and the religious.[55]

There are some important cognitive symmetries common to both the Christian and the sociological perspectives on sociocultural life.[56] These revolve around the basic Christian imperative about being in but not of the world. We would argue that the classical debates about the differences between the natural and social sciences, notably in Germany, may fruitfully be seen in these terms. More broadly, the whole problem of involvement versus detachment is something which is, culturally speaking, an Occidental one. As many social scientists from Weber onwards have taught us, this problem and the pristine Christian solution to it – i.e., being in but not of the world – came to a head in the religious context with the rise of Protestantism. We are not arguing here for a direct historical continuity between the development of Protestantism and the development of sociology (although there probably are elements of such an idea worthy of exploration). What we are saying is that in ideal-typical form the required stance of the sociologist conforms to the 'in-but-not-of' Christian dictum. As within the history of Christianity, so within the discipline of sociology there are acute versions of this requirement. A good example is that mode of inquiry known as participant observation – or its more subtle and demanding successor, ethnomethodology (which is, of course, much more than a mode of inquiry).

There are, then, two different respects in which this characteristic of the sociological consciousness (being 'in-but-not-of') makes its appearance in modern social-scientific circles: the religious-cultural and the methodological. Lying mid-way between Christian observations on what Martin calls the 'schizoid' stance of the sociologist[57] and the methodological strictures about scientific procedure in sociology are observations such as those of Chomsky, who speaks, in the context of linguistics, about the problem of 'psychic distance'. Although Chomsky is speaking specifically about the problems we encounter in grasping scientifically the principles governing such a fundamentally taken-for-granted phenomenon as language and linguistic ability, the notion of psychic distance – the capacity to distance ourselves from something which is seemingly extremely familiar to us – is, of course, a common feature of the sciences of man. And yet we know relatively little about the foundations and nature of analytic-psychic distance. Undoubtedly Berger is correct, and very importantly so, in remarking that 'the social sciences have become so much part of the intellectual scene taken for granted that sometimes the sociological enterprise itself can become for an individual an excellent method of avoiding any existential encounter with the social reality within which he is located'.[58] (The *degree* to which this is true is naturally a matter for empirical inquiry.) Within the history of sociology only Simmel consistently addressed the problem of distance, presumably under the influence of Hegel – to whom the matter was crucial in connection with his conception of alienation. Husserl-inspired ideas within sociological phenomenology and ethno-methodology that center upon 'the suspension of the natural attitude' are also obviously relevant to the problem of distance. In effect the purposes of bracketing and suspending the natural attitude can be considered as functionally similar to the specifics of the training of a psychoanalyst – including, of course, the analysis of the candidate-analyst.

The phenomenon of 'sociological insulation' minimizes the problem of distance in one major respect. For those sociologists who have become psychically insulated from encounters with existential reality in the sense intended by Berger – that is in confronting the basic issues of meaning in sociocultural life – will tend to experience few problems connected with achieving optimal distance, particularly if they have technical and methodological intellectual equipment to guide them 'through' (and insulate them from) the perceived surface of sociocultural reality. The phenomenal world is for them basically a field of objects to be studied, conceptually arranged, abstracted from, and so on. This kind of sociologist, again ideal-typically, manages to isolate his or her sociological role from his or her other role contexts in such a way that the phenomena he or she confronts sociologically are not of the same class as those which he or she confronts in non-sociological roles. Or, as is frequently the case, insulation is a diffuse characteristic of the personality structure; in which case the routine of the sociologist is an extension of his or her 'natural' inclinations. In the former case sociological problems are located within specific cognitive settings, 'guarded', for example, by institutional and personal work routines – sociocultural experience is separated from sociological experience.[59] In the second case, the repression – in the Freudian sense – of concern with 'ultimacy' is made to constitute the core of the sociological attitude.[60] The degree to which these are satisfactory solutions to the problem of attaining analytic distance (more accurately, getting round it) depends very much on one's views about the goals and aims of sociological inquiry and also the branch of sociology in which one is involved.

One of the major problems of any science concerns that of attaining ontological depth. We characterize the attainment of ontological depth as a process of going deeper and further into sociocultural reality, such that we find 'deep' factors which account for the basic phenomenon in which we are sociologically interested. Thus some sociologists would argue that sociology suffers from so much conceptual confusion and fuzziness precisely because it has not cut deeply enough into sociocultural reality – that it has not got beyond or behind the readily observable and/or measurable. The main point to be made is that there are a number of ways of getting to this 'reality'. We will mention only two here. The first procedure essentially involves a series of abstractions from sociocultural reality. One proceeds in terms of a continuous search for underlying variables – on the basic principle that underlying one variable is always another. In principle, then, 'reality', be it all a highly abstract conception of reality, is obtainable through these processes of analytic regression. The hypothetical end-point of such an endeavor is a two-fold sociological reality. One of these realities is, again in principle, at the very depths of man's ontic state – way 'underneath' the empirical realities of everyday perceived reality. In great contrast, the way in which this deep reality is expressed is in a highly abstract theoretical reality. To put it another way, the referents of this kind of sociology are deeply embedded in sociocultural reality, while the symbolic modes of expressing that reality are, so to speak, way 'above' phenomenal, sociocultural reality.

In contrast to this style there is an orientation to the problem which involves a very different tack. This involves what one might call ontological probing, probing through surface reality to the 'deep structures' which generate that reality. A major example of this kind of approach is to be seen in the work of some ethnomethodologists who attempt to demonstrate that, while things are not what they seem, there are, nevertheless, universal principles of sameness about the apparent *lack* of sameness in everyday reality.

Manifestly the scientific goals of these approaches are not in principle ultimately dissimilar – but they are different in their procedures. The first, the abstractive, does not take everyday, phenomenal reality very seriously; whereas the second takes this reality as its very point of departure. In contrasting these two approaches – which are invoked merely to illustrate some extreme cases in contemporary sociology – we can, hopefully, now see the problem of reality conceptions or, more important, the sociologist's contribution to reality conceptions as being far more complex than has been suggested by Berger.

Sociology in the Future

What then can we say in more constructive vein about the stance of the sociologist at this point in historical time? Geertz has effectively argued that Mannheim's Paradox about the relationship between social science and the validity of ideologies should be circumvented, rather than tackled in its own terms – that we should eschew the problem. In fact Mannheim himself said as much towards the end of *Ideology and Utopia* when he argued for an essentially pragmatic orientation to the problem of the relationship between 'sociology and society'. The interesting link between Mannheim's recommendation in this respect and the philosophical pragmatism of people such as Dewey and James has been neglected – Stark being a major exception.[61] We might also note that Simmel's justification for the 'validity' of sociology was based on not dissimilar grounds – that it was functionally effective.[62] Simmel's position in this respect does of course run counter to the widely-accepted recommendations of the Popperian school, approximating what Popper calls instrumental conceptions of theory and validity.[63]

What is presently needed is a sociology which transcendentally relates sociological thought as a reality to 'the world' which lies outside sociology as a reality. In such connections, as we have already hinted, we can learn from some developments in modern theology. We suggest that in terms of the Mannheim-Scheler debate some contemporary theology leans very much in the Schelerian direction – in the direction of what one might call futuristic, but historically informed, transcendentalism.[64] The so-called Theology of Hope argues very much in terms of hopes for the future based on trajectories of change inherent in the present.[65] This stance contrasts with the predictors, forecasters and planners who tend to argue in terms of extrapolations, which we can by knowing in part control. What we are advocating amounts to a precarious synthesis of probabilities and possibilities.

The Theology of Hope rests considerably on Marxian ideas, notably those of Ernst Bloch. Epistemologically and gnosiologically, the key theme of Marx's work which bears on the present essay is that which is presented by the idea of 'overcoming'. Marx maintained that in his time philosophy was overcoming religion and that philosophy in turn had to be overcome by a social-scientifically guided form of political action – the allegedly 'voluntaristic' elements of which were later spelled out more definitively – and very problematically – by Lenin and Lukács.[66] If only by implication, much of Marxist thought has held to the position that the final phase in the series of cognitive overcomings appears in the genuinely socialist or communist society – when interpretation and analysis of sociocultural life become fused with sociocultural life itself (or, better, the former 'disappear into the latter'). This, from a sociological standpoint, is essentially a scenario of a tacit society – one in which people merely act, and there is no functional need for reflexive social science. In this scenario there is no need for social-science as *culture*;

indeed there may be no room for any kind of culture – which ironically is precisely where yet again the end-of-ideology planners and predictors converge with the implications of certain features of Marxism. Although it should quickly be added that far more emphatic conceptions of a cultureless society are openly advanced by the 'anarcho-subjectivist' schools of thought and their academic interpreters. Roszak echoes some prominent modern sentiments: '. . . (T)he primary purpose of human existence is not to devise ways of piling up ever greater heaps of knowledge, but to discover ways to live from day to day that integrate the whole of our nature by way of yielding nobility of conduct, honest fellowship and joy'.[67] This prescription is made in the context of denigrating 'the myth of objective consciousness', which for Roszak is almost synonymous with what he takes to be 'official' conceptions of scientific method. Roszak goes on to argue that what is important is 'that our lives should be as *big* as possible, capable of embracing the vastness of those experiences which though yielding no articulate, demonstrable propositions, nevertheless awake in us a sense of the world's majesty'.[68]

As arguments along the plane of contention about scientific procedure there would of course be no need to take Roszak seriously, notwithstanding his attempt to seek intellectual legitimation through the invocation of Polanyi. But Roszak's views are, clearly, part of the reality which sociologists have to contend with and these same views suggest an attempt to de-mythologize science as a whole. The apparent seriousness of variants of this perspective in conjunction with other cultural tendencies which deny the validity of analysis and interpretation (sometimes backed up very misleadingly by appeals to dialectical rationality) have posed to sociology formidable challenges. It may well be that the excesses of later 1960s are waning. But, on the other hand, it seems clear that the views expressed by the likes of Roszak *do* reflect one particularly resilient trend in modern societies, namely that of increasing individuation, a process which of course amplifies, and which probably has been the empirical foundation of the subjectivism which has been so prominent in some sections of the academy in the Western world in recent years. Hence planning at the level of individuals – individuals developing their own life-cycle plans; planning for revisability of self; planning experience; planning for death – is a phenomenon that calls for extensive sociological sensitivity. (Although such tendencies were more than hinted at long-ago by Durkheim, Weber and Simmel.) Insofar as societies and individuals are becoming increasingly future-oriented then sociology itself has to become more seriously so than heretofore. Insofar as there are shifts against the idea of there being any canons of scientific inquiry and of objective culture then sociologists have to adapt positively, but not yieldingly, to the situation.

Our two main proposals are that sociology should be adequate to the task of comprehending the becoming sociocultural world, and that it should be capable of maintaining analytic distance from its subject matter. In adumbrating these proposals we are particularly heedful of Parsons' application to the sociocultural field of Freud's maxim: 'where *id* was there shall *ego* be'.[69] This application implies that societies, as well as individuals, tend to become increasingly 'manifestful', that is reflexive in terms of their relationship to past and future. In turn social science, in order to maintain analytic distance has to 'keep-ahead' of long-term processes of sociocultural manifestation. To advocate a teleonomic sociology may be dangerous – given that the word almost certainly evokes memories of the invocation of mysterious prime-movers in the work of nineteenth-century social scientists and that it was one of the major symbols of attack on structural-functionalism in the 1950s and 1960s. We use the term here mainly to convey the ideas of purposefulness and means-ends relationships. Thus a teleonomic sociology is one which is concerned with routes to goals, goals which are preferably not 'ultimate', but always 'penultimate'. A teleonomic sociology is one which is concerned with realistic possibilities, with end-constrained becoming. Following Whitehead, we regard becoming as ontologically prior to being – as more real than being, which is essentially an abstraction from becomingness.[70] The future is, however, regarded as combinatorial – as composed out of a mixture of historical and contemporaneous sociocultural tendencies. Thus change is not simply a process of unfolding – as in some evolutionary and neo-evolutionary perspectives.

In this combinatorial project sociology is a vital ingredient. Sociology assists in the making of the future, particularly in terms of its cultural significance. Probably the most significant switch in emphasis in comprehension of how human societies function and change during the modern period has been the realization that culture (or what some call cultural codes) has to be regarded as an absolutely central component. Sociology is part of culture, in that it pivots upon the presentation of ideas. The kernel of the notion of positivism, as it issues in modern thought from Hegel, is that positivism involves accepting that which is posited in the immediacy of given arrangements and configurations. In its vital, inevitable dimension of culturality sociology has the choice – or rather its practitioners do – of accepting that which is posited or, on the other hand, of taking its cultural role in a transcendent, critical mode. It must be emphasized, however, that the latter phrase only makes

substantive sense – can only be more than a rhetorical gesture – if it
is fleshed-out with more specific perspectives. The perspectives most
suited to the task are, we would argue, the civilizational and what
Martins has called the 'historicophilosophical'.[71] These are needed as
crucial supplements to the futuristic perspective that we have already
indicated. The three in combination enable sociology to be transcendent
and critical. In effect, the civilizational and the historicophilosophical
perspectives are, as interpreted here, two sides of the same coin.

The civilizational perspective provides transcendence, and in a sense
criticism also, by its being rooted in a context wider than the single
society.[72] It commits analysis to a frame that is sensitive, *inter alia*, to the
longevity of matrices of ideas; to the manner in which particular sets of
ideas typically relate to each other; to the recurrence of combinations of
ideas and social circumstances in an anthropological perspective, and –
not least – to the ways in which analysis of societies has been conducted
in a wide variety of sociocultural and historical circumstances. In sum, it
inhibits what has become so typical of much of modern social science –
namely, obsession of the latter with here-and-now empirical immediacy
within societies. The historicophilosophical perspective includes within
its transcending and critical facilities: an emphasis upon time and
temporality; a concern with the balance between historical uniqueness
and universalism; a commitment to interpretation of the long-term
meaning and significance of sociocultural processes; and an interest in the
nature of what man-in-society is preoccupied with and capable of in
long-term perspective.

The thrust of the immediate commentary is in pointing to the need for
a fuller understanding of the implications of being a sociologist in our
time and in the future. More directly we are concerned with the
differential survival capacities of types of sociology and adjacent
intellectual pursuits in terms of epistemological stances and relationships
to 'the world'. Thus what has been said thus far posits a delicate balance
between being in but not of the world, between being engaged with but
yet marginal to the sociocultural order.

The Possible and the Probable

In his controversial essay in philosophical biology (*Chance and Necessity*),
Jacques Monod emphasizes the complexity of the relationship between
invariance and teleonomy. The 'invariance content' of a particular
species 'is equal to the amount of information which, transmitted from

one generation to the next, ensures the preservation of the specific structural standard'. Teleonomy, on the other hand, basically implies the 'subjective idea of "project"' – that project essentially 'consisting in the transmission from generation to generation of the invariance content characteristic of the species'.[73] As Monod argues, the cornerstone of 'the scientific method' has been the postulate that nature is objective – 'the systematic denial that "true" knowledge can be reached by interpreting phenomena in terms of final causes – that is to say, of "purpose"'. On the other hand, natural science could not have been established solely on this premise, for 'it still needed the strict censorship implicit in the postulate of objectivity – pure and impossible to demonstrate. For it is obviously impossible to imagine an experiment proving the nonexistence anywhere in nature of a purpose, of a pursued end'.[74] In any case objectivity 'obliges us to recognize the teleonomic character of living organisms, to admit that in their structure and performance they decide on and pursue a purpose'.[75]

Monod refers to the relationship between objectivity and purpose as constituting a 'profound epistemological contradiction'. In this connection it is important to note that in various ways the objectivity/subjectivity relationship lies at the very core – constitutes the pivot – of some of the most salient paradigmatic disputes in contemporary sociology. This is not to say that there is a straightforwardly homologous relationship between biological objectivity-invariance and subjectivity-teleonomy, on the one hand, and sociological objectivity and subjectivity on the other hand. What is at issue in the present context is the bearing which such 'contradictions' have on the general problem of 'the future'.

There are two major reasons for approaching this field via the work of a philosophical biologist. First, the relationship between biology – in the broadest sense – and the social sciences has become quite a central feature of the modern intellectual scene. Second, and more important in the present context, the relationship between the biological idea of teleonomy and social-scientific ideas concerning subjectivity raises a number of vital questions revolving around such themes as collective and emergent purpose, macro-subjectivity, and so on. The nature of that relationship – between teleonomy and subjectivity – is, however, problematic; since sociologists who have adhered most closely to subjectivism tend to lean upon such ideas as individual praxis, individualistic voluntarism, and so on. Moreover they have frequently mounted their analytic styles in direct opposition to concepts having 'the taint' of biological origin. The most conspicuous manifestation of this in the recent history of sociology is the voluntaristic critique of the teleological elements in functional and structural-functional sociologies. It would not be profitable here to rehearse the details of that phase of the history of sociology. But one aspect of the controversy has to be mentioned. The basic idea of end-orientedness, which constitutes the pivot of all forms of teleological account and all notions of teleonomic processes, has clear affinities with concepts such as praxis, subjective purpose and so on. But the use of teleological modes of explanation of micro processes or events in reference to macro processes or attributes jars against the modern stress upon the primacy of individual or small-group praxis, although it should be emphasized that straightforwardly teleological *explanations* have hardly been utilized in sociology since the prevalence of vitalistic and animistic theories in the nineteenth century. Certainly they play little or no part in contemporary Parsonian theory – against which the 'teleological charge' has so often been directed. Such ideas – particularly as propagated in the second half of the nineteenth century – have tended to assume that invariance was safeguarded, ontogeny guided and evolution oriented 'by an initial teleonomic principle'[76] – as for example in Spencer's unknowable force. This Monod rightly characterizes as an animistic projection, not worthy of serious modern consideration.

Thus in sociology as such teleological ideas have been addressed in two principal modes, both constituting variations on the theme of introjecting an entelechy of purpose into the societal entity. First, as in the debate of the late 1950s and early 1960s, there has been the worry about trying to account for particular phenomena in terms of system needs or purposes. Second there has been the older, but related, issue of mysterious forces operating continuously over historical time. However, to abandon teleonomic ideas completely under the pressure of some current sociological fashions may well deny sociologists the possibility of gaining any significant leverage on the major trajectories of sociocultural change.

Although their interesting and challenging contributions to the general problem of future possibilities are highly sensitive to such factors as unintended consequences of purposeful action and causal relationships (particularly 'everyday' *beliefs* about causal relationships), which may strongly inhibit the achievement of desirable states of affairs, Bell and Mau veer strongly in the direction of a pure volitional model of sociocultural change.[77] Bell and Mau propose a 'new sociology' would 'take man into account, and give him priority over new institutions'.[78] In effect, if 'we' stop worrying very much about what constrains us and spell-out what 'we' want then we stand a very good chance of obtaining the latter, and avoiding that which seems undesirable. This is undoubtedly something of a caricature of the Bell-Mau position; but the general objection can still be responsibly made: in Monod's terms, Bell and Mau seem to be seeking release from both invariance and teleonomy. Invariance implies objective constraint upon realistic choice of desired states of affairs, while teleonomy implies a 'future pull' suggestive of factors which in the conventional voluntaristic perspective would presumably be regarded as severely restrictive in respect of change trajectories. In a word both concepts would be regarded as deterministic.

Along these lines crucial questions arise in connection with the well-trodden theme of the relationship between determinism and voluntarism, which cannot be fully re-explored here. However, some aspects of the problem must be referred to. Voluntariness clearly has internal constraints, quite separately from the usual voluntaristic claim that man can if he so chooses more or less free himself from the chains of sociocultural 'forces' – either by 'decisional wager' or by arguing that external constraints are susceptible to and dismissable in terms of the fallacies of misplaced concreteness or reification. Thus even a pure ideationist approach to the study of the future needs as one of its major components a comprehension of cognitive structure and process; not only in the obvious sense as exhibited in the various schools of cognitive anthropology, but also in the more general and, perhaps more fundamental, area of the relationship between perceptions and counter-perceptions; that is, of the symbiotic relationships between cultural givens and counter-cultural alternatives. In this latter respect arguments made concerning the need for 'countersystem models' and 'negative values' in sociological analysis more or less ignore the problem of the degree to which negations of existing states of affairs are – by definition – severely constrained by those latter states.[79] To parade the virtues of opposing an existing phenomenon is to grant to that phenomenon a considerable 'say' in developing one's preferences. Such preferences are necessarily couched in direct reference to the oppositional target, which thereby becomes the pivot of one's analysis for the framing of alternatives. Naturally one is always, as a matter of degree, a cognitive victim of the sociocultural system or systems in which one dwells – but this very circumstance has to constitute part of the general strategy of mounting what Waskow has called 'possidictions'.[80]

For all the current talk about the need to negate that which already obtains in industrial societies there seems to be relatively little awareness on the part of modern sociologists of the actual phenomenal aspects of sociocultural changes – the amalgams of individual ideas, perceptions, and so on – notwithstanding some strands of thinking in this direction in the (by now highly heterogeneous) Marxian tradition,[81] and in a few relatively isolated areas of sociology. In particular we know very little either from an historical or a sociological point of view about restoration after an objectively discernible break in a society's historical trajectory. Neither do we know much about the phenomenality of attempts to correct – before, during or after the 'event' – states of affairs which are deemed undesirable or stressful by social individuals or collectivities (save for some small-group psychological contributions).

A major contention which emerges from such considerations is that one of the major pejoratively regarded ideas of sociology almost certainly needs modified resurrections. We refer to the concept of *homeostatis*. Apart from the fact that the latter concept has been so heavily criticized for its having been taken out of the (sociologically suspect) biological realm, the brunt of the objection to its relevance to sociology has been its implication that sociocultural systems are inherently disposed, without intervention, to some kind of self-corrective process. It is presumably its lineage connection with such themes as the cunning of reason and the hidden hand which has also helped to make the notion of homeostatis so suspect. Moreover, many would say: what can be the point of reintroducing such a notion at precisely that point in time when to many it seems that in numerous respects societies in the modern world are internally and externally imbalanced, in terms of relationships between culture and nature; man and his technological environment; social institutions and population size; the individual and society; and so on? But the idea of objective (as opposed to phenomenal, subjective), automatic societal regulation – insofar as it has existed in modern sociology – is seemingly less controversial a notion than it used to be. But in any case we ought to regard 'everyday' subjective attempts at regulation as part of a process of regulation. Surprisingly, this conception received very little attention in the heyday of debate concerning homeostatis, equilibrium, and so on. However, many of those working in the concrete planning and futures area clearly recognize the significance of this – particularly in respect of the role of the professional evaluative researcher. To this extent there is wide, but not of course total, agreement upon what amounts to a loose position concerning the unity of theory and practice. On the other hand, much remains to be done in respect of spelling out both the structure and the substance of that unity. In this connection it is appropriate to invoke

Churchman's comment that 'perhaps one of the most ridiculous manifestations of the disciplines of modern science has been the creation of the so-called social sciences' which have tended to adhere to mechanistic ideals relating to the objective empiricism perceived within the physical sciences.[82] But as Jantsch points out, in invoking Churchman: 'Neither the old analytical nor the younger phenomenological schools of social science tell us how to conduct our social life. . . . The vigorous development of a critical sociology . . . does not yet provide the building blocks for a normative social science.'[83]

Jantsch argues:

Exploratory forecasting, which starts from today's level of knowledge and explores future feasibilities and probabilities, has to match *normative forecasting*, which implies the delineation of goals of the future and their translation into missions and tasks for scientific and technological development. Only the combination of both in a 'bi-polar' view leads to technological forecasting fitting into a non-deterministic framework; exploratory forecasting alone is a deterministic concept.[84]

The key phrase 'to match' gets only skeletal treatment in Jantsch's book. However, his emphasis upon the role of anthropology as the 'organizing language' for discussion at the 'purposeful level' relates closely to the basic ideas expressed in the present context.

There is no doubt that the many demands which have recently been made for a sociology sensitive to historicity, temporality, openness to wide ranges of future alternatives – above all a sense of *becomingness* – are justified in view of the long-drawn out commitment, notably in the 1940s, 1950s and early 1960s to preformist views concerning the unfolding of elemental sociocultural givens. The necessitarian basis of the latter has certainly now been heavily corrected, if not 'overcorrected', by the interventionist implications of the newer perspectives. And yet the contributions of those like Jantsch or, in more strictly sociological terms, of Etzioni, which try to inject interventionism or voluntarism into a preformist or necessitarian intellectual context ought to be regarded as only the beginning of a thorough discussion of the relationship between constants and innovations. What, in particular, needs to be accomplished is a deeper comprehension of the limits of sociocultural variation. This, it is here argued, is a problem which is almost always confounded by a lack of analytic sensitivity to the problem of the level of abstraction at which debates about futures are conducted. One of the most conspicuous straw men in modern sociology has almost certainly been the charge that structural-functional theory essentially presents a static conception of sociocultural systems – that insofar as change is acknowledged it is in terms of the development of features of human societies sown in the distant evolutionary past. But this charge has overlooked the virtues of synchronic forms of analysis. Sensitivity to synchronic problems must be a vital component in discussion of futures, in that it provides potentially firm guidelines to what is socioculturally possible. This is definitely not to say, for example, that the functional imperatives of the structural-functional scheme constitute the only way of tackling this kind of issue, although some analytic tools of that kind are clearly necessary.

Much, but by no means all, of the work on futures carries the inbuilt assumption that the future is – virtually by definition – different from the past. It is in this connection that the abstraction problem comes to a head. For while we can readily acknowledge that at a low level of abstraction – at the level of surface impression – most aspects of our life are changing (leisure patterns, technology, art and popular culture, and so on, almost *ad infinitum*), many things appear on close inspection to be much less novel. And in any case the alleged novelty of many phenomena of a relatively concrete and tangible kind resides not so much in genuine innovation but in quantitative change, expressible notably in terms of logistic or exponential growth curves (which is not to deny the relevance of the relationship between quantitative and qualitative change). In view of such considerations the central analytic problem becomes that of producing criteria by and in terms of which empirical phenomena should be identified.

Two examples may suffice to indicate the virtues of such an approach. The first example has to do with trends in respect of socio-legal control relative to crime and deviant behavior; while the second concerns trends in the broad area of religion and cultural symbolization. Both of these problem areas have, like many others, been treated by those who specialize in them as if there were definite discernible shifts over periods of developmental time, such that modern societies appear to be very different from other previous – including extant pre-industrial – circumstances. And yet in both cases the *fusion of sociological and anthropological insights* has in very recent years thrown considerable doubt on the credibility of such views.

Recently evolutionary ideas concerning socio-legal systems, such as those advanced by Durkheim and Maine, have been attacked on the grounds that primitive societies manifest functional analogues of certain aspects of Western civil and criminal, public and private law. This kind of claim rests, as Sally Moore puts it, on the fact that there are social problems which *all* societies have in common.[85] Thus the typical contrast between self-help and collective obligation in primitive societies, on the one hand, and official enforcement and individual obligation in industrial societies, on the other hand, has been greatly exaggerated. In modern societies we have various forms of collective economic liability in such cases as business corporations, insurance companies and labor unions. There have also been — heretofore unsuccessful — legislative moves to introduce collective obligation and liability in the 'war' against so-called organized crime.[86] But in any case to those who would argue that criminal liability is a completely different matter in Western societies as compared with pre-industrial societies Moore replies that analysts frequently commit the fallacy of comparing incomparables. For example:

Retaliatory vengeance killing between groups is not at all equivalent to criminal penalty. What is equivalent . . . is the kind of individual assessment of character inside corporate groups which can lead ultimately to expulsion or execution. This exists as much on an individual basis in pre-industrial society as in any complex one.[87]

Such cogent arguments require that we develop adequate comparative conceptual tools — tools which revolve around choices, for which no *strict* methodological guidelines can be provided, concerning the level of abstraction at which one should work. In turn the development of benchmarks for comparative work enable us not merely to put novelty into proper perspective, but more important to elaborate universal variable features of all societies. In the particular area of socio-legal control and deviance the need is to comprehend systematically those social and cultural factors which constrain the size of the 'gap' between controlling status-roles and the status-roles of those who are controlled.[88] The basic idea is that there are limits of social psychological and sociocultural tolerance of the size of the gap, and that modern societies are under considerable pressure to reduce its size; in directions which, in fairly *abstract* terms, bear significant similarities to circumstances obtaining in primitive societies — such as the increasing conversion of criminal norms into civil norms and a blurring of distinctions between official, centralized socio-legal controllers and individual deviants.

The second illustration can be stated more briefly, since the basic idea to that obtaining in the socio-legal sphere is similar. Some students of religion in modern societies — notably Bellah — have observed interesting similarities between primitive religion and the 'religion' of the former. This is not to say that religion in modern societies manifests a return to what Bellah calls 'primitive monism'. But, on the other hand, the modern world has 'simply no room for a hierarchic dualistic religious symbol system of the classical historic type'. It is argued that 'an infinitely multiplex' world has replaced a 'simple duplex structure'.[89] This second, modern characteristic bears similarities to the primitive situation, in that although it contrasts with the latter in not manifesting a homogeneous, undifferentiated thought-world it nevertheless *is* a sociocultural context in which beliefs and associated practices are related to particular situational circumstances, in which distinctions between religion and magic are not as clear cut as in 'transitional' societies, and so on. It might also be fruitfully added that a number of anthropologists have recently advanced strong arguments to the effect that primitive belief systems manifest more 'cognitive virtues' than has been conventionally recognized – for example in their accounts of situations of social and psychological strain.[90]

Neither of these examples have been invoked on a basis of 'primitivism'. And neither imply cyclical conceptions of sociocultural change. Both point, on the other hand, to the need for historical and cross-cultural comparison in the assessment of possibilities and probabilities. This in two respects. First, alternative futures should take strongly into account previous circumstances that in some sense seem to have worked. It is in this connection that the abstraction issue is crucial – for we may be able to obtain general guidelines concerning feasible futures even though the latter will be substantively dissimilar from the historically experienced. (This is to say rather more than that we should 'learn from history', for it asks for sociological history – and historiography – of a rather special kind.) Second, we may hope to learn more about the dynamic factors which, as it were, push and pull institutional sectors in particular directions.

There are of course sociological traditions of widely differing kinds which have been sensitive to the idea that there are constant factors of change which in some sense bring sociocultural systems 'back' in substantively different forms and in different parametric terms to older, previous states of affairs. The classic example is the relationship between primitive communism and post-capitalistic communism in Marxist historiography.

We need more sensitivity to problems of a historiographical nature, based upon sociological considerations. Full and complete acknowledgment of the choicefulness of social man is not at all incompatible with ideas which have affinity with that of an overall guiding purpose. That purpose does not have in any sense to be of the mysterious kind developed by nineteenth century evolutionists. Nor does it have to be based upon ideas concerning ideological or cultural consensus. Monod argues that 'ideas which have the highest invading potential are those that *explain* man by assigning him his place in an immanent destiny, a safe harbor where his anxiety dissolves'.[91] Hardly sociological language! But many futurists, without using such 'metaphysical' language, do seem to work in the same spirit. A social-scientific translation of a term like 'immanent destiny' is *possible*. The drift of sociocultural, and technological and economic, change has been expressed far too objectivistically. The increasing concern with subjective values and beliefs among futurists in the last few years has begun to correct this imbalance. But the two approaches have to be woven together much more elaborately than heretofore. Therein lies potentially a social-scientific version of 'destiny' — not necessarily a destination, but a direction of change which is in line with assessed constraints.

NOTES

1. This chapter in part issues from ideas expressed in Nettl and Robertson, *International Systems and the Modernization of Societies*, op. cit., esp. Part I.
2. This essay was completed before many of the more recent contributions to the 'Kuhn debate' were published. Cf. Martins, 'The Kuhnian "Revolution" . . .', in T. J. Nossister et al. (eds.), *Imagination and Precision in the Social Sciences*, London, 1972, pp. 13–58. Of particular relevance to these problems: Jürgen Habermas, *Theory and Practice* (trans., J. Viertel), Boston, 1973.
3. Cf. Gerard Radnitzky, *Contemporary Schools of Metascience*, Chicago, 1973 (3rd edn.).
4. *New York Times*, 5 January 1970, p. 39.
5. Stanislav Andreski, *Sociology as Sorcery*, London, 1972.
6. Robert N. Bellah, 'Religious Evolution', *American Sociological Review*, XXIX (June 1964), pp. 358–74. (This crucial essay has influenced many of the ideas presented in this book.)
7. Gino Germani, 'Secularisation, Modernisation, and Economic Development', in S. N. Eisenstadt (ed.), *The Protestant Ethic and Modernization*, New York, London, 1968, pp. 346–50.
8. For a highly relevant extract from Comte's work see Auguste Comte, 'Plan of the Scientific Operations Necessary for

Reorganising Society', in Philip Rieff (ed.), *On Intellectuals*, Garden City, New York, 1969, pp. 248–82.

9. Cf. Louis Schneider, *Sociological Approach to Religion*, New York, 1970, pp. 148–50.

10. We do not enter here into the problematic relationship between sociology and ethics in Comte's work. The relationship between the views of Saint-Simon and Comte has long been as issue of controversy. Our remarks are based on: (a) Comte's insistence on the autonomy of social science in relation to Saint-Simon's tendency to treat social science as an application of mathematics; (b) the disjunction in Saint-Simon's work between scientific administration and his vision of a 'New Christianity' – in contrast to Comte's attempt to integrate logically both the culture and the organizational principles of the emergent societal pattern. See the very useful introduction by Markham to Henri de Saint-Simon, *Social Organization: The Science of Man and Other Writings* (ed. and trans. by Felix Markham), New York, 1964, pp. xi–xlix.

11. For a partial survey of the end-of-ideology thesis, see Chaim I. Waxman (ed.), *The End of Ideology Debate*, New York, 1968.

12. Merton's famous statement on the differences between American and (continental) European sociology should still be regarded as the major backdrop to this: Robert K. Merton, *Social Theory and Social Structure*, Glencoe, 1949, pp. 440 ff. On the more general theme of anti-intellectualism in America: Richard Hofstadter, *Anti-Intellectualism in American Life*, New York, 1962; and Christopher Lasch, *The New Radicalism in America 1889–1963*, New York, 1967, esp. pp. 280–349.

13. Notably in the case of Daniel Bell. See Bell, *The End of Ideology*, New York, 1960; and Bell (ed.), *Toward the Year 2000: Work in Progress*, New York, 1967. (This is not of course the first time that a sociology of knowledge argument has led a sociologist into a policy-oriented position. Karl Mannheim's transition is probably the best example of the twentieth century.) See in particular Daniel Bell, *The Coming of Post-Industrial Society*, New York, 1973. Bell's more recent ventures into cultural sociology illustrate clearly our point concerning the near-inevitability of sociologists having to take stands on cultural and religious issues: Bell, *The Cultural Contradictions of Capitalism*, op. cit.

14. It should be pointed out that one of the men most closely involved with the end-of-ideology thesis, Edward Shils, has written one of the few penetrating analyses of the general cultural significance of

sociology in the modern period. See Edward Shils, 'The Calling of Sociology', in Talcott Parsons et al. (eds.), *Theories of Society*, Vol. II, New York, 1961, pp. 1405–48.

15. Space precludes discussion of a notable sense in which the end-of-ideology theorists have perhaps turned out to be correct: There has been a conspicuous anti-ideological thrust in many of the left-wing radical movements of the modern period. The latter are in a Mannheimian sense frequently more utopian than ideological. (Karl Mannheim, *Ideology and Utopia*, New York, 1936. Cf. Clifford Geertz, 'Ideology as a Cultural System', in David Apter (ed.), *Ideology and Discontent*, New York, London, 1964, pp. 47–76.) However, such a concession to the end-of-ideology position does not obviate the point that they seriously underestimated the range of potential dislocations of modern societies – ironically this has partly to do with a 'Marxian' focus on economic-class variables.

16. See Roland Robertson, 'Societal Atributes and International Relations', in Jan Loubser et al. (ed.), *Explorations in General Theory in Social Science*, Vol. I, New York, 1976, pp. 713–35.

17. Cf. the classic debate about analytical versus dialectical rationality between Sartre and Lévi-Strauss: Claude Lévi-Strauss, *Savage Mind*, London, 1965, pp. 254–69.

18. For various aspects of late 1960s developments see, *inter alia*, Daniel and Gabriel Cohn-Bendit, *Obsolete Communism: The Left-Wing Alternative*, London, New York, 1969; Norman Birnbaum, *The Crisis of Industrial Society*, London, Oxford, New York, 1969; Alain Touraine, *Le Mouvement de mai ou le communisme utopique*, Paris, 1968; and Alexander Cockburn and Robin Blackburn (eds.), *Student Power*, London, 1969. For a highly suggestive description of some particularly American trends of the late 1960s see Gary Wills, 'The Making of the Yippie Culture', *Esquire*, LXXII (November 1969), pp. 135 ff. (Since these words were written in 1970 there have been many signs of a 'left drift' among sociologists. In turn, there has been a mid-1970s conservative reaction. See in particular Sheldon S. Wolin, 'The New Conservatism', *New York Review of Books*, XXIII, 1, 5 February, 1976, pp. 6 ff. For a viewpoint that marks the transition from late 1960s to 1970s thinking, see Barrington Moore, Jr., *Reflections on the Causes of Human Misery*, New York, 1972.)

19. Of course the mandarinate attributes of social scientists were noted long ago. The 'savant syndrome' has been strongly continuous in France from Saint-Simon to Raymond Aron. Institutionalized social science in Britain was conceived under the 'planist wisdom' of the

Webbs – in the form of their brain-child, the London School of Economics. In America Edward Ross denounced (on grounds echoing Marx very strikingly) philosophy and all but highly specialized, administrative thought around the same time. See Edward A. Ross, *Social Control*, New York, 1901. See, for example, Bell, *The Cultural Contradictions of Capitalism*, op. cit.; Zygmunt Bauman, *Culture as Praxis*, London, 1973; and a number of works of the Frankfurt school.

20. We take up the theme of sociological change and cultural change in relation to the sociology of knowledge below, pp. 20 ff.

21. The modern varieties of concern with such matters were in part anticipated in the mid-1960s. See, *inter alia*, W. G. Runciman, *Relative Deprivation and Social Justice*, London, 1966; and Peter Laslett and W. G. Runciman (eds.), *Philosophy, Politics and Society*, Third Series, Oxford, 1967.

22. See in particular Edward Suchman, *Evaluative Research*, New York, 1967. For connections between the Marxism conception of *praxis*, critical theory and applied sociology, see the recent work of Paul Lazarsfeld. The latter's attitude towards 'traditional' critical theory is to be seen in P. F. Lazarsfeld, *Main Trends in Sociology*, London, 1973, pp. 57 ff.

23. K. R. Popper, *The Open Society and Its Enemies*, London, 1962 (fourth edition), Vol. II, p. 212. Cf. John H. Goldthorpe, 'Theories of Industrial Society; Reflections on the Recrudescence of Historicism and the Future of Futurology', *European Journal of Sociology*, XII, 2 (1971), pp. 263–88.

24. Cf. W. W. Bartley, III, 'Karl Barth', *Encounter*, March 1970, pp. 46–9. Bartley notes that Popper grants an 'irrational basis to rationality'.

25. Cf. Kurt Baier and Nicholas Rescher (eds.), *Values and the Future*, New York, 1969; and Wendell and James M. Mau (eds.), *The Sociology of the Future*, New York, 1971.

26. See pp. 28 ff., infra.

27. See Daniel Bell, 'Twelve Modes of Prediction', *Daedalus* (Summer, 1964), pp. 845–80, for varieties of prediction.

28. Among the more important books on concrete prediction are: Bell (ed.), op. cit.; Robert Jungk and Johan Galtung (eds.), *Mankind, 2000*, London, 1969; Victor C. Ferkiss, *Technological Man: The Myth and the Reality*, London, 1969; Herman Kahn and Anthony J. Wiener, *The Year 2000*, New York, 1967; C. S. Wallia (ed.), *Toward Century 21*, New York, 1969, Herman Kahn and B. Bruce-

Biggs, *Things to Come*, New York, 1972. Cf. Andrew M. Greeley, *Religion in the Year 2000*, New York, 1970.

29. The symbiotic relations between dominant and counter-cultures have been illustrated considerably in the development of black militancy in America. See for example, Lewis M. Killian, *The Impossible Revolution?*, New York, 1968; Charles Keil, *Urban Blues*, Chicago, 1966.

30. Many aspects of this orientation and its tactical and strategic correlates were dramatically illustrated in the trial of the 'Chicago 7–8', which may be regarded as the paradigm of many subsequent 'authority-radical' confrontations. Cf. Alfred Willener, *The Action-Image of Society*, London, 1970; and William A. Gamson, *The Strategy of Social Protest*, Homewood, Ill., 1975.

31. Polanyi, op. cit., p. 164.

32. Cf. T. J. Fararo, 'The Nature of Mathematical Sociology: A Non-Technical Essay', *Social Research*, 36 (Spring 1969), pp. 75–92. More elaborately, see Thomas J. Fararo, *Mathematical Sociology*, New York, 1973.

33. See, *inter alia*, Harold Garfinkel, *Studies in Ethnomethodology*, Englewood Cliffs, 1967; Paul Filmer et al., *New Directions in Sociological Theory*, London, 1972; and Roy Turner (ed.), *Ethnomethodology*, Harmondsworth, 1974.

34. See, for example, Norman Pittenger, *Alfred North Whitehead*, Richmond, Virginia and London, 1969; Ralph E. James, *The Concrete God*, New York, 1968.

35. Peter L. Berger, *The Sacred Canopy*, Garden City, New York, pp. 45 ff.

36. See, *inter alia*, Burkart Holzner, *Reality Construction in Society*, Cambridge, Massachusetts, 1968; and Peter L. Berger and Thomas Luckmann, *The Social Construction of Reality*, Garden City, New York, 1966.

37. This is particularly true of the difference between the old and the new sociologies of knowledge. We should not, however, ignore the important bridges between the two provided above all by Alfred Schutz. Retrospective significance within the domain of the sociology of knowledge has been accorded in particular to George Herbert Mead; but Simmel's crucial contributions have been insufficiently acknowledged.

38. Holzner, *Reality Construction in Society*, op. cit., p. 15.

39. Cf. Talcott Parsons, 'An Approach to the Sociology of Knowledge', in Parsons, *Sociological Theory and Modern Society*, New York, 1967,

pp. 139–65; Peter L. Berger, *A Rumor of Angels*, Garden City, New York, 1969. Here again Simmel is very relevant. He was the first radical, sociological relativist. Cf. Alfred Mamelet, *Le relativisme philosophique chez Georg Simmel*, Paris, 1914.

40. See Peter L. Berger, 'Toward a Sociological Understanding of Psychoanalysis', *Social Research*, 32 (Spring 1965), pp. 26 ff. See also Philip Rieff, *The Triumph of the Therapeutic*, London, New York, 1966; and John R. Seeley, *The Americanisation of the Unconscious*, New York, 1967.

41. We refer, of course, to diverse forms of therapy and psycho-analysis which have proliferated in recent years – notably in the U.S.A.

42. For an interesting discussion of the lack of reflexivity in many post-Cartesian theories of knowledge see Edward Pols, 'Polanyi and the Problem of Metaphysical Knowledge', in T. Langford and W. Poteat (eds.), *Intellect and Hope*, Durham, 1968, pp. 58–90. The conventional notion of reflexivity relates very closely to our idea of sociological transcendence, and contrasts considerably with Alvin W. Gouldner, *The Coming Crisis of Western Sociology*, New York, 19701. Our position has much in common with Herminio Martins, 'Time and Theory in Sociology', in John Rex (ed.), *Approaches to Sociology*, London, 1974, ch. 12. In the present chapter we do not emphasize historicity as a component of sociology as much as Martins; but this theme is exhibited in some of our later chapters.

43. See Charles Madge, *Society in the Mind: Elements of Social Eidos*, London, 1964.

44. See Robertson, *The Sociological Interpretation of Religion*, op. cit.

45. See especially Peter L. Berger, *The Precarious Vision*, Garden City, New York, 1961; Berger, *The Sacred Canopy*, op. cit.; Berger, *A Rumor of Angels*, op. cit. Cf. David Martin, *The Religious and the Secular*, London, 1969, esp. chs. 3, 5, 6 and appendix. See also David Martin, *A Sociology of English Religion*, London, 1967, concluding chapter; and Berger, *Invitation to Sociology*, Garden City, New York, 1963.

46. Berger, *The Precarious Vision*, op. cit., pp. 10–11.

47. Ibid., p. 85.

48. Ibid., p. 204.

49. See Peter L. Berger and Richard J. Neuhaus, *Movement and Revolution*, Garden City, New York, 1970. The conservative thrust is even more in evidence in Berger et al., *The Homeless Mind*, op cit.

50. Ralf Dahrendorf, *Essays in the Theory of Society*, Stanford, London, 1968, pp. 19–106.

51 Cf. John R. Seeley, 'Thirty-Nine Articles: Toward a Theory of Social Theory', in Kurt H. Wolff and Barrington Moore, Jr. (eds.), *The Critical Spirit: Essays in Honor of Herbert Marcuse*, Boston, 1967, pp. 150–71. On concepts in relation to differing empirical contexts, see Robertson and Taylor, *Deviance, Crime and Socio-Legal Control*, op. cit.

52. Berger, *The Precarious Vision*, op. cit., pp. 216–17. That view would seem to be severely contradicted by the philosophy and sociology of Simmel; for he produced a system that persuasively shows that life itself produces transcendence-of-life – that one can simultaneously take life seriously and not be compromised by it. See in particular Rudolph H. Weingartner, *Experience and Culture*, Middleton, Conn., 1962.

53. Berger, *A Rumor of Angels*, op. cit.

54. For a suggestive exposition see Richard A. Fenn, 'Max Weber on the Secular', *Review of Religious Research*, 10 (Spring 1969), pp. 159–69. More generally, see the excellent H. H. Bruun, *Science, Values and Politics in Max Weber's Methodology*, Copenhagen, 1962.

55. See Robertson, *The Sociological Interpretation of Religion*, op. cit.

56. Cf. Harold K. Schilling, *Science and Religion*, London, New York, 1963. See also Ian G. Barbour, *Issues in Science and Religion*, London, 1968; and Barbour, *Myths, Models and Paradigms*, New York, 1974.

57. Martin, *A Sociology of English Religion*, op. cit.

58. Berger, *The Precarious Vision*, op. cit., p. 13.

59. Highly relevant to this part of the discussion is Nettl's distinction between those dealing with ideas of quality and those focusing upon ideas of scope. See J. P. Nettl, 'Ideas, Intellectuals, and Structures of Dissent', in Rieff (ed.), *On Intellectuals*, op. cit., pp. 53–122.

60. Cf. Becker, *The Denial of Death*, op. cit.; and Liam Hudson, *Contrary Imaginations*, Harmondsworth, 1966. Cf. Roland Roberton, 'Toward the Identification of the Major Axes of Sociological Analysis', in Rex (ed.), op. cit., ch. 5.

61. Werner Stark, *The Sociology of Knowledge*, London, 1958, pp. 307–28. See also C. Wright Mills, 'Methodological Consequences of the Sociology of Knowledge', *American Journal of Sociology* (1940–1), pp. 316 ff.

62. See Nicholas J. Spykman, *The Social Theory of Georg Simmel*, Chicago, 1925.

63. See Karl A. Popper, *Conjectures and Refutations: The Growth of Scientific Knowledge*, 1965 (second edition), pp. 107 ff. It must be emphasized that Simmel held to the view that sociology was only

one of a number of modes – or in his terms 'worlds' – of comprehending life. Thus on his view sociology should *not* ideally clash with religion, philosophy, art or other 'worlds' that he mentions. For Simmel, sociology was characterized by its being abstractive and typifying. See in particular Georg Simmel, *On Individuality and Social Forms* (ed. Donald N. Levine), Chicago, 1971, Part I.

64. See Stark, *The Sociology of Knowledge*, op. cit., esp. pp. 339 ff.
65. See in particular Jürgen Moltmann, *The Theology of Hope*, New York, 1967; Ernest Bloch, *Man on His Own* (trans. E. B. Ashton), New York, 1970; Martin E. Marty and Dean G. Peerman (eds.), *New Theology No. 5*, New York, London, 1968, esp. the papers by Braaten, Pannenberg, Metz and Cox.
66. Wellmer rightly criticizes Marx, Engels, and later Marxists for failing to attend to 'the question of the connection between the organizational forms of the revolutionary movement and the goal of the revolution on the level of principle . . .' Albrecht Wellmer, *Critical Theory of Society* (trans. John Cumming), New York, 1974, p. 123.
67. Roszak, *The Making of a Counter Culture*, op. cit., p. 233.
68. Ibid., p. 234. Cf. Roger Poole, *Towards Deep Subjectivity*, London, 1972.
69. Talcott Parsons, 'Social Science and Theology', in W. Beardslee (ed.), *America and the Future of Theology*, Philadelphia, 1967, p. 156. Somewhat similar ideas are to be found in the work of G. H. Mead, where the influence of Hegel is clearly at work. Cf. G. H. Mead, 'Evolution Becomes a General Ideal', in M. H. Moore (ed.), *Movements of Thought in the Nineteenth Century*, Chicago, 1936.
70. See Alfred North Whitehead, *Process and Reality*, Cambridge, 1929; Pittenger, op. cit.
71. Herminio Martins, 'Time and Theory in Sociology', op. cit.
72. See in particular Benjamin Nelson, 'Civilizational Complexes and Intercivilizational Encounters', *Sociological Analysis*, 34, 2 (Summer, 1973), pp. 79–105.
73. Jacques Monod, *Chance and Necessity: An Essay on the Natural Philosophy of Modern Biology* (trans. Austryn Wainhouse), London, 1972, p. 24.
74. Ibid., pp. 30–1.
75. Ibid., p. 31.
76. Monod, op. cit., p. 33.
77. Wendell Bell and James M. Mau (eds.), *The Sociology of the Future*,

New York, 1971. In particular see Bell and Mau, 'Images of the Future: Theory and Research Strategies', in ibid., pp. 6–44.

78. Wendell Bell, 'Epilogue', in ibid., p. 334.
79. Gideon Sjoberg and Leonard D. Cain, 'Negative Values, Countersystem Models, and the Analysis of Social Systems', in Herman Turk and Richard L. Simpson (eds.), *Institutions and Social Exchange: The Sociologies of Talcott Parsons and George C. Homans*, Indianapolis and New York, 1971, pp. 212–29.
80. Arthur I. Waskow, 'Looking Forward: 1999', in Jungk and Galtung (eds.), *Mankind 2000*, op. cit., pp. 78–98.
81. Habermas's work has relevance to this theme. See in particular Jürgen Habermas, *Toward a Rational Society* (trans. Jeremy J. Shapiro), London, 1971, esp. ch. 6; Habermas, *Legitimation Crisis* op. cit.
82. C. West Churchman, *Challenge to Reason*, New York, 1968, p. 85 – as quoted in Erich Jantsch, *Technological Planning and Social Futures*, London, 1972, p. 226. Even more directly relevant to the present essay is C. West Churchman, 'Epilogue: The Past's Future: Estimating Trends by Systems Theory', in George J. Klir (ed.), *Trends in General Systems Theory*, New York, 1972, pp. 434–43.
83. Jantsch, loc. cit. That may be a somewhat rash statement in light of Habermas's more recent work.
84. Ibid., p. 48.
85. Sally Falk Moore, 'Legal Liability and Evolutionary Interpretation: Some Aspects of Strict Liability, Self-Help and Collective Responsibility', in Max Gluckman (ed.), *The Allocation of Responsibility*, Manchester, 1972, p. 74.
86. See Donald R. Cressey, *Criminal Organization*, London, 1972.
87. Moore, op. cit., p. 94.
88. This constitutes the central theme of Robertson and Taylor, op. cit.
89. Bellah, *Beyond Belief*, op. cit., p. 40.
90. See below, ch. 7.
91. Monod, op. cit., p. 155. Cf. Becker, *Escape from Evil*, op. cit.

Chapter Three

Weber, Religion and Modern Sociology

Each of us knows that what he has accomplished will be antiquated in ten, twenty fifty years. . . . Every scientific fulfilment . . . *asks* to be surpassed.

Max Weber

One is disappointed in trying to find theoretical significance in the recent sociology of religion. The external flourishing of the discipline was not accompanied by theoretical progress. On the contrary, compared to Weber's and Durkheim's view of religion as the key to the understanding of society, the state of theory in the recent sociology of religion is, in the main, regressive. . . . The awareness of the central significance of religion for sociological theory [has been] lost — in the sociology of religion as much as in other branches of sociology.

Thomas Luckmann

There is a sense in which Weber's own tragic death at the early age of 56 is symbolic of the incompleteness of his work; but I think, given the intellectual situation of his time, it is exceedingly unlikely that Weber would have presented a symmetrically rounded perfection at all. In my opinion it is not his primary significance that he created finished products, but that he began things.

Talcott Parsons

These statements strikingly point-up the issues involved in assessing Max Weber's direct and mediated contributions to modern sociology.[1]* It would be readily accepted by many sociologists of religion that much of Weber's contribution remains as important as ever. It is his name which still gets most mention in many general books on the sociology of religion; a large proportion of the themes which preoccupy modern sociologists of religion were first crystallized by Weber; and there are still a number of areas where it is clearly thought that Weber's analysis is

---

* Notes for this chapter begin on p. 90.

as valid today as it was at the time of writing. However, Luckmann's observations on the condition of the sociology of religion are undoubtedly less true now than at the time that they were first published in 1963. The last few years have witnessed an increasing number of attempts to clarify and elaborate fundamental theoretical issues in the sociology of religion; and to relate these to more general sociological problems. The rapid increase of interest in cultural change; tradition; individual and collective identity structures; the continuities between religion and science; and so on, suggests that the traditional concerns of the sociology of religion are being reabsorbed into the mainstream of sociology. Moreover, as in Weber's time, the relationship between the social-scientific analysis of religion and the study of religion by historians and theologians is quite close. Clearly these changes on the analytic side are not autonomous – in part they reflect and arise in response to social and cultural changes in the wider society. In this wider-societal respect it is striking that the kinds of cultural problem about which sociologists such as Weber, Simmel and Durkheim wrote so much seem to be similar to those which preoccupy modern sociologists. However, the degree to which the study of religion and associated themes is 'Weberian', 'Durkheimian', or whatever, is another question – one which gets some attention here.[2] The move on the part of the sociology of religion to a more central position in contemporary sociology and the injection of greater theoretical sophistication into the study of religion will form the backdrop to the present evaluation of the significance of Max Weber's contribution to our comprehension of religious phenomena.

However, it must be emphasized that our discussion is not directed merely toward the relevance of Weber's work for the modern study of *religion*. Certainly that is part of the overall exercise; but, in line with Luckmann's observation with which we began, our explorations have to do with the more general issue concerning the relevance of Weber's writings to modern sociology in-the-large. We regard the separation of Weber's sociology of religion from his other foci of analytic and empirical interest as a most unfortunate occurrence in the history of the social sciences. It follows that we are constrained to attend to the links in Weber's life-work between 'religious' and 'non-religious' themes. We commence with a discussion of some general features of Weber's studies of religious matters, which we briefly relate to Weber's analytic style as an investigator of social and cultural phenomena. We move then to a consideration of the Protestant Ethic thesis, in an attempt to illustrate with respect to one of Weber's most well-known studies some of the ways in which the Weberian sociological ethos has been distorted. This is followed by a consideration of Weber's work on the church/sect theme, which is, of course, closely related to the Protestant Ethic thesis. Our next section focuses upon the theme of secularization and theodicy, at which stage the need for revision of Weber's work is strongly emphasized. In the last of our main sections the central topic is the idea of meaning as it appears in Weber's sociology. Of all motifs and stances that modern sociology has inherited from Weber this topic, surely, is the most cited. On the other hand, of prominent Weberian themes it is certainly the least analyzed. We claim that no adequate comprehension of Weber's sociology is possible without coming to terms with Weber's conception of meaning. The themes of theodicy and meaning are, of course, quite intimately connected; and it is through utilization of these, informed by some of the leads contained in Weber's work on Protestantism and capitalism and on church and sect, that we believe Weber's sociology can be most fruitfully sifted for modern relevance.

There is no attempt in what follows to itemize or draw-up a catalogue of Weberian assets. The themes chosen are, we believe, among the most central for assessing the general significance of Weber's sociology of religion. Some themes which were important to Weber – such as prophecy; and the relationship between religion and sexuality – are hardly discussed at all; others – such as the nature of charisma, and the relationship between religion and social stratification – are subsumed under our main categories; while still others are pursued in depth in chapters that follow.

General Features of Weber's Approach to Religion

A basic feature of Weber's sociology as a whole must be emphasized from the outset. Weber was committed to a form of empirical concreteness in his work which is characteristic of only a small proportion of modern sociological theory, but he was clearly not an empiricist in the sense of 'letting the facts speak for themselves'. It is true also that he occupied himself for extended periods with technical discussions of concepts and analytic delineations; while his historical-empirical work was undertaken in terms of broad generalizing theses and a highly developed sense of accounting for the social and cultural phenomena which he picked out for detailed scrutiny. Weber was, of course, also explicitly concerned with general methodological questions. However, in spite of these broadly theoretical interests the fact remains that Weber was above all concerned with the empirical and concrete;

and the epistemic gap, or distance, between empirical reality and sociological construct was small in his work compared with much of what is now regarded as genuine sociological theory. Parsons, in spite of his great substantive indebtedness to Weber's sociology, has been one of the latter's keenest critics in this respect; and we shall see that problems arising from Weber's attitude towards theoretical abstraction and generalization are central to any consideration of the contemporary relevance of his sociology of religion.[3]

Closely related to Weber's commitment to empirical concreteness was his apparent lack of interest in elaborating an *a priori*, general-theoretical schema – neither for sociocultural life as a whole nor for the domain of analysis with which we are focally concerned here, namely the sociology of religion. That is not to say that no general standpoint or analytic mode can be discovered through close inspection. The critical point is that Weber neither produced a master sociological program, nor did he commit himself to a definitive position on the fundamental operative principles of sociocultural systems. To be sure, he did present his own methodological principles, and frequently drew attention to pivotal processes, notably that of rationalization. Compared, however, with a Durkheim or a Simmel, Weber's conception of sociology was liberally diffuse; while in comparison with those two sociologists his substantive generalizations were uncoordinated.[4]

Roth has succinctly characterized the structure of Weber's analyses of religion as having been 'built . . . around the relation of *religions* to their organizational carriers (functionaries), and to the status groups and classes supporting them'.[5] The distinctively sociological nature of Weber's contribution to the study of religion is highlighted here. Weber was directly concerned with the differential propensities of social groups in respect of adherence to certain forms of religious belief. His was a highly original ocontribution in its sustained focus on the relationship between social variables and religious doctrines.

The sociological connections which Weber made between religious belief and the groups which developed and adhered to religious beliefs and, equally important, the social vehicles which developed and promoted beliefs were intimately related to Weber's rather problematic emphasis upon the autonomy of religious need. Roth, Lichtheim, Schumpeter, and others have convincingly argued that this emphasis was not in principle at odds with Marx's conception of religion as 'the sigh of a creature in distress' and 'the opium of the people'.[6] It is rather that Weber had a different evaluative orientation to religion – an orientation which had both sociological and extra-sociological aspects. ('Evaluative' does not here necessarily mean autonomously value-judgemental. That is a question which we will touch later.) More important, Weber, because he regarded religion more 'constructively' than Marx, was disposed to inquire systematically into the *minutiae* of the processes and social mechanisms by and through which religion was elaborated, preserved and attenuated. Weber 'respected' religion sufficiently to wish to know the details of its various forms; whereas Marx, diagnosing religion as an impediment to the attainment of 'true' sociality, tended to consign it to the status of a psycho-cultural reflex.[7] But these differences do not obviate similarities in the analytic approaches of Marx and Weber; for both saw religion as constituting a mode of adaptation and accommodation to the exigencies and contingencies of sociocultural life.

Weber's claim concerning the autonomy of individual religious need and of religious culture rested upon, first, the postulated striving for salvational meaning (at least in the areas of the 'world religions'); and, second, upon the crucial category of religious specialists. The first of these is, in the form which Weber gave it, problematic; but the second is less ambiguously of great sociological significance. The stress which Weber put upon religious specialists is an excellent example of his greater sophistication in the treatment of religion in comparison with his sociological predecessors and contemporaries. The notion of religion as autonomous has often been taken, notably by certain Marxists, to mean that religious ideas operate immanently – that they change at what, in rigid Marxist terms, is the superstructural level. An interpretation of Weber along those lines yields a depiction of his holding to a neo-Hegelian position. The choice, however, is not between on the one hand, the autonomous development of ideas as such and, on the other hand, the determination of ideas by material or even social-relational factors. Weber's notion of elective affinity has often been invoked to advance the claim that a once-and-for-all sociological choice does not have to be made.[8] But the critical consideration here is that even in the least differentiated societies there have been or are groups of individuals who, and collectivities which, specialize self-consciously in the production, dissemination and preservation of beliefs and symbols. Thus in sociological terms a claim as to the relative autonomy of ideas may have to mean only that ideas are self-consciously produced, sustained and modified.[9] Actually, the notion of alienation as developed by Marx embraces a not dissimilar idea.[10] Weber (again like Marx) tended to eschew interest in what we would now call patterns of cultural change, where the interest is in the objectively discernible nature of change at the cultural level. In that he appeared to agree with Marx's pejorative comment: 'So-called *objective* historiography consisted precisely in conceiving historical relations separate from activity.'[11] Weber's failure to deal with the 'logic' of change at the level of objective, substantive rationality in modern societies is a matter deserving close attention.[12]

Another central feature of Weber's study of religion and one which is closely connected to the idea of religious autonomy is his emphasis upon processes of rationalization. What Roth calls 'theological elaboration' was for Weber very much a case of striving for ration-ethical consistency.[13] It was, on Weber's view, in Calvinism that rational-ethical consistency was most completely obtained in the Western world. As Parsons has paraphrased Weber's conclusions as to the characteristics of Calvinism, the ultimate resolution of the problem of meaning 'depends upon relations between an absolute, all powerful God, whose "motives" are in principle inaccessible to finite human understanding, and a creation, including man, which is absolutely and completely dependent on his will'.[14]

Weber's work on religion may be described as a mixture of empirical propositions and historically grounded conceptual distinctions, these being linked together by the intertwined interests in salvational religions and the differential levels of development of the Oriental and Occidental worlds. In turn these latter foci were permeated and guided by philosophical and 'metaphysical' concerns with the bases of action in the modern world. In this respect Weber's program was closely in line with the mainstream of German thought as it had been cast since the early nineteenth century, crystallized most clearly in the themes of praxis and meaningful action. Closely bound-up with these characteristics is the unwillingness on Weber's part to define or conceptualize 'religion'. Sociological orientations to problems of definition and conceptual-ization are always conditioned by substantive interest, and in Weber's case it is clear that he was not directly interested in religion *per se*. His leading interests were in the broader issues which we have briefly adumbrated thus far. His preoccupation with processes of rationalization – and, more broadly, intellectualization – in the religious sphere in itself severely limited the range of religious phenomena which could have attracted his analytic attention. He was above all interested in religious-cultural traditions of lasting and visible societal importance. Hence his relatively few observations on religion in primitive societies; his scathing attitude towards individualistic, diffuse religious tendencies in industrial societies; his lack of interest in conversion and syncretism; his relative neglect of the religious reformer, as opposed to the prophet (who created) and the priest (who preserved and taught) – all these evidence

his highly specific interests within the range of religious phenomena.[15]
However, given Weber's usual sensitivity to conceptual distinctions and
his ideal-type methodology we may still express some surprise at and
criticism of his calculated unwillingness to define religious phenomena.

Undoubtedly one of the major intellectual reasons for Weber's failure
– or rather unwillingness – to define religion is embedded in his
commitment to (to a significant degree his creation of) that style of
analysis known as *Religionssoziologie*. *Religionssoziologie* was in Weber's
hands a mode of study which regarded religious phenomena in their
objective social aspects; and which saw these phenomena as manifested
collectively in a society or a civilizational complex. Typically
Religionssoziologie was the work of 'non-believers', the major figures of
the period adhering to this way of analyzing religion including Simmel,
Sombart, and Weber himself. The *a prioristic*, functional approach of
Simmel evidences the dominant characteristic of *Religionssoziologie* rather
more unambiguously than does the orientation of Weber.[16] In the
broader German tradition of *Religionswissenschaft* many analysts were
Christian believers – their major predicate being the *sui generis* nature of
religion as individually experienced.

In many respects Schleiermacher may be regarded as having founded
this tradition, in the early nineteenth century. In the early part of the
twentieth century the *Religionswissenschaft* school included Scheler and
Otto; and the tradition has sustained very strong phenomenological
features, as in the work of Wach, Van der Leeuw and Eliade. A
distinctively phenomenological slant had been mediated temporally
through the *verstehen* approach of Dilthey, a circumstance which points
up the slightly ambiguous nature of Weber's position in terms of the
Religionswissenschaft/Religionssoziologie relationship. In this connection it
is fruitful to note the views attributed to Weber's friend Ernst Troeltsch
by a practitioner of *Religionswissenschaft*, Joachim Wach. In attacking
neutrality about religion, Troeltsch 'characterized an unlimited
relativism by stating that a weakly constituted natural history has
become identified with empathy (Nachfühlung) for all other characters
together with a relinquishing of empathy for oneself, with scepticism
and playful intellectualism, or with oversophistication (Blasiertheit) and
a lack of faith. It will be asked if an open hostility is not more appropriate
to the subject of religion than this noncommital attitude.'[17]

Given such division within and interpretation of the field of study,
Weber's reluctance to get involved in definitions of religion cannot be
entirely condemned, for it might have meant him seeming to adopt a
form of definitional essentialism, of saying what religion really is, and,

therefore, of embracing the *sui generis* religious predicate. Admittedly Durkheim in his sociologistic commitment did say what religion 'really' was – without embracing such a position – but in Weber's intellectual context there was no easily discernible position between the view which circumstantially denied the internal validity of religious experience and belief *per se* (as did Durkheim) and the religiously based position of the *Religionswissenschaft* position. (In any case Durkheim differed from Weber in being hostile to the dominant religion of his own society, namely Catholicsm.) Weber's ambivalence in these matters is highlighted further by his own statements about his lack of religious 'music'. That is, he claimed to be immune to the religious experience – in great contrast to the prominence in his family network of religiously committed women. The relationship between those close to him who were 'religiously musical' and his own conviction about the historical significance of religion is particularly important (although psychohistorical interpretation in this case – and, we believe, in other cases – is exceedingly dangerous.)[18]

The Protestant Ethic Thesis

The greatest continuity between Weber's sociology of religion and modern sociology as a whole is to be seen in issues arising out of the Protestant Ethic thesis. Not only is the thesis still discussed in its own terms, it has been re-formulated and extended by a number of social scientists. In spite of periodic attempts to call a moratorium, the heart of the problem – the origins and the sociocultural dynamics of mature industrialism – is still very high on the agenda of social science. It has, however, probably become a little less interesting for sociologists of religion *per se*. The latter have, during the past twenty years or so, addressed much more the issue of the extent and degree of secularization of modern societies, a theme which was diffusely prominent in Weber's work. If fact, even though Weber seemed to take extensive secularization for granted, it could be viably argued that the secularization theme is more in line with Weber's thought – at least as far as Western societies are concerned – than the almost obsessional interest in the extra-religious consequences of religious affiliation.[19] In fact the larger amount of work self-advertized as related to the Protestant Ethic thesis has probably been undertaken by sociologists with no obvious interest in the study of religion as a distinctive problem-area, nor even in the sociology of culture as a more general field of inquiry.[20] It is probably for that reason that so many of the (mainly American) survey studies of the relationship between 'religion' and dependent variables, such as actual or aspirational upward social mobility, attitudes towards work, educational and scientific achievement, and so on, have paid only fleeting attention to the details of Weber's arguments. The same kind of assessment holds for much of the work undertaken during the past twenty years on the underpinnings of economic development. The general idea that economic development is significantly dependent upon non-social-structural and non-technological factors has indeed been consistently credited to Weber.[21] But few of those who have worked on problems of economic development in recognition of the importance of Weber's work have actually attempted either to undertake their inquiries in a Weberian spirit or systematically transcend Weber's contributions. A particularly conspicuous example is to be seen in the work of McClelland – who, while stating that his work should be seen as continuous in relation to Weber, nevertheless argues and presents data in terms of a direct connection between motives, or need-achievements, and economic institutional structure.[22] This clearly contravenes Weber's emphasis, at least in the Christian-civilizational content, upon religious culture (puritanist Protestantism) constraining individuals to adapt to economic situations in specific and unique modes, leading both to a reinterpretation of the significance of economic activity and a modification (a rationalization) of the pristine doctrinal culture itself; the overall impact of such changes becoming manifest as a new economic 'spirit'. Structures are transformed under the aegis of the resulting 'spirit of capitalism' – an ethos which, according to Weber, eventually becomes detached from its original, strictly religious matrix.[23]

The fact that a great proportion of the work done under the rubric of the Protestant Ethic thesis is not 'Weberian' should not of course lead us automatically to dismiss it. One of our tasks is indeed to probe the degree to which Weber's interpretations and findings have been surpassed. McClelland, to continue with our example of work on the underpinnings of difference in the economic development of societies, emphasizes the ways in which Protestantism restructured personal relations, notably within familial contexts. He argues that 'it seems reasonable to interpret Weber's argument for the connection between Protestantism and the rise of capitalism in terms of a revolution in the family leading to more sons with high need for achievement'.[24] We doubt very much whether dedicated students of Weber's work could seriously entertain such an interpretation. That is not to say that the idea of examining the familial consolidation and perpetuation of pristine

Puritanist activism is social-scientifically unimportant, but rather that the thrust of Weber's argument was in a different direction. McClelland himself actually argues that 'the events Weber discusses were probably only a special case of a much more general phenomenon – that it was *n* Achievement as such that was connected with economic development, and that the Protestant Reformation was connected only indirectly in the extent to which it had influenced the average *n* Achievement of its adherents'.[25] Weber, in contrast, was interested, *inter alia*, in the origins of a specific form of what McClelland calls 'the need for achievement'; what individuals and groups differentially do with their (differential) 'needs for achievement'; and the social-structurational consequences and the cultural ramifications of the subjective interpretations of 'the need for achievement'. Needless to say, the latter is not a Weberian category, but there can be not great exception to arguing that it bears a resemblance to something in which Weber was indeed interested.

The crucial point is that McClelland gets Weber's priorities wrong, almost in reverse. And yet there are those who regard work of that kind as standing in a relation of substantive continuity with Weber's sociology. Yinger, for example, claims that McClelland's work 'is illustrative of a line of questioning, growing out of Weber's work, that is concerned with the transformative capacities of different religions'.[26] We have seen, however, that that is precisely what McClelland is not interested in. (Indeed, it is doubtful either whether Weber had any particular interest in economic growth *per se* – any more than did Marx.) But to be genuinely interested in 'the transformative capacities of religions' does, surely, constitute a *Problemstellung* stemming directly from Weber's work. It has quite often been argued that Weber was 'really' interested only in the specifics of the transformative capacity of Western Protestantism – that Weber's work was deliberately (and very problematically) 'skewed Westward'.[27] On the other hand, his general interest in processes of religious rationalization obviously suggests the appropriateness, even in his terms, of considering the transformative capacities of developments other than that precipitated by the Protestant Reformation. Moreover, since Weber was very much concerned with non-economic correlates and consequences of different religious traditions – even though economic action is the major focus of the essay, *The Protestant Ethic and the Spirit of Capitalism* – we can safely enter the judgement that recent interests exhibited in the political consequences of the Reformation, in the longer-established focus on the scientific consequences of the development of Protestantism, and so on, are directly relevant to problems raised by Weber.

We must repeat that the kinds of criteria which we here use to acertain 'Weber-relevance' are not intended as standards for assessing social-scientific quality in universalistic mode. Rather, we are concerned to trace the relevance of Weber's studies of religion to modern sociology. Many studies are 'Weber-relevant' on their own say-so, which – as with our McClelland example – are only in the present context invokable *en passant*, to illustrate where we think the boundary between relevance and non-relevance should be drawn.

The present state of the debate about the Protestant Ethic thesis and its potential for new forms of research has been extensively reviewed recently by, *inter alia*, Robertson, Eisenstadt, Nelson and Little.[28] Thus we would only be engaged in a duplicatory exercise were we to assess the state of the debate at this juncture. However, in view of these recent summations and commentaries, plus new substantive contributions to the debate, we may note three particularly important tendencies. The first of these is basically negative in relation to Weber's own work, the second positive, and the third of a hybrid nature. The relatively negative thrust has to do with Weber's insistent rejection of the idea that what he called the 'temporary external historio-political situation' of Protestants had a significant bearing upon their religio-economic orientation. Weber was of course convinced of the relatively autonomous status of the process of rationalizing theological elaboration, and it is that view which certainly guided his arguments in *The Protestant Ethic and the Spirit of Capitalism*. And yet in other parts of his work on religion Weber emphatically attends to social-to-cultural flows of impact – one of the outstanding examples being the essay on religion and social stratification (divided in English translation into 'Castes, Estates, Classes and Religion' and 'Religion of Non-Privileged Classes').[29] The view that religions may have innovative economic impact in part by virtue of their being placed in marginal, peripheral positions has found support in a number of recent studies.[30] In any case that view does not have to rest its case on the simple phenomenon of structural marginality or subordination – the more sophisticated version of the argument being that marginality in conjunction with particular religious cultural dispositions is productive of economic, and indeed more wide-ranging, forms of cultural change. In fact that kind of proposition is not at all inconsistent with Weber's emphasis upon particular forms of sectarianism being absolutely central in effecting change in consciousness, definitions of identity, and so on (with which we deal later). Unlike Troeltsch, Weber said little about the social-locational aspect of sects as opposed to the cultural aspect.

Second, we turn to possibilities for definitely positive developments.

along Weberian lines. These, in our view, center upon the transformative capacities of particular religious-cultural traditions. Eisenstadt, Bellah and Nelson have been among the main proponents of this stance.[31] Eisenstadt has drawn attention to the impact of Protestantism upon political aspects of early modern societies, notably in effecting differentiation of societal sectors and promoting individualistic conceptions of citizenship. Nelson, in stressing the dangers of seeing the political realm as the major spill-over agency in civilizational change, tends to emphasize the cultural realm. He argues that 'Weber might have spared us [from many of the grossly misleading interpretations of his work] if he had placed more explicit stress on the changes in the structures of experience, conscience and consciousness'.[32] The thrust of this type of advice is in the direction of expanding our notions of the range of impact of Protestantism – but more generally, and more significantly, it suggests the need for detailed analyses of changes in consciousness that have had, or are in the modern condition likely to have, trajectoral salience at the levels of societal and civilizational change. The two most promising themes in this respect would seem to be: first, the balances between what we now call, following Parsons, particularism and universalism and ascription and achievement; and, second, structures of identity and consciousness as they relate to participation in or, as a matter of degree, withdrawal from the political and economic centers of modern societies. The first theme continues Weber's interest in phenomenal criteria of evaluation and inclusion/exclusion. The second refers directly to a theme which Weber did not actually develop as such, but which is a corollary of many of his interests, such as his contrast between asceticism and mysticism – namely the relationship between identity and authority, particularly the political aspect of that relationship. It can readily be seen that each of Weber's types of authority implies a congruent form of identity definition. We would suggest that one possible starting point for such inquiries should be the proposition that authority problems arise when there is a break between definitions of personal and collective identities.[33]

The final possibility for development from the basis of The Protestant Ethic thesis takes-off in one sense from the theme which we have just discussed – namely the identity/authority relationship. The paradigm case is Swanson's *Religion and Regime*.[34] Opinions differ as to the degree to which Swanson works in a relatively pro- or anti-Weber spirit. Certainly in *prima facie* terms Swanson's program is very different from that of Weber; for he sets out to show why some societies or subsocieties turned Protestant and others remained Catholic – as determined by the nature of legitimacy codes of authority and the locus of political decision-making. But for those not committed to 'he-was-always-right' interpretations of Weber, such an approach is much more sensitive to the relationship between micro- and macro-aspects of societal change than the latter. (Moreover, as he himself was at pains to argue, Weber was concerned to demonstrate in *The Protestant Ethic* only one aspect of the development of modern societies.) In any case problems related to the connection between self-monitoring and collectivity or societal monitoring are eminently Weberian themes – themes which can fruitfully be explored in terms suggested by Weber, namely that civilizations and societies within civilizational complexes differ in the nature of the 'coding' of relationships between the individual and the collectivity; the small-scale and the large-scale; the citizen and the state; and so on.[35]

Church and Sect

The conceptual distinction between church and sect has probably been even more cultivated by specialists in the sociology of religion than has the Protestant Ethic thesis.[36] In this case, too, the Weberian idea has been deployed so frequently that from time to time there have been calls for a moratorium – although it should be said that the direct inspiration for the church/sect theme has been much more the work of Troeltsch than Weber. As with other Weberian topics, this is partly due to the vagaries of translation – for until 1968 the major source in the English language for understanding Weber's ideas about types of religious collectivity and relationships between religious forms and wider societal settings was Weber's short essay, 'The Protestant Sects and the Spirit of Capitalism', whereas Troeltsch's *The Social Teaching of the Christian Churches* had been easily accessible to the English-speaking since 1931. This lag in access to Weber's work has had the consequence of divorcing, particularly for non-German readers, the Protestant Ethic thesis from the elaboration of sectarianism and churchliness. Failure to attend to the latter has been one major factor in the use of gross categories of religious affiliation in testing hypotheses about the differential secular impacts of variation in religiosity. The fact that the 1950s witnessed a gain in sophistication through attempts to dimensionalize religiosity (in particular separating the social from the cultural aspects of religion) can hardly be credited to any increase in understanding of Weber's coordination of gross forms of religious affiliation (Protestant, Catholic, Jew, and so on) with the church/sect distinction. Only a few sociologists – such as Berger, Demerath and Johnson – have been sensitive to these matters: Berger and Demerath in casting sectarianism and churchliness as forms of processual variation within any religious collectivity, Johnson in addressing the affinities between certain forms of American Protestant sectarianism and dominant cultural values (as well as probing the links between types of prophecy and the church/sect distinction).[37]

It is a moot point whether greater knowledge of Weber's work would have made any fundamental difference to the deployment of the church/sect distinction. To be sure, there might have been less puzzling over the degree to which the distinction as a putative typology of religious collectivities (or as a sociological characterization of 'church/society' relationships) is applicable beyond the sphere of dominantly Protestant societies. For Weber does make it clear that, quite apart from the concrete occurrence of 'churches' outside Christianity in Islam and Lamaist Buddhism (plus more restricted manifestations in Mahdism, Judaism and ancient Egypt), the church/sect dialectic is not to be seen as inherent solely in the social dynamics of Christian civilization.[38] In that respect the degree to which we classify Martin's pathbreaking utilization of the church/sect relationship in universalistic mode as 'Weberian' is problematic – for Martin's work, as presented, is not explicitly inspired by Weber.[39]

Thus the extensive use of the church/sect distinction and the attendant ideas which have been developed through almost continuous controversy since the 1920s do not really have a Weberian base. The base has been more Troeltschian than Weberian. (It has often been noted that Weber 'passed' the church/sect theme to Troeltsch). Interestingly this may well account for what genuinely progressive developments have taken place in this problem area. The relatively circumscribed, specific nature of Troeltsch's exposition of the sect and church modalities made it an easily communicable intellectual package.[40] To be sure, that narrow inspirational base has led to a large number of scholastic, logic-chopping essays; but on the other hand the attempt to escape the Medieval and Reformation confines of the Troeltschian exposition has undoubtedly been mainly responsible for the production of a number of contributions which focus upon the complexity of modern sociocultural systems in relation to the simplicity of the church/sect distinction. It may well have been the case that had the corpus of Weber's writings on religion been confronted more comprehensively before the 1960s, the large amount of work on religious sects in the 1950s and 1960s might not have been accomplished – a circumstance which has both advantages and disadvantages.

The work inspired by the church/sect distinction has been notable for its failures – in comparison with Weber – to consider the general nature of religious governance, which was addressed by Weber most specifically in his discussions of hierocracy, caesaropapism and theocracy, and the individuated forms of religiosity which Weber examined in terms of the category of mysticism.[41] This has meant that much of the work on developing typologies of religious orientations has, at least in its reference to Western societies, concentrated upon understanding the organizational dynamics of different types of religious collectivity. It could be argued that this has not been undertaken in a Weberian spirit, in that the major thrust of Weber's writing on church and sect and related themes had to do with the wider-societal ramifications of the sectarian and the churchly thrusts. On the other hand, much of that work has seemingly been concerned to explore the internal functioning of religious collectivities in a way which is consonant with Weber's more general interest in the modalities of modern organizations. Thus those students of religion who have attended to the variation in relationships between doctrine and polity in religious collectivities have in most cases been working along a 'Weberian path', and in so doing have enhanced both our knowledge of the internal dynamics of religious organizations and the organizational characteristics of, what Etzioni calls, normative organizations in general.[42] Few have gone so far, however, as Harrison in attempting to build-upon and revise Weber's multiconceptualization of rational-legal bureaucracy in specific reference to a religious organization (the American Baptist Convention).[43]

Weber did, of course, tend consistently to associate charisma and charismatic authority with religion. The governance-type hierocracy and the concepts of the routinization of charisma and office charisma were closely related to his general interest in the ways in which the mundane and 'ordinary' was and could be transcended.[44] His own ambiguity about (and seeming ambivalence toward) the degree to which routinized charisma was 'really charisma' is reflected in the work of some modern analysts of religious sects (most notably Bryan Wilson) who see in many forms of sectarianism a kind of mirror-image attempt to hold tenaciously to a vehicle of insulation from materialistic rationalism – more technically, instrumental or formal rationality).[45] To that extent the imbalanced concentration by sociologists of religion on sects, as opposed to churches, reflects – if it has not clearly been inspired by –

Weber's tendency to see charisma and worldly transcendence as endangered by the inflation of *Zweckrationalität*. Thus the view that sects are really more genuinely religious than other collective modalities of religion has found a strong expression in the sociology of religion, particularly from the time of publication of Niebuhr's book on the bases of denominationalization.[46] While, as we have remarked, it is doubtful whether there has been a direct continuity from Weber to the modern period in this respect, it is almost certainly the case that the religious matrix of charismatic authority as sketched by Weber (following a long line of previous scholars) has been influential in sustaining the ethos that religion is most appropriately studied in its 'purest form'.[47]

The question of what is 'really' or 'interestingly' religious from a sociological standpoint can be seen in the context of Weber's work to relate closely to Weber's analyses of religion and social stratification. Weber himself did not – unlike Troeltsch – get deeply into the links between the church/sect typology and the religious dispositions of different social strata and classes. Because Weber wanted to avoid economic-determinist theories of differential religiosity (which was not simply a matter of philosophic choice, but one based in his view on empirical evidence), he was seemingly not prepared to state, as many after him have done, that sectarianism is basically a lower-class phenomenon.[48] His view, as expressed frequently in his writings, was that each of the major religious traditions had been primarily developed by distinctive status groups – in the case of Christianity by itinerant artisans and journeymen. Weber's insistence upon the basically 'lower-middle class' social dynamic of Christianity was, of course, systematically integrated with his emphasis upon the ethical-compensatory significance of that doctrinal tradition, and in particular of the puritan and pietist Protestant sects within it. When allied with his further characterization of rural magic in contrast to urban religiosity (another clear-cut example of the quite close relationship between Marxian and Weberian thought) we can recognize the very specific and rather unique conception of religion to which Weber adhered. The confluence of his desire to escape essentialism in his definition of religion and his parametric interest in differential trajectories of civilizational and societal change resulted in a definition of religion which has only infrequently been grasped by would-be Weberians and deployers of his insights and thematic preoccupations.[49]

Nevertheless it is clearly the case that the style in which many recent analyses of sectarian movements have been undertaken echoes Weber in respects that go beyond those previously mentioned. In one way or

another the themes of relative deprivation and alienation have appeared
many times in the development of the study of religious sects. Although
the terms themselves appear only *en passant* in Weber's work, we can see
clearly via Parsons' excellent account of Weber's theory of religion that
what Parsons calls a focus on the 'propensity to alienation' was
prominent in Weber's thinking;[50] while the associated idea of relative
deprivation was at the heart of Weber's whole idea of compensation
ethics, and in particular was expounded in his essay on 'Religion of Non-
Privileged Classes'.[51] (That essay, for all its brilliance, provides one of the
'best' examples of Weber's not infrequent inconsistency: '[Among] the
privileged strata, the need for salvation . . . is remote. . . . A religion of
salvation may very well have its origin within socially privileged
groups'!)[52]

The collectivities which Weber explicitly addressed and named as
sects were those which were characterized above all by their emphasis
upon a voluntary principle of membership in an association of
religiously qualified persons. The inner-life of the collectivity was
marked by intensive and extensive participation – tending toward what
is frequently called the priesthood of all believers – a form of
participation which required frequent demonstrations of religious
qualification. Both internally and externally a premium was placed upon
discipline and self-control – the principle of asceticism. The ideal-typical
sect was, moreover, of the kind which contributed through the
manifestation of such characteristics to the wider development of a
historically unique form of self-control: 'The ascetic conventicles and
sects formed one of the most important historical foundations of modern
"individualism". Their break away from patriarchal and authoritarian
bondage, as well as their way of interpreting the statement that one owes
more obedience to God than to man, was especially important.'[53] Weber
insisted, however, that 'in modern times' all phenomena originating in
religious conceptions succumb to the 'characteristic process of
"secularization".'[54] He observed that in America demonstration of
certified 'sect' membership has operated as a basis of economic-credit
worthiness: 'Sect membership meant a certificate of moral qualification
and especially of business morals for the individual . . . in contrast to
membership in a "church" . . . which lets grace shine over the righteous
and the unrighteous alike.'[55] However, this generalized impact of
sectarian religion was as subject to atrophy as any other religious
phenomena: 'Today the kind of denomination (to which one belongs) is
rather irrelevant. It does not matter whether one be Freemason,
Christian Scientist, Adventist, Quaker, or what not.'[56] Weber goes on

to argue that in America at the turn of the century other purely secular forms of association were replacing the sect, offering 'the member the . . . claim for brotherly help on the part of every brother who had the means'.[57]

There are, clearly, grounds for arguing that in terms of the general drift of Weber's interests – as summated in such motifs as secularization, disenchantment, the 'iron-cage' of modern rationalism, the individuated forms of religion, and so on – a 'faithful Weberian' would not in our period be studying religious collectivities *qua* religious collectivities. Insofar as religiosity would be focused by the faithful modern Weberian it would have to be in terms of the character of individuated religion, perhaps under the two-stranded conceptual sponsorship of charisma and mysticism. There has been a strong tendency among students of religious collectivities to encapsulate part of the Weber-Troeltsch thrust in this respect by their use of the type-concept 'the cult'. But the latter has dangled uneasily in typological displays as a form 'of unorganized organization' and has not been accorded the 'respect' which has been given to the more clearly collective vehicles of religiosity, such as the church, denomination, established sect and 'ordinary' sect.[58] The recent revival of interest in mysticism as a neglected element in the Weber-Troeltsch schema will not, hopefully, atrophy through attempts to include it in new dynamic typologies of religious collectivities.[59]

Weber's discussion of sects in early twentieth-century America suggests, moreover, that his observations indicate sociocultural development along very secular paths. In terms of modern sociological interests his insistence on sect membership as a vehicle of interpersonal certification evokes considerations which have centrally to do with the concept of identity. Sect membership, as presented by Weber, constituted a form of social identification.[60] The information-saving function that some sociologists now accord the concept of identity overlaps with Weber's notion of certification. The point that we wish to make, then, is that in a very important respect some, perhaps the vast majority, of Weber's sociology-of-religion insights and findings are not most appropriately pursued now in sociology-of-religion terms. A clear exception to this prescription would, of course, be sociological studies of a definitely historical nature – studies which focus on religious phenomena when those phenomena were still clearly religious in character, and not like so many phenomena in the contemporary world (for Weber) secular emanations or outcomes of religious developments. In that perspective a major research program would fruitfully be guided by the questioning of the degree to which past periods were as religious as conventional (including Weberian) wisdom has it.[61] There has been a diffuse tendency among many of those who have debated the various facets of the modern secularization thesis to question both the extent of the religiosity of the past and the areligiosity of the present. That involves in effect a quite profound scepticism about Weberian historiography; and we would be in a much better position to sift Weber's sociology as a whole (not merely his studies of religion) were we to settle on a more solid perspective in that respect.

When we consider Weber's refusal to countenance the idea that the development of the spirit of capitalism (or even of the religious groups that according to him initiated it) could be accounted for in terms of the structural marginality of various forms of Protestantism, in comparison with his almost equally strong insistence that the cultural patterns and structural features of modern societies (which had in significant part been produced by previous 'theological elaboration') were non-religious, the need for re-examination becomes particularly acute.[62] The various forms of functionalism which have developed in the sociology of religion have clouded this desideratum – for the erection of definitional signposts pointing toward man's 'ultimate concerns' as the centerpiece of the study of religion has tended to make religion a 'non-variable'.[63] That is to say, since all men and women (individually and collectively) are deemed to have ultimate concerns (which constitute 'religion') in equal proportions there can be no serious problematic concerning degrees of religiosity. There are signs that this tortuously expressed standpoint is on the wane, and that energies are at least being reallocated in the understanding of the ways in which 'ultimate concerns' are expressed. This does hold out promise for a serious study of the modes of transformation of the 'higher' forms of substantive culture – higher in the sense of being presumptively the most profound and impactful.

Thus, in spite of our earlier suggestions concerning the affinity between certain characteristics of the modern study of religious sects and the interests in such expressed by Weber, we must insist that Weber himself was basically interested in a vast and complex range of issues centered upon the cultural foundations, cultural trends and forms of consciousness of modern society. More specifically, his concerns might be called *microcultural*, in the sense that it was the dynamics of the link between culture and the individual, including the nature of identity, which was his leading preoccupation.[64] However, Weber did not directly address the problematic of conversion, which is clearly central to such a microcultural focus – a matter to which we return in a later chapter.

The Protestant Ethic thesis and the deployment of the church/sect distinction were intimately connected in Weber's work, to a degree which has been greatly neglected among those who have interpreted and/or claimed to use his ideas. The separation of the two themes has probably led to a more intensive exploration of each than would have been the case had they been developed as an integral whole. On the other hand, lack of attention to their interdependence has amplified neglect of Weber's leads with respect to such themes as processes of identification and the sociocultural bases of the modern conception of conscience and modes of consciousness.[65] Nelson cogently argues that 'Weber had a deep insight . . . into the central importance of the conflict between "universalism" and "particularism" posed by the Deuteronomic commandment on usury and its odyssey in the Christian West.'[66] In these terms Nelson grasps a trajectory of Weberian thought which has hardly been touched by sociologists of religion. Speaking specifically of the history of Christian Europe, but nevertheless directing his thoughts much futher, Nelson argues that 'the *makings* of cultures [are] the *makings* of minds working with *mechanisms of conscience* in its multiple senses – its formalized canons, arguments, justifications, criteria, and reasons'. The key summating term which Nelson uses is that of *matrices of decision*[67] – a phrase which resonates with Weber's concern with authority, legitimacy, ethics and laws – above all with action.[68]

Such then are some of the major features of Weber's work on the church/sect theme. If we ask whether in a more general sense – that is, more general than Weber's specific interests – we have progressed with respect to our comprehension of types of religious collectivity, in terms of the relationship between social vehicles of religiosity and the settings in which they arise and persist, the answer must surely be in the affirmative. In particular, since the time of Weber and Troeltsch we have gained empirical knowledge and sharper analytic tools in two interdependent spheres of inquiry. First, exploration of the relationship between doctrine and polity has facilitated a much more sophisticated appreciation of variability in the degree to which religious sects are insulated from or vulnerable to external circumstances. In Weberian terms this variability can be expressed as having to do mainly with types and degrees of inner-worldliness and the idea that there are varieties of paths and directions toward 'salvation' within the Western religious complex. Second, recent work – both empirical and analytic – has led to refinement of the either/orness of the Weber-Troeltsch distinction. Both Weber and Troeltsch were clearly aware of such need for refinement. In particular the concept of the denomination as a major type of collectivity (in terms of religion/society relationships) has been increasingly seen as a modality involving differentiation of the religious from non-religious roles.[69] That is obviously very relevant to Weber's ideas concerning the autonomy of rational-legality *vis-à-vis* its original religious base. The denominational type of collectivity as presently characterized thus helps us to focus a Weberian puzzle: Does the secular autonomy of the work ethic involve the entire demise of the religiously-cast notion of work as God-ordained? Does formal rationality triumph over substantive rationality?

Secularization and Theodicy

Seen in this light it becomes apparent that, even though many individual themes have been taken from Weber by sociologists of religion, 'Weberian' sociology of religion has a slender base. In one sense this is not surprising. Nor is it in an even more important sense possible for there to be a Weberian sociology of modern religion. Weber himself declined to delimit the sphere of religion and yet all of his writing on trends in the modern era suggest strongly that 'religion' was unimportant. Secularization was taken for granted. Those central features of the modern world that had sprung from a religious matrix – which meant virtually all of them (as much for Weber as for Durkheim) – had attained autonomy, their own logic of change.[70] Yet, and the caveat is crucial, the phenomenal grounding of action in the modern world remained highly problematic for Weber. For all his talk of types of rationality and processes of rationalization, Weber lacked a systematic conception of types and trajectories of rationalization – even though he analyzed processes of rationalization in several societal spheres.[71]

Weber did, nevertheless clearly, recognize that there were in modern societies what Hill has called an 'incipient source of conflict' between substantive and formal rationality – between the values of democracy and the logic of bureaucracy, between conceptions of substantive justice and legal formalism, and so on.[72]

Thus the problem of rationalization at the level of *Wertrationalität* suggests a genuinely Weberian *Problemstellung*. On the other hand, it can be said that Weber himself evaded that issue, or at least remained highly uncertain on the question. Another, we believe more viable, interpretation has to do directly with Nelson's conception of matrices of decision. Speaking in his essay, 'Religious Rejections of the World and Their Directions', of the triumph of 'the cosmos of natural causality',

Weber argues that 'the intellect . . . has created an aristocracy based on the possession of rational culture and independent of all personal ethical qualities of man'.[73] A central feature of the modern condition, at least for 'the most modern' within it, is that of senselessness – 'if this cultural value is to be judged in terms of its own standards'. The ontic pivot of senselessness and that which is most alien to religious thought is the senselessness of death, which 'has seemed to put the decisive stamp upon the senselessness of life itself'. In contrast to the peasant, the feudal landlord and the warrior hero (which are the particular examples cited by Weber) modern 'cultivated' man striving for self-perfection has no natural life-cycle. Modern man – or at least modern 'cultivated man' – cannot absorb all of the available culture, he can only select from different cultural spheres. (That is a theme which ran through much of the work of Weber's associate, Simmel.) He is unable, then, to become what Weber calls 'satiated with life' – he can only become 'weary of life'. 'There is no guarantee that this selection has reached an end that would be meaningful to him precisely at the "accidental" time of his death. He might even turn his back to life with an air of distinction: "I have enough – life has offered (or denied) all that made living worthwhile for *me*." '[74] Speaking still of the unfolding of inner-worldly attitudes, Weber argues (in a way that echoes much nineteenth century, particularly Marxian, thinking about the alienative quality of culture) that all culture can appear as a form of freeing man from the natural life cycle (a circumstance re-presented in Bellah's suggestion that life has come to be regarded as an infinite possibility thing).[75] Culture becomes increasingly, on the other hand, in Weber's view burdened with guilt: it is 'a locus of imperfection, of injustice, of suffering, of sin, of futility'. The devaluation of life implicated in such circumstances calls forth a 'salvation' response of an other-worldly kind – a response, says Weber, which is '*more alienated* from all structured forms of life . . . by confining itself to the specific religious essence'.[76]

Weber thus 'puts down' religion (as indeed he does with respect to youthful quests for meaningfulness in 'Science as a Vocation'). In spite of his declining to define 'religion' in his comparative historical studies he, like many subsequent social scientists, tended on occasions to use 'religion' as a pejorative term. Religion, in almost Marxist terms, becomes a form of alienation. As in Marx – and indeed in a very different sense in Durkheim – religion, for Weber, had done its historical work. For Marx (but even more so for Engels) the historical role of religion had been in the broadest sense political; it has been the culturally available means for the expression of needs and desires. For Durkheim religion had facilitated – had been the historical basis of – reflexiveness and logical thought. For Weber religion had been historically about the problem of meaning – but in a special sense, that modern Weberians would do well to examine in more detail than is possible here. One critical issue is that it is only certain categories of social individuals, under specific social-structural conditions who are liable to have a problem of 'general' meaning. For Weber the problem of general meaning (what is life, terrestrially and cosmically about and for?) could only be cultivated 'among strata who are economically carefree'. The development of mystical tendencies in Western-type contexts is doomed to failure, says Weber in one crucial passage, because 'in the midst of a culture that is rationally organized for a vocational workaday life, there is hardly any room for the cultivation of acosmic brotherliness. . . .'[77]

Such statements lead directly to consideration of the extent to which modern life is rationally organized for vocational work in such a way as preclude ongoing, viable concern with problems of what we have here called 'general' meaning. That question will be looked at more fully in the next chapter. Here we may note that Weber seems to have believed, in an almost Calvinist manner, that the busy-ness of modern life precluded preoccupation with the *raison d'être* of life and death;[78] except, that is, for the 'economically carefree'. The latter idea Weber generalized to the point of arguing that 'in keeping with the law of marginal utility, a certain concern for one's own destiny after death generally arises when essential earthly needs have been met. . . .'[79] This, of course, raises the whole question of the degree to which release from preoccupation with 'essential earthly needs' is so widespread in many modern societies that the category 'the economically carefree' has come to be applicable to a majority of the population. Certainly, the recent concern with death and dying in widely-purchased books and other mass media, as well as in the thanatological interests of medical experts, psychologists and sociologists, suggests that Weber's views need to be re-examined. In haste, it must be added, however, that the modern concern with death and dying appears to constitute a rationalization of thanic concerns – a systematic planning for death. Thus in an important respect a problem of general life-meaning becomes an object of rationalization. However, the fact that we can contain this phenomenon of planning for, and attempting to accept the facticity of, death within Weberian terms does not obviate the proposition that in modern life the problems of 'ultimate reality' are receiving much attention.

In Weber's terms the problem of meaning had been 'solved' in primitive societies simply because it did not exist. (Those who presently speak of the restoration of meaning as if individuals in primitive and traditional societies led or still do lead 'meaningful' lives would do well to grasp this.)[80] In the historic societies, the societies of the world religions, there were various theodical 'solutions' to a specific range of problems of meaning. Broadly speaking, one can discern in the overall context of Weber's work an emphasis upon two major categories of general meaning problems – those, on the one hand having to do with injustice and suffering, and those, on the other hand, which relate to the *raison d'être* of life itself and the connection between the life-cycle of individuals and the course of history. It is the former that have mainly to do with theodicy. The major – that is the most rational – solutions to the theodical problems in broad historical perspective were dualism, predestination and that which 'was peculiar to the religiosity of Indian intellectuals'. The latter Weber heralded both for its consistency and its 'extraordinary metaphysical achievement'. It combined 'virtuoso-like self-redemption by man's own effort with universal accessibility of salvation, the strictest rejection of the world with organic social ethics, and contemplation as the paramount path to salvation with an inner-worldly vocational ethic'.[81] In effect it cuts across both Weberian categories of sociocultural meaning.

Acknowledging fully that Weber stressed the confinement of such a world-view to a particular stratum and also his emphasis upon the proliferation of symbol spheres and associated societal sectors in modern societies as making it extremely difficult for modern man to obtain such cognitive totality, there still remains a puzzle. Why did Weber not confront fully the possibility of new and diverse forms of theodical solutions and/or 'rational metaphysics' in modern societies? Why was such an idea seemingly rejected? Of course, the premature death of Weber always compounds problems of interpretation. But the fact remains that on the whole the comments he made about the cultural trends of his own time were very much of the negatively critical type. Thus part of the difficulty here inheres in Weber's ever-present concern with rationality and his lack of serious interest in aspects of Western development that evidently were not part of the positive mainstream of historical rationalization. On the other hand, as we shall see, we may find clues to this problem in more personal aspects of Weber – characteristics of his personal-intellectual quest that have substantive sociological implications.

Berger argues that 'the illiterate peasant who comments upon the death of a child by referring to the will of God is engaging in theodicy as much as the learned theologian who writes a treatise to demonstrate that the suffering of the innocent does not negate the conception of a God both all-good and all-powerful'.[82] In contrast to such a view we should note that Weber said relatively little about what we now often call the 'everyday life' of the individuals and groups to whom he was referring in his studies of religion – except in the respect that he interpreted the life of the Calvinist in terms of what their life must psychologically have been like, given what we 'know' about their 'official' religious beliefs and 'their' socioeconomic circumstances. (But when addressing Islamic predestination beliefs he engages, for no clearly stated reason, in a different kind of reconstruction.)[83]

Insofar as the theme of theodicy is still part of the sociology of religion and of sociology in the large, we can see that its presence simultaneously confirms and denies Weber. Confirmation is witnessed in the ease with which the very invocation of the term resonates with 'Weber-centricism'. Denial occurs, obversely, in the failure to celebrate a Weberian problematic. The fact is we know little about the phenomenal structure of 'mainstream', as opposed to relatively sectarian theodicies of the modern world. The theodicies and theodical 'solutions' about which we do know quite a great deal, therefore, are of a kind which a modern Weberian would probably find of only marginal interest.[84] The one major proviso that we would enter is that if Bellah's characterization of the modern world – particularly the late twentieth-century U.S.A. – as being phenomenally regarded as a site of 'infinite possibility' has more than rhetorical viability, the distinction between sectarian and mainstream breaks down. That scenario suggests the dictum: 'we are all sectarians now'. The proliferation of 'new' religious, therapeutic and 'life-guide' doctrines in recent years is in part confirmative of the scenario. Continuing research of the kind initiated by Bellah is clearly very relevant to problems pointed up by Weber.[85]

In an oblique respect some elements of stratification theory touch on the theodicy issue, particularly where the focus is upon the notion of distributive justice; but that kind of study rarely gets into either the significance of 'big' idea systems or the microculturality of stratification systems (that is, the operation at the level of individuals of particular phenomenal theories of stratification).[86] It is something of a sociological tragedy that although Weber's work on what we now call social dimensions of stratification has directly or indirectly been so highly influential in modern sociology, the cultural aspects of stratification which Weber pursued even more thoroughly have rarely been central to the work of stratification theorists.[87]

Before we can come to terms with the nature and structure of theodicies and theodical solutions in the modern world much has to be done in order to obtain more analytic consistency than that which Weber reached. The need for such does not, we emphasize, arise simply from the fact that Weber himself was clearly inconsistent on this matter, but also, as we have in part already suggested, because there are a number of features of the modern world which emphatically require analysis in terms deriving from the study of theodicies. After all, we owe to Weber much of our modern conceptual apparatus for discussing such themes as authority, legitimacy and the like; and although Weber did not get very far in linking the theodicy issue to these matters of *Realpolitik*, our reading is that in the general overview of Weber's work the 'soft' themes deriving from his study of religion are intimately connected to the 'hard' themes of politics and economics. To be sure, all sociologists – from undergraduates upwards – know that Weber linked these 'soft' and 'hard' themes in *historical* contexts, notably in *The Protestant Ethic and the Spirit of Capitalism*, but few seem to recognize their connections at the conceptual level, as part of a battery of analytic tools. And even if Weber himself did not in any sustained manner link theodicy to modern stratification or to authority and power; or did not fully connect his own great historical interest in casuistry and conscience to his observations on the sociocultural pluralism of the modern world – even if these, and other such relationships, are not to be found in detail in Weber's work we must surely note the 'elective affinities', and use them as best we can.

The most insightful comment on Weber's work on theodicies has been presented by Obeyesekere, mainly in reference to Weber's essay, 'Theodicy, Salvation and Rebirth'.[88] There are, as Obeyesekere notes, at least three senses in which Weber used the concept theodicy. First, Weber employs the term in its classic sense – deriving from theology and precipitated into general use by Leibniz in the early eighteenth century – as meaning a vindication of God's providence in view of the existence of evil. Second, Weber uses the term 'to refer to the existential need to explain suffering and evil'.[89] Third, he speaks of theodicy as the resolution of such existential needs in moral terms. The first and second uses differ in that one pivots on God, while the other refers to suffering as such. The third use is clearly out of line with the first and second – in that it is concerned with theodicy as a form of coping with a strain, whereas the first two refer to strains requiring a form of coping (in the one case a satisfactory form of vindication of God's omniscience, omnipotence and benevolence; in the other, an adequate legitimating account of evil and suffering). More specifically, the disjunction between the first and third senses is, as Obeyesekere argues, particularly acute: 'In sense (*a*) *karma* cannot result in a theodicy; yet according to Weber, *karma* is one of the theodicies (*c*).'[90] Moreover Weber also sees monotheism as a rationalizing resolution of theodicy at some points in his work. Indeed he seems to argue that whereas Islamic monotheism created a need for theodical resolution which never yielded a satisfactorily rational theodical solution, Calvinism constituted a rational theodical solution by virtue of its extreme monotheism.[91]

Aside from Weber's weakness in the area of cross-cultural methodology (which we noted at the beginning of this essay), we can again see in these ambiguities and inconsistencies Weber's problems concerning his encapsulation in the main trajectory of Western history, which provided his 'window on the world'. Thus when he analyzed non-Occidental contexts a different conception of theodicy appears in Weber's work, based on the universal need to account for suffering as such, rather than suffering in relation to *God's* existence.

These matters are crucial in coming to terms with the relevance of Weber's sociology of religion to modern sociology. They have of course to be cleared-up simply in order for historical sociologists to study the past and anthropologists to study 'their' present. But as far as modern societies are concerned, the danger arises that partly because of Weber's inconsistencies and partly because of the failure to appreciate the general-theoretical significance of Weber's studies of religion, we will neglect to study personal and cultural rationales, and fail to comprehend modes of accommodation to stress as genuine sociological problems – problems that to date have been sequestered on a fragmented basis in such sub-disciplinary areas as the sociology of deviance, the sociology of religion, the sociology of (ideological) politics, and so on. Perhaps the resurgence of interest in life-cycles, death, ageing and the more diffuse phenomenon of 'identity voyages' signals another set of substantive opportunities to place the theodical and salvational issues that Weber raised firmly on the sociological map.

One of the most revealing of all passages in Weber's work is to be found in his essay on theodicy:

In one form or another [the problem of theodicy] belongs everywhere among the factors determining religious evolution and the need for salvation. Indeed a recent questionnaire submitted to thousands of German workers disclosed the fact that their rejection of the god-idea was motivated, not by scientific arguments, but by their difficulty in reconciling the idea of providence with the justice and imperfection of the social order.[92]

Thus Weber thought that 'the problem of theodicy' was, at least in

Christian contexts, the matrix from which sprang the demise of religion itself. If we place that proposition alongside Weber's theses concerning 'the modern proletariat's . . . consciousness of dependence on purely societal factors' and the supplanting of religion by 'other ideological surrogates' we can reasonably entertain the interpretation that Weber conceived of the idea of *the secularization of theodicies* and theodical solutions.[93] Although Weber himself did not integrate the concepts of theodicy and salvation – in spite of their frequent proximity in his essays on religion – such has clearly to be done before we can accomplish much along the lines indicated here. In turn, there is no doubt that such cannot be accomplished without attending to the problem of change at the level of substantive rationality.

Meaning

As vast numbers of sociologists have emphasized 'meaning' lay at the heart of Weber's sociology and of his life-philosophy generally. We should recall that Weber tied meaning very closely to his delineation of action. In fact 'meaning' tended only to make sociological sense for Weber in reference to its actional significance. And, *vice versa*, action was constituted, in contrast to mere behaviour, by its subjectively meaningful significance. For a number of schools of sociology Weber's emphasis upon subjective meaning has not simply been unproblematic, it has been unequivocally stamped with approval as being the paradigmatic form of interpretive sociology. Unfortunately what Weber meant by meaning has not been adequately discussed by Weber *aficionados*. The major exception is the critique offered by Schutz and subsequent elaborations of Schutz's work. Weber did not, as Schutz rightly argued, excavate the foundations of social knowledge and the phenomenal attribution of meaning.

There is no doubt that, in Parsons' words, 'Weber postulates a basic "drive" toward meaning and the resolution of . . . discrepancies [between normative expectations and actual experiences] on the level of meaning, a drive or tendency which is often held in check by various defensive mechanisms, of which the pre-eminent one [relevant to his sociology of religion] is that of magic.'[94] Meaning for Weber had, then, very much to do with making sense of sociocultural circumstances, with a heavy emphasis upon cognitive coping with the contingencies and exigencies of such – as developed in his work in terms of the concept of rationalization. Weber also sketched empirically a path leading from

primitive states of magic and ritual, where, as Parsons puts it, the quest
for meaning was 'held in check', to a highly modern, intellectualist
situation in which a *Sinnzusammenhang* (meaning complex) became, so
to speak, autonomously generative of quests for meaning.[95] This is the
circumstance, indicated above, in which culture becomes radically
divorced from man's organic life-cycle.

Weber clearly held to what we call an intellectualist position in
relation both to 'everyday' action and experience and to general cultural
change. In order that we may avoid exaggerating this interpretation we
may invoke Bendix's attempt to temper this tendency in Weber's work:

Weber did not ignore the fact that a great deal of human behaviour is
inconsistent or unreflective. He was fully aware that men seldom articulate their
principles with the kind of 'last-ditch' consistency that he expected of himself
and that he thought necessary for conceptual clarity. He also knew that in
ordinary life men do not examine the usages in which they persist by
'unreflective imitation.' But he wanted to emphasize that his sociology would
deal with men as 'cultural beings' and that much of what men in a society take
for granted even in their most routine behavior actually involves basic beliefs
and assumptions without which they cannot function. *In his sociology of religion he
set himself the task of formulating clearly these underlying principles and assumptions.*[96]

If, as we believe we should, we accept Bendix's summation, an
important set of issues is opened with respect to the relationship between
putative Weberian sociology of 'religion' and other kinds of inquiry
into 'deep cultural' phenomena. For a start, we are presented with the
idea that all men and women operate in terms of basic beliefs. But how
and in what sense is this accomplished? The form in which that idea was
mediated to modern sociology by Parsons was not Weberian, as Parsons
himself has freely admitted. It was Parsons' criticism that Weber lacked
an adequate conception of total action systems, which view led
eventually to Parsons' conception of cultural systems being conceived
cybernetically, as forms of controlling beliefs, values and symbols (with
values getting most analytic attention).[97] And it is this view which has
been the object of so much recent criticism. However, even though
Weber adhered to a more discrete conception of clusters of meaning
systems than that which Parsons subsequently erected, the fact remains
that Weber did see contentful beliefs and values of the 'doctrinal' type as
the principal ideational features of sociocultural life.

One very important exception to this judgement has to do with an
aspect of Weber's thought to which Eisenstadt has recently drawn
attention, centered upon Weber's concept of *Wirtschaftsethik*.[98]

Eisenstadt has embryonically developed that idea in terms of *codes*, most specifically with respect to the codal nature of continuities in tradition. Weber had considerable difficulty with, and has been criticized for, his conceptualizations of traditional action and traditional authority. Recent attention to continuities in tradition has highlighed relatively permanent features in the operation of societies and civilizations over very long periods of time. Thus aspects of Weber's work, ranging from the notion of status ethics to his typology of paths and directions to salvation, might appropriately be recast in terms which have nothing directly to do with doctrinal belief systems and contentful *Weltanschauungen*, but are seen to constitute sociocultural 'habits' with respect, for example, to modes of interpersonal interaction; perceptions of the locus of power in large and small collectivities; the handling of the relationship between self and society and so on. On that reading the differential development of doctrinal traditions – most notably in respect of the Occidental/Oriental divergence – so central to Weber's life-work takes on a somewhat different complexion; demanding in particular a 'codal', as opposed to a 'contentful' delineation of the historic starting points in the major trajectories of global change. Or, to put the matter in another way, the Weberian concept of tradition needs to be elaborated so as to carry connotations other than 'non-changeful' or 'change-resistant'.[99]

Weber was always at pains to contend that the content of a religious doctrine 'can never be treated as a simple reflex of the social position of its proponents (particular their *Interessenlage*)'[100] – but it seems that in veering so much towards 'theological elaboration' he failed to see, or at least to make clear, that there are bases of thought which have neither to be of the interest type nor of the cognitive-solutional type. In that respect the tradition of inquiry that issues from the interests of such French scholars as Durkheim and Lévy-Bruhl supplies a contrasting approach to the study of meaning (one which does indeed, to varying degrees, neglect cultural content).[101] This, by now heterogeneous, tendency involves paying unwavering attention to the social grounding of the ways in which men and women think, which in turn has, of course, important implications for the kinds of belief system to which men will be differentially attracted. This has been particularly well indicated by Swanson (in his attempt to show the social-structural underpinnings of the variation between immanent and transcendent religious doctrines) and Douglas (in her analysis of the relationship between social-structural variation and ritual).[102] Weber, according to Bendix, 'explicitly rejected the attempt to interpret social structures as wholes. . . . For him sociology was a study of understandable behaviour of individuals in society, and collectivities do not act.'[103] The point is not, however, whether societies or smaller collectivities 'act' but whether the structuration of social relations in itself has constraining effects of a cognitive nature; and conversely whether cognitive codes affect forms of structuration.[104]

Thus, at the very minimum, Weber's emphasis upon the doctrinal manner in which individuals rationalize (and we use this word deliberately to illustrate some leakage between Freudian and Weberian notions) their circumstances needs to be supplemented with analysis of the nature of their social relations in their own social context. (It is worth considering the point that in his discussions of Islamic and Oriental process of rationalization Weber did perhaps veer toward a use with quite close affinity to that of Freud.) The existence of a traditional culture plus a tendency for men to comprehend, to make sense of, their circumstances is simply not a sufficient set of beginning tools. We need to know more about the *how* – that is, how men think.[105] And this is precisely the kind of question that has been preoccupying some sociologists and social anthropologists for many years. Weber, unlike Durkheim, had a slender phenomenal epistemology upon which to build.

This is one of the reasons we may invoke in being sceptical of Weber's tendency to think that man always acts, however implicitly and unreflectingly, from basic beliefs. As we have said, we do not for a moment doubt that men and women act from premises; but that is not at all to say that 'big culture' is effectively the same in its impact for all subscribing individuals. Cultural resources are used in different ways by different people – and the notion of a free-floating cognitive-solutionism, motored by a concern with ethical consistency, is simply not sufficient to explain why men believe what they do and the way in which meaning is attributed to the world (cosmic or 'merely' terrestrial). Weber's general idea that religious innovations had typically arisen along stratificational lines but then, once elaborated, had rapidly diffused across such lines is certainly not sufficient for modern sociological needs – although it clearly remains a useful and influential analytic tack. The implicit theory of relative deprivation to which Weber adhered, particularly in his analyses of Western Christian developments, has certainly proven fruitful in many areas; but has tended in the hands of some social scientists to degenerate into tautology: what people believe is a consequence of their being deprived of that which they say they want. Weber's synthetic emphasis upon elective affinities   and   actor-interpretation-of-situation   certainly   absolves *him* from the charge of tautologous reasoning in that respect. Yet that same feature of his work is open to serious challenge. For he constantly asked the question: in the context of 'official' doctrine what are the kinds of meaningful interpretations that relevant individuals would accomplish in relation to their actual social situation? Nowadays a growing number of students of religious change pay equal attention to 'everyday' beliefs and study the relationship between those and 'big cultural' doctrines. It is only in such terms, for example, that religious-cultural change in Africa can be fruitfully studied.[106] This involves paying systematic attention to the closely related themes of the phenomenality of syncretism and conversion; major desiderata of modern sociology which will, unfortunately, not be met by cashing Weberian analytic checks.

Parsons is certainly right when he argues that for Durkheim religious ideas 'were in the main treated negatively'.[107] (Although we must never forget that Durkheim attributed an enormous primordially creative significance to religion.)[108] But in then implying that Weber addressed the problem from the actor's point of view of 'not merely *how* the world works, but *why* in a teleological sense' Parsons misleads us. To be sure, Weber did address the teleological issue and, moreover, he did equate 'whyness' with the problem of 'real' (or 'general') meaning. (*Why* is there suffering, death, and so on?) But, unlike Durkheim, Weber seemed not to think that *how?* questions were to do directly with the problem of meaning. Weber's use of the old German notion of the disenchantment of the modern world focused specifically on the proposition that in principle, all *how?* questions could now be answered and so the world was becoming meaningless. Belief that howness could be consummated eradicated whyness. Or, to put it another way, the demise of the question *why?* promised the demise of general meaningfulness.[109] That interpretation is closely related to the idea of the strengthening of formal rationality and the weakening of substantive rationality. It also needs to be said that there may well be a disjunction between, on the one hand, Weber's tendency to talk of the demise of *why?* meaning at the level of the 'general' *meaning of life* and, on the other hand his *defining action as a universal sociological category*. Action is meaningful by virtue of its teleological, means-ends nature, according to Weber. In this sense, *why?* meaning is ubiquitous; social action is only conceivable in terms involving the question *why?* Clearly, Weber had two senses of meaning in mind here; but he did not spell them out.

Weber's intolerance of inconsistency – in a sense his tendency, as pointed-up in Sartre's observation on Mauriac, 'to play God to his

characters' (an inbuilt trap of nearly all *verstehen* stances, from Weber
himself to modern phenomenology) – prevented him from seeing that
how? and *why?* questions could be phenomenally (that is to say
empirically-subjectively as opposed to 'ideal-typically') fused in modern
belief systems. The combination of the how? and the why? in various
embryonic scientific-religious movements of Weber's own time
(Spiritualism, Christian Science, Theosophy and the like) might have
provided the clue to empirical possibilities.

Bendix correctly notes that Weber had 'a reasoned conviction that
some conflicts among men are due to an opposition of ultimate values
that no amount of clarification can undo. . . . A man cannot consistently
adhere to more than one . . . system of belief and actions.'[110] How, then,
do we account for the phenomenon of syncretism? How do we account
for conversion? (Unless we were seriously to believe that men
completely switch belief systems in one moment – or to adhere in
discussing conversion only to the religious injunctions concerning
change of personality; being, that is, reborn, a subject upon which
Weber did dwell considerably.)

The situational application of beliefs developed in respect of why?
questions seems in Weber's view to have resulted over historical time in
the growing paramountcy of how? questions, the modern end-point of
inner-worldliness. The why? questions that inevitably arise in the
modern condition lack a coherent cultural base and are thus, in a sense,
arbitrary or mere reflexive quests for meaning, mounted against
prevailing howness and instrumentalism. (We should note that in *The
Protestant Ethic*, 1904–5,[111] Weber spoke more positively of the
possibility of 'new prophets' or 'a great rebirth of old ideas and ideals'.)
Comparisons and contrasts between Weber and Marx are called for in
this connection. Weber appears to have accepted Marx's brand of
historicism (in the Popperian sense) to the extent that industrial societies
are unique; and moreover, to have adhered to a more substantive
agreement with Marx, to the effect that what is sometimes now called
objective culture met its demise in advanced industrial societies. Of
course Weber flavored the situation very differently from Marx as far as
'evaluation' is concerned. And the contrast can be seen very much in
terms of their different attitudes towards the significance of work and in
their different conceptions of action. Marx, of course, saw work activity
as ultimately the most meaningful activity. In a complex argument –
which we will not reproduce here – Marx saw work in its potentially
socialist setting as intrinsically satisfying. Weber, on the other hand,
regarded industrial work as characterized by routine – and as far as

capitalist societies were at issue Marx and Weber agreed – in all modern types of society. Thus, for Weber, work-activity still left men open to the asking of why? questions, but without a solid cultural base. (Scientific work – notably social-scientific praxis – was very meaningful for Weber.) How? questions prevailed and for many led in their own logic to what for Weber was the futility of instrumental forms of self-realization.[112] Thus the crucial contrast between Marx and Weber pivots on the degree to which the quest for why? meaning is eradicable. For Marx such was clearly possible, in terms that suggest an intimate connection between phenomenal, everyday quests for meaning and the meaning of history. Marx, of course, saw the truly socialist society as consummative of the end of history. Man in that condition 'finds himself' and is no longer susceptible to alienative restlessness.

There remains a large cluster of problems in that stance, not the least being the problematic role of instrumental or administrative rationality in the Marxist scenario. And some of those relatively unaddressed questions are precisely those which worried Weber, finding crystalline form in the projection of inevitably-bureaucratic socialism. Weber and Marx differed fundamentally over the degree to which they conceived of the possibility – or the likelihood – of man being synchronized with his social-structural circumstances. Much of Weber's case was mounted on the nature and consequences of the disparity between what we often nowadays call, on the one hand, the ideal and on the other hand, the actual. The modern situation was seen by Weber as fragmented vertically and horizontally into series of conflicting ideals (relating to substantive rationality) and segmented actualities (governed by special-purpose modes of instrumental, or formal, rationality). Life was either a matter of routine or one of cultural restlessness. And it was in reference to that circumstance that Weber's emphasis upon meaningful action as a prescribed response or personal solution should be viewed. Again, as with many (probably the vast majority) of the concepts and sociological ideas of the classic sociologists, we have to regard Weber's themes and definitions as heavily tinged with, often grounded in, philosophic commitment. This is well-illustrated via the contrast that Weber made between the classic Puritan conception of (meaningful) calling and the modern condition under which a calling is imposed upon us, a 'calling' which tends to degenerate into habit. 'Genuine' action for Weber is defined as such by its meaning-full quality, a mode of conscientious, responsible transcending of the modern iron-cage. This tendency in Weber has often, of course, been noted in terms of his emphasis upon the charismatic breakthrough as the principal modality of sociocultural change (a form of the 'caesarial' conception of change). That has been the ground upon which the allegation of Weber's position as a precursor of decisionism and fascism has been rested. It is certainly not an interest of our essay to pursue that point, but it should and must be said that the position that Weber reached – better, the position in which through agonized reasoning and living he placed himself – has a very strong existentialist flavor. What Sartre says of Weber's friend Jaspers has more than passing relevance to Weber himself:

Between the two World Wars the appearance of a German Existentialism . . . corresponds – at least in the work of Jaspers – to a surreptitious wish to resuscitate the transcendent. Already – as Jean Wahl has pointed out – one could wonder whether Kierkegaard did not lure his readers into the depths of subjectivity for the sole purpose of making them discover there the unhappiness of man without God . . .

Jaspers, mute on Revelation, leads us back – through discontinuity, pluralism, and impotence – to the pure formal subjectivity which is discovered and which discovers transcendence through its defeats. Success, indeed, as an *objectification*, would enable the person to inscribe himself in things and finally would compel him to surpass himself . . . One will never go beyond pessimism; one will have a presentiment of reconciliation while remaining at the level of an insurmountable contradiction and a total cleavage.[113]

We do not need to assent to Sartre's motives or flavoring in order to see that the comment is applicable to Weber – notably in respect of such themes as the charismatic breakthrough in routinized circumstances and the consequent ambivalence about the death of religion, indeed the death of God. (Two of the German intellectuals whom Weber deeply respected – Nietzsche and Marx – become particularly relevant at this point; in that in applying Sartre's observation to Weber, instead of to Jaspers, we see the impact respectively of the notions of the death of God and praxial overcoming.)

It is remarkable – although perhaps still insufficiently emphasized – that so many intellectuals of Weber's period were preoccupied with meaning and in particular with what Ernest Becker called 'Real meaning',[114] an issue that had a number of critical ramifications. The relationship between analytic meaning and analyzed (or to-be-analyzed) meaning; the problem of relativism; the attainability of a secure Archimedean point for non-relativistic, non-encapsulated analysis – these and other associated matters commanded the baseline attention of Weber, Simmel, Lukács, Mannheim, Scheler, Jaspers, Wittgenstein, Husserl and many others. The proposed solutions – negatively or positively stated – veered off in many directions. What, however, virtually all of the German and Central European tacks had in common was their concentration on meaning as making cognitive or cognitive-moral sense. Nowadays 'meaning' and 'meaningfulness' cover not merely that phenomenon but also such aspects of life as the attributes of social relationships (e.g., 'to have a meaningful relationship'); personal attributes such as 'a sense of purpose': predictability; and so on. Clearly the notion of meaning has become exceedingly fuzzy, particularly in folk sociology. What in fact are often now called problems of meaning would more adequately be expressed as problems of being, of which problems of meaning – sensefulness – would be conceptualized as a subset.

Of the major intellectuals of the classic period only Durkheim and his associates were fully appreciative of this kind of idea. For they readily saw that what we now often call 'meaning' has very much to do, for example, with the quality and structure of social relationships. Weber's intellectualistic stance constrained him to overload problems of cultural meaning in pinpointing the 'troubles of the age' with the problematic nature of being. To be sure, as we have had occasion to remark, he clearly saw that much of the problem of cultural meaning derived from a lack of synchronicity in the life-cycle of individuals (and associated factors). He, like Marx and Durkheim, recognized that much of the problem of cognitive or cognitive-moral meaning arose from social-structural sources. But, unlike Durkheim, Weber did not explore positively the phenomenon of social integration in its 'meaningful' aspects, except obliquely via charisma and mystical belonging.

Some of Weber's characteristics in these respects may be attributed to his attitude toward ritual and his sharp distinction between magic and religion. Although he declined to define religion, we know clearly that one of its allegedly central features for Weber was its anti-magical nature. Closely related to these relevant attributes of Weber's sociology were his diffuse, negative image of tradition, and, we believe, his relatively negative attitude toward ritual. Parsons in fact argues that 'it may well be suspected that traditional action is the principal category in Weber's thinking where ritual is to be found hiding'.[115] He goes on to argue (not very convincingly) that there is a close affinity between the conceptions of Durkheim and Weber on the function of ritual; although there is no doubt at all that what Parsons calls 'Weber's focus of empirical interest' prevents our being conclusive on this matter. It was by reason of Weber's commitment to discerning paths and trajectories of civilizational change, with particular reference to the East/West differential, that he lumped together concepts such as magic, tradition, ritual and sacredness. The definition of the sacred as that which is unalterable, and the tendency to bind ritual with magic together cloud our vision of salient problems of modern sociological analysis; as do certain aspects of Weber's attitude toward mysticism.

We must emphasize strongly our recognition of Weber's analytic rationale. His main aim was to comprehend the evolution of Western societies in relation to other civilizational complexes. But those who would today deploy Weberian insights for purposes other than this would be well-advised to be wary in accepting Weber's delineations and associations. And even if the spirit of inquiry *is* Weberian in the sense of contributing to our understanding of sociocultural evolution, we would run a severe risk in blocking-off from our domains of positive empirical focus all that seemingly has to do with ritual, magic and the like in the Weberian senses. Weber conveys very successfully the idea that historically magical ritualism has constituted a closure on social action and human potential, whereas religion (particularly in the West) has constituted openness and a sense of unrealized, but realizable potential. However, as we have frequently remarked, "religion" for Weber had done its work (at least for the time being). Successive generations of sociologists have avoided the question that left Weber so puzzled. To be sure there has been much talk about 'ultimate problems' and the phenomenal need for individuals to take care of them. And some sociologists of religion have seen in the resurgence of interest in spiritual matters a return to religion. (Weber certainly anticipated such a development, but tended to regard it as out of the mainstream, to be symptomatic of the sense of unintelligibility of modern life.) Still others, in neo-Durkheimian mode, have elevated the idea of civil religion to the status of the sacred, focusing core of social life – that which constitutes the operative locus of meaningfulness, the attachment beyond-the-immediate.[116] It may well be that Weber would have eventually accorded that idea some significance. It is no accident that the idea of civil religion has found most modern favor in the U.S.A. and undoubtedly it rests in large part upon the related ideas of voluntariness (in the sense that America is basically a society of immigrants) and eschatological hope – two central characteristics of the Protestant-sect contribution to Western history emphasized by Weber. But that picture in the later part of the twentieth century will not suffice without further probing of the ways in which the life-cycles of individuals are maneuvered. The resurgence of interest in death (particularly in American society), involving what has been described as the increasing tendency to see death as 'a wall rather than a door', surely portends a constraint to establish relatively institutionalized (in this context, *ritualized*) forms of approach to death. In fact, the increasing attention being paid to the phenomena of ageing and old-age as a state in itself bear partial witness to just such a pressure.

All that we seek to establish here is that in the spirit of Weber's concern with meaning (including his preoccupation with theodicy and theodical solutions) such questions as those which we have skeletally indicated need to be more widely diffused in modern sociology, and the appropriate connections between heretofore separate subdisciplinary domains accomplished. But, on the other hand, the Weberian package of ritualism and traditionalism (given ultimate root in magic) still leads to an averting of the eyes from what men and women may actually be self-consciously devising. The *anti*-ritual religious tendencies that Weber discerned and tapped so brilliantly over the course of Occidental history have indeed been continued in our own time – as the recent history of Roman Catholicism amply demonstrates. But the modern demise of religiously-based ritual does not mean an end of ritual *per se*. Merton's elaboration of bureaucratic ritualism as a mode of adjustment of the rational-legality that so preoccupied Weber, long-ago sensitized sociologists to such a proposition. More profoundly, in the modern context some social scientists have begun to show us how important – if highly problematic – is the phenomenon of psychological and social-solidarity boundary maintenance in modern life.[117] In one important sense this is a distinctively Weberian theme, for as we have indicated the religious origins of 'brotherly love' were central to Weber's work; and, as Nelson has so cogently shown, represented for Weber a key aspect of the 'sociocultural march' toward universalism in the Western world. But in order to capitalize upon that grossly neglected aspect of Weber's sociology and history we have to revise, if not actually dispense with, his negative attitude toward ritual; and weave our modern knowledge of symbolic meaning into his theses. The study of particularity within universality needs to be studied with due sensitivity to the operation of ritual in modern life. Perhaps such can commence in terms of probing the degree to which Weber often used 'ritual' in the sense of 'legalistic'. We do know that Weber was greatly influenced by legal categories and ideas (as in his characterization of action in the teleological form of a means-ends schema; and in his emphasis upon the methodological connection between cause and meaning). Indeed what, under Merton's influence, sociologists of the modern period came to call (bureaucratic) 'ritualism' is best seen as a form of legalism. By way of contrast it is in an anthropological sense that we need now further sensitization to ritual in modern sociology.

Weber's orientation to meaning, meaningfulness and intelligibility is an extremely complex one – demanding much more attention than it has received either here or elsewhere. The core difficulty lies, as we have intimated, in the relationship between his analytic insistence upon meaningfulness as the centrepiece of sociological study (action as the basic unit of analysis) and his interest in the meaningfulness of the world (particularly the modern industrial world). It is in the latter respect, even more than the former, that Weber was an anti-positivist. Weber stands in a very unique position *vis-à-vis*, on the one hand, the phenomenological school as it became manifested sociologically in the work of Schutz and on the other hand, the logical positivists of the Viennese Circle. The microphenomenologists have cut meaning down to size and have made it a 'local' matter of small-scale, interactional negotiation. To be sure, Schutz's criticism of Weber concerning the latter's failure to detail the ways in which inter-individual meaning is established is legitimate – but on the other hand transsituational or 'external' meaning has been lost by most of modern sociological phenomenology and its offshoots. Weber's failure to coordinate his abstract conceptions of action-as-meaningful with his concrete studies of complexes of meaning is in a sense partly responsible for this – something for which, although in different terms, Parsons criticized Weber many years ago. The Viennese solution was, of course, to rule 'metaphysical' matters out of analytic court, as being not proper matters for scientific analysis (for some not 'proper matters' at all). Weber, of course, did not suggest that it was the task of social science to assess the validity of doctrinal or metaphysical systems (quite the opposite) – but they were undeniably for him central features of sociocultural life, demanding sociological comprehension in terms of their impact and their origins. Interestingly Weber's interest in casuistry and conscience overlaps with certain concerns of Viennese philosophy;[118] just as his observations on the cultural fragmentation of the modern world – the parceling-out of human life – overlaps the phenomenological concern with finite provinces of meaning. The spirit of Weber's preoccupations leads, however, to the comprehension and overcoming of – not the analytic celebration of – discontinuity and casuistry. The program initiated by Gerth and Mills in their discussions of symbol spheres and vocabularies of motive follows that lead.[119] As we have indicated, we doubt whether such a program can be adequately followed through without forceful use of Durkheimian ideas concerning the relationship between social structuration and cognitive style, nor without a greater sensitivity to the dynamics of symbolization. On the other hand, the latter kinds of thrust need to be enhanced in the directions initiated by Weber.

In the spirit of the quotations with which we began, we offer no summation or conclusion. We would only wish to emphasize one point. Historical sociology will continue to be inspired directly by Weber; but perhaps the most fertile aspect of Weber's work in relation to general sociology lies in seeing the sequences and divergences that were central to his quest to comprehend civilizational change as sets of variables for the analysis of modern societies; that is, in effect, to look for 'historical variations in the present'. We have in recent years learned increasingly of the dangers of drawing sharp distinctions between the allegedly traditional and the allegedly modern. Certainly considerable revision of Weber is necessary in order that we would be able to address systematically the modern 'equivalents' of traditionalism, magic, ritual, theodicy, mysticism and so on. But yet that would indeed be in the spirit of Weber's work; for he was most interested above all in the relationship between factors which are inhibitive of change and those which generate change.

Our aim has not in any sense been to mount a general critique of Weber nor to argue for Weberianism. The latter is, we have tended to argue, an elusive idea (in view of the openendedness of Weber's social science). The former would, at least for our present purposes, be self-defeating. This because Weber's relationship to his own products constitutes a large reservoir of very important sociological conundra. It might be said in comparing the two classic sociological giants that whereas Durkheim provided a coherent sociological program, Weber provided an incoherent set of problems? (The redundancy in the latter phrase is deliberate. Of course, problems are such by virtue of their appearing initially unintelligible.) Weber's inconsistencies in themselves provide an important set of sociological *Problemstellungen*. Weber's life and work persistently require us to address the relationship between the situational and the transsituational; between the material and the ideal; between 'the iron-cage' and the 'transcendental thrust'; between 'ordinary man' and Protean man and woman; between asceticism and mysticism and so on.

Finally, again we argue that Weber's sociology of religion is misinterpreted if modern sociologists see it as having to do directly and only with religion. We force empirical reality if we make certain

features of the modern world 'religious' in order that we can bring
Weber's insights and concepts to bear upon them. We forestall
wide-ranging analysis of matters of cultural change, new definitions of
identity and selfhood, codal continuities, and so on, if we think that what
was said of religion in the past has no relevance to 'the secular' in the
present and the future.

NOTES

1. The present essay is an updated and elaborated version of the
   author's presentation at the Lancaster Conference on Max Weber
   and Religion in 1970. It pursues in detail a small cluster of issues
   raised on that occasion.
2. Cf. Robertson, *The Sociological Interpretation of Religion*, op. cit., ch.
   2 and *passim*.
3. In particular, see Talcott Parsons, *The Structure of Social Action*,
   New York, 1949, ch. XVI; 'Introduction' to Max Weber, *The
   Theory of Social and Economic Organization* (edited Talcott Parsons,
   translated A. M. Henderson and Talcott Parsons), New York,
   1947, pp. 8–29; and 'Introduction' to Max Weber, *The Sociology of
   Religion* (trans. Ephraim Fischoff), Boston, 1963, esp. pp. lxiii ff.
   The centerpiece of the analytic-methodological critique of Weber
   implied here is his use of ideal types. Their mixture of 'sociologic',
   'psycho-logic' and empirical facts made it particularly difficult for
   Weber to operate consistently in cross-cultural exercises. They
   were neither strictly analytic nor strictly empirical. Moreover, they
   were heavily structured by an injection of Weber's own parametric
   assumptions revolving around the notions of rationality and
   rationalization. This means that all uses of ideal types in Weberian
   mode have to be carefully examined for the degree to which they
   embody such motifs. For detailed analysis of related matters, see
   Bruun, op. cit.
4. Which is a main factor in the claim that there has been no
   Weberian school of sociology, even though there are many who
   claim to start from Weberian premises. Cf. Julien Freund, *The
   Sociology of Max Weber* (trans. Mary Ilford), New York, 1968. Of
   course, some of the uncertainty about Weber's overall sociology or
   overall social science relates to the fact that his death came at a
   relatively young age and during an intellectually fertile period.
   That Weber had a program is *much* less in doubt than the question

of whether he had a general 'theory'. Cf. Benjamin Nelson, 'Max Weber's "Author's Introduction" (1920): A Master Clue to his Main Aims', *Sociological Inquiry*, 44(4), 1974, pp. 269–78.

5. Guenther Roth, 'Introduction to Max Weber, *Economy and Society* (trans. and ed. G. Roth and C. Wittick), I, Totowa, 1968, p. lxxi.

6. Ibid., p. lxxi ff.; George Lichtheim, *Marxism: An Historical and Critical Study*, London, 1961, p. 385; Joseph Schumpeter, *Capitalism, Socialism, and Democracy*, New York, 1962, p. 11; More generally see Anthony Giddens, *Capitalism and Modern Social Theory*, Cambridge (England), 1971, esp. Part 4. Cf. Benjamin Nelson, 'Weber's Protestant Ethic: Its Origins, Wanderings, and Foreseeable Futures', in Charles Y. Glock and Phillip E. Hammond (eds.), *Beyond the Classics?* New York, 1973, ch. 2.

7. Such comments certainly do not do full justice either to Marx's conception of the significance of religion or to that of Weber. Marx and Engels both accorded a creative, or a constructive, role to religion in the history of societies which subsequently became capitalized. On the other hand we will argue below that Weber was very much less appreciative of religion as a societal phenomenon than is frequently assumed by modern students of religion. For contrasting views on the degree of agreement between Marx and Weber see Giddens, op. cit., and Raymond Aron, *Main Currents in Sociological Thought*, II, New York, 1967, p. 262. For some provocative comparisons of Marx's and Weber's attitudes towards religion see Bryan S. Turner, *Weber and Islam*, London, 1974, especially ch. 11.

8. Some Weberists are often keen to decry the use of natural-scientific imagery in the work of Durkheim. It is interesting to note, therefore, that the term 'elective affinity' derives from chemistry. Goethe used it for the title of a novel, partly to indicate his concern with the relationship between choice and compulsion. See Victor Lange, 'Introduction' to J. W. von Goethe, *Elective Affinities* (trans. Elizabeth Mayer and Louise Bogan), Chicago, 1966, pp. v–x.

9. For a case of low-level differentiation which nevertheless manifests a degree of specialization, see Godfrey Lienhardt, *Divinity and Experience*, Oxford, 1961. One of Weber's major essays on this issue is his 'Gods, Magicians, and Priests', in Weber, *The Sociology of Religion*, op. cit., ch. 2.

10. Karl Marx, 'On the Jewish Question' and 'Contribution to the Critique of Hegel's Philosophy of Right', in T. B. Bottomore (ed.), *Karl Marx: Early Writings*, London, 1963, pp. 1–40 and 41–60.

Weber's affinity with Marx is brought out even more specifically in the latter's comment on Luther: 'Luther . . . liberated man from external religiosity by making religiosity the innermost essence of man. He liberated the body from its chains because he fettered the heart with chains', ibid., pp. 52–3.

11. *K. Marx and F. Engels on Religion*, London, 1958, p. 80. Comment by Marx in margin of manuscript of *German Ideology*, cited by editors of the Institute of Marxism-Leninism of the CCPSU, 1955.

12. See below, pp. 191 ff. Full realization of this lacuna I owe to Rainer Baum, although the theme arises in the work of Habermas. Systematic concentration upon patterns of cultural changes need *not* involve neglect of what Marx called 'activity' or what we might now call social-structural factors. Possibly, Weber's eagerness to avoid the charge of Hegelianism played a part in *his* seeming reluctance to get into this area of inquiry, although his brother, Alfred, had no such problems. (But there were other important factors – some of which we discuss later.) For a very relevant comparison of Popper and Kroeber with respect to the problem of *autonomous* cultural change, see Herminio Martins, 'The Kuhnian "Revolution" and its Implications for Sociology', in T. J. Nossiter et al. (eds.), *Imagination and Precision in the Social Sciences*, London, 1972, pp. 42 ff. See, more generally, David Bidney, *Theoretical Anthropology*, New York, 1967 (second edition), pp. xi–xii.

13. Roth, in Weber, *Economy and Society*, loc. cit.

14. Parsons, 'Introduction' to Weber, *The Sociology of Religion*, op. cit., p. xlviii.

15. Cf. Joachim Wach, *Sociology of Religion*, Chicago, 1944, pp. 341–70. Durkheim and his immediate school can in historical perspective be regarded from an objectivist standpoint as subscribers to a form of *Religionssoziologie*.

16. Georg Simmel, *The Sociology of Religion* (trans. Curt Rosenthal), New York, 1959.

17. Troeltsch quoted by Joachim Wach, *The Comparative Study of Religions* (ed. Joseph M. Kitagawa), New York and London, 1958, p. 8. (The significance of this remark was brought home to me by Ninian Smart, *The Sociology of Religion and the Sociology of Knowledge*, Princeton, 1973, p. 64.) Wach divided *Religionswissenschaft* into hermeneutics, the study of religious experience, and the sociology of religion. It is of the greatest importance to note that Wach and others focusing on the experience of religion insisted that one

had to 'know religion' before one got into comparative work. Weber said the *opposite*: Weber, *The Sociology of Religion*, op. cit., p. 1.

18. A number of works have highlighted the personal characteristics of Weber. We are only concerned with the latter here to the extent that they have *direct* relevance to the sociological problems that he tackled. Rather than seeing Weber's personal characteristics and the nature of his private relationships as shaping his substantive intellectual work, we prefer only to focus upon these when they can clearly be regarded as matters of categorizable sociological relevance. See, *inter alia*, Edward Baumgarten, *Max Weber, Werk und der Person*, Tübingen, 1964; Karl Jaspers, *Max Weber, Politiker, Florscher und Philosoph*, Munich, 1958; Marianne Weber, *Max Weber*, Heidelberg, 1950; Arthur Mitzman, *The Iron Cage: An Historical Interpretation of Max Weber*, New York, 1970; Martin Green, *The Von Richtofen Sisters*, New York, 1974. One of the most judicious and informative of such explorations is Donald G. MacRae, *Max Weber*, New York, 1974.

19. Weber's comments upon secularization and the closely related theme of disenchantment appear most frequently in his essays 'Science as a Vocation', 'The Protestant Sects and the Spirit of Capitalism', and 'Religious Rejections of the World and Their Directions' — being chs. V, XI, and XII of Gerth and Mills, op. cit. See also Max Weber, *General Economic History* (trans. Frank H. Knight), New York, 1961, esp. p. 270.

20. This is, of course, a large claim — one which cannot be adequately substantiated here. Operationally, the claim can be expressed by contending that even though many of the hundreds of items listed in Eisenstadt's bibliography of writings on the Protestant Ethic thesis are indeed inspired and guided by definite interests in religious and cultural change and the impact of such, there are even more scattered throughout the academic journals of the past thirty years that have no such inspiration or guidance. That is not to say in a Weberist fashion that they *ought* to be so inspired or guided. See S. N. Eisenstadt (ed.), *The Protestant Ethic and Modernization*, New York, 1968, pp. 385–400. Cf. Andrew M. Greeley, 'The Protestant Ethic: Time for a Moratorium', *Sociological Analysis* XXV, 1 (1964), pp. 20–33; and Richard L. Means, 'Weber's Protestant Ethic Thesis: The Ambiguities of Received Doctrine', *The Journal of Religion* XLV, 1 (January, 1965), pp. 1–11.

21. But see Robertson, *The Sociological Interpretation of Religion*, op. cit., pp. 189–90. For a suggestive critique of Weber on Islam that

emphasizes the social-structural variables invoked by Weber, see Turner, op. cit.

22. David C. McClelland, *The Achieving Society*, Princeton, 1961.
23. Max Weber, *The Protestant Ethic and the Spirit of Capitalism* (trans. Talcott Parsons), New York, 1930, esp. pp. 181–2. See also Max Weber, *General Economic History*, loc. cit.
24. McCelland, op. cit., p. 49.
25. David C. McClelland, 'The Achievement Motive in Economic Growth', in Bert F. Hoselitz and Wilbert E. Moore (eds.), *Industrialization and Society*, The Hague, 1963, p. 77.
26. J. Milton Yinger, *The Scientific Study of Religion*, New York, 1970, p. 390.
27. Roland Robertson, 'Theoretical Perspectives for Future Research in Comparative Civilizations', *Comparative Civilizations Bulletin*, Summer, 1974, pp. 9–13. Cf. the emphasis upon Weber's interest in *universal* history in Nelson, 'Author's Introduction', op. cit. Weber originally entitled the series of lectures published as *General Economic History*: 'Outlines of Universal Social and Economic History'.
28. Robertson, *The Sociological Interpretation of Religion*, op. cit., pp. 169–81; Eisenstadt in Eisenstadt (ed.), op. cit., pp. 3–45; Nelson, 'Weber's Protestant Ethic . . .', op. cit.; David Little, *Religion, Order and Law*, New York, 1969.
29. Weber, *The Sociology of Religion*, op. cit., chs. VI and VII. Cf. Talcott Parsons, 'Comentary on "Religion as a Cultural System"', in Donald R. Cutler (ed.), *The Religious Situation, 1968*, Boston, 1968, p. 693.
30. Robertson, *The Sociological Interpretation of Religion*, loc. cit. Interestingly, Weber seems to make a concession in this direction with respect to the nobility in Scotland and in France. ('Max Weber on Church, Sect and Mysticism', *Sociological Analysis*, 34, 2 (Summer, 1973), p. 143.)
31. See notes 28 and 29; Robert N. Bellah, 'Reflections on the Protestant Ethic Analogy in Asia', in Eisenstadt (ed.), op. cit., pp. 243–51. Cf. Stephen R. Warner, 'The Role of Religious Ideas and the Use of Models in Max Weber's Comparative Studies of Non-Capitalist Societies', *Journal of Economic History*, 30, 1 (May, 1970), pp. 74–87.
32. Nelson, 'Weber's Protestant Ethic . . .', op. cit., pp. 86–7.
33. See Roland Robertson and Burkart Holzner (eds.), *Identity and Authority*, Oxford, forthcoming.

Weber, Religion and Modern Sociology 95

34. Guy E. Swanson, *Religion and Regime*, Ann Arbor, 1967. (Of course, there have been debates among historians about Swanson's thesis and findings. For example, see 'Reevaluating the Reformation: A Symposium', in *The Journal of Interdisciplinary History*, I, 3 (Spring, 1971), pp. 379–446.)

35. Some of these matters receive further attention below. On codes and their relationship to Weber's conception of *Wirtschaftsethik* see S. N. Eisenstadt. 'The Implications of Weber's Sociology of Religion for Understanding Processes of Change in Contemporary Non-European Societies', in Glock and Hammond, op. cit., ch. 3; and S. N. Eisenstadt, *Tradition, Change and Modernity*, New York, 1973, pp. 133–5 and 320–7. On civilizational complexes see Benjamin Nelson, 'Civilizational Complexes and Intercivilizational Encounters', *Sociological Analysis*, 34, 2 (Summer, 1973), pp. 79–105.

36. For recent surveys of the history and present state of church/sect typologizing, see Robertson, *The Sociological Interpretation of Religion*, op. cit., ch. 5; and Michael Hill, *A Sociology of Religion*, London, 1973, chs. 3 and 4. See also Allan W. Eister, 'H. Richard Niebuhr and the Paradox of Religious Organization: A Radical Critique', in Glock and Hammond, op. cit., ch. 8; and Roland Robertson, 'On the Analysis of Mysticism: Pre-Weberian, Weberian and Post-Weberian Perspectives', *Sociological Analysis*, 36, 3, 1975, pp. 241–66.

37. Peter L. Berger, 'The Sociological Study of Sectarianism', *Social Research*, 21 (Winter, 1954), pp. 467–85; Peter L. Berger, 'Sectarianism and Religious Sociation', *American Journal of Sociology*, 64 (1958–9), pp. 41–4; N. J. Demerath III, *Social Class in American Protestantism*, Chicago, 1965; Benton Johnson, 'Do Holiness Sects Socialize in Dominant Values?', *Social Forces*, 39 (May, 1961), pp. 309–16; Benton Johnson, 'On Church and Sect', *American Sociological Review*, 28 (August, 1963), pp. 539–49. See also Roland Robertson, 'The Salvation Army: The Persistence of Sectarianism', in Bryan Wilson (ed.), *Patterns of Sectarianism*, London, 1967, pp. 49–105; and Stephen D. Berger, 'The Sects and the Breakthrough into the Modern World: On the Centrality of the Sects in Weber's Protestant Ethic Thesis', *Sociological Quarterly*, 12 (Autumn, 1971), pp. 486–99.

38. Weber, *Economy and Society*, op. cit., p. 1164. Cf. Robertson, *The Socioloigcal Interpretation of Religion*, pp. 95 ff.

39. David Martin, *Pacifism*, London, 1965. (See Roland Robertson

review of ibid., *British Journal of Sociology*, XVII (June, 1966), pp. 204–5.) Compare the radically different position of Bryan R. Wilson, *Magic and the Millennium*, London, 1973.

40. Ernest Troeltsch, *The Social Teaching of the Christian Churches* (trans. Olive Wyon), New York, 1931. There is little doubt that the simplicity of Troeltsch's presentation has been exaggerated. He did have an embryonic conception of the denominational form of religion and of what are often now called established or institutionalized sects.

41. Both Weber and Troeltsch thought that mysticism would be the dominant religious form among the educated strata in the twentieth century. Cf. 'Max Weber on Church, Sect and Mysticism', op. cit. For full discussion, see the next chapter.

42. Amitai Etzioni, *A Comparative Analysis of Complex Organizations*, Glencoe, 1961.

43. Paul M. Harrison, *Authority and Power in the Free Church Tradition*, Princeton, 1959. Cf. Kenneth Thompson, *Bureaucracy and Church Reform*, Oxford, 1970. The general historical background to this kind of issue is sketched in J. Milton Yinger, *Religion in the Struggle for Power*, Durham, NC, 1946.

44. For Weber on hierocracy see Weber, *Economy and Society*, op. cit., pp. 1164–6, 1118–81, 1190–1200. Cf. Vatro Murvar, 'Max Weber's Concept of Hierocracy', *Sociological Analysis*, 28 (Summer, 1967), pp. 69–84.

45. See in particular Bryan Wilson, *Sects and Society*, London, 1961; Wilson (ed.), *Patterns of Sectarianism*, op. cit.

46. H. Richard Niebuhr, *The Social Sources of Denominationalism*, New York, 1929. Cf. Eister, in Glock and Hammond (eds.), loc. cit. The idea is, however, very much older than that. See the following chapter.

47. For Weber on charisma, see particularly Weber, *The Theory of Social and Economic Organization*, op. cit., pp. 358–91. For the Christian-religious basis of charisma and the ramifications of this in Weber's work, see Hill, *A Sociology of Religion*, op. cit., chs. 7 and 8, esp. pp. 144 ff. See also Michael Hill, *The Religious Order*, London, 1973.

48. The most important correctives to the view that sectarian religion is simply a stance of the economically deprived have been advanced by Bryan Wilson in many publications.

49. Benjamin Nelson characterizes Weber's work as having overall significance in terms of its focus upon 'comparative historical

differential processes and patterns': 'Sciences and Civilizations, "East and West": Joseph Needham and Max Weber', in *Boston Studies in Philosophy of Science*, XI (ed. R. S. Cohen).

50. Parsons, 'Introduction' to Weber, *The Sociology of Religion*, op. cit.

51. Weber, ibid., ch. VII.

52. Weber, op. cit., p. 101.

53. Weber, 'The Protestant Sects and the Spirit of Capitalism', in Gerth and Mills (eds.), op. cit., p. 231.

54. Ibid., p. 307.

55. Ibid., p. 305.

56. Ibid., p. 307.

57. Ibid., p. 308.

58. Cf. Roy Wallis, 'Ideology, Authority, and the Development of Cultic Movements', *Social Research*, 41, 2 (1974), pp. 299–327.

59. See the six articles, three on Troeltsch and three on Weber, in *Sociological Analysis*, 36, 3 (1975).

60. See Burkart Holzner and Roland Robertson, 'Identity and Authority: A Problem Analysis', in Robertson and Holzner (eds.), op. cit., ch. 2.

61. Important beginnings have been made, *inter alia*, by Peter Laslett, *The World We Have Lost*, London, 1966; and Keith Thomas, *Religion and the Decline of Magic*, New York, 1971. See also David Martin, *A Sociology of English Religion*, London, 1967; and Martin, *The Religious and the Secular*, London, 1969.

62. Weber, *The Protestant Ethic and the Spirit of Capitalism*, op. cit., p. 40. Weber is actually very ambiguous on the respective priorities of what in his main essay (ibid.) he called 'the permanent intrinsic characer of ... religious beliefs', on the one hand, and the 'temporary external-historio-political situation', on the other hand. For more on this point see Robertson, *The Sociological Interpretation of Religion*, pp. 26–7 and pp. 169 ff.

63. It is particularly ironic that a work that heralds Weber's great modern relevance should be so un-Weberian in its delineation of religious phenomenon, i.e., Luckmann, *The Invisible Religion*, op. cit.

64. In that we do agree with Luckmann's argument about the interests of Weber and Durkheim being centered on *identity* (ibid.).

65. Cf. Benjamin Nelson, 'Self-Images and Systems of Spiritual Self-Direction in the History of European Civilization', in Samuel Z. Klausner (ed.), *The Quest for Self-Control*, New York, 1965, pp. 49–103.

66. Benjamin Nelson, *The Idea of Usury*, Chicago, 1969 (second edition), p. 237.

67. Ibid., pp. 230–1. See also pp. 239–45.

68. It is illustrative of Weber's very unique interest in the significance of different religious forms that he argued that 'the *consistent* sect gives rise to an inalienable personal right of the governed against any power. . . . Such freedom of conscience may be the oldest Right of Man . . . at any rate it is the most basic Right of Man.' (Emphasis added.) Weber, *Economy and Society*, op. cit., p. 1210. (Many of the movements *now* characterized as sects are very 'inconsistent'.)

69. See Talcott Parsons, in Parsons et al. (eds.), *Theories of Society*, Glencoe, 1961, p. 251.

70. One of the central differences between Weber and Durkheim was that the latter saw a 'smoother' continuity between religious and 'post-religious' culture. Moreover, that difference relates very closely to the restricted conception of tradition in Weber's work. Under a neo-Weberian influence the relationship between tradition and modernity was regarded in contrast terms. Had students of cultural, social and societal change paid more attention to Durkheim this by-now-obvious mistake would not have been made. See in partiuclar Emile Durkheim, *The Elementary Forms of the Religious Life* (trans. J. W. Swain), New York, 1961, pp. 462–78. Weber tended to regard the significance of charisma as breaking the bond of tradition; whereas for Durkheim there was no such catalyctic agency – which makes the Parsonian tendency to see an intimate connection between charisma and Durkheim's conception of the sacred very precarious. Cf. C. K. Yang, 'Introduction', to Max Weber, *The Religion of China* (trans. Hans H. Gerth), New York, 1964, p. xliii.

71. Although see his emphasis upon the other-wordly Indian theodicy in contrast to the inner-worldly Calvinist theodicy; and *The Religion of China*, op. cit., ch. VIII.

72. Hill, *A Sociology of Religion*, op. cit., p. 153. Cf. Jürgen Habermas, *Toward a Rational Society* (trans. Jeremy J. Shapiro), London, 1971, esp. ch. 6.

73. In Gerth and Mills (eds.), p. 355. Criticisms of Weber's intellectualist approaches to religion are offered in Robertson, *The Sociological Interpretation of Religion*, op. cit., esp. ch. 6.

74. In Gerth and Mills (eds.), op. cit., p. 356.

75. Robert N. Bellah, 'Religious Evolution', *American Sociological*

Review, XXIX (1964), pp. 358–74. Bellah seemingly regards the situation much more in a mode of approval, in contrast to Weber's negative attitude.

76. In Gerth and Mills (eds.), op. cit., p. 357.

77. Ibid.

78. On the repression of concern with death: Becker, *The Denial of Death*, op. cit.

79. Weber, *The Sociology of Religion*, op. cit., p. 140.

80. Consider, for example, Berger et al., *The Homeless Mind*, op. cit.

81. In Gerth and Mills (eds.) op. cit., p. 359. The details are in Max Weber, *The Religion of India* (trans. Hans H. Gerth and Don Martindale), Glencoe, 1958.

82. Peter L. Berger, *The Sacred Canopy*, op. cit., p. 53.

83. Rather surprisingly, in his critical survey of Weber on Islam Turner does not give attention to this problem.

84. Bryan Wilson has probably done more than any other sociologist to enhance our comprehension of modern *religious* theodices. See in particular *Magic and the Millennnium*, op. cit. (Wilson does tend to regard himself as a Weberian.)

85. The relative paucity of good anthropological materials in his time must, of course, be invoked as a small 'excuse' in noting Weber's insensitivity to actual, everyday life in the societies that he studied. However, it is clear that his interest was in the 'big' philosophic ideas. The critical literature is by now enormous. By way of example we note only: Yang's criticism that Weber failed to notice 'the drastic difference between Taoism as a philosophy and Taoism as a religion' (Yang, op. cit., p. xxxiv), and the related failure to note sectarian prophetic movements in Taoist history; and recent work on the relationship between Buddhism and so-called magical-animism – what Smart calls 'sub-Buddhism' (Smart, op. cit., p. 31). Generally this problem relates to Weber's inability to link heterodoxy to syncretism.

86. Cf. An important contribution which points the way to some degree: Stanislaw Ossowski, *Class Structure in the Social Consciousness*, London, New York, 1963. See also the work of Louis Dumont. Rawls' recent and much debated book on justice suffers from a lack of concern with Kantian theodical problems. John Rawls, *A Theory of Justice*, Cambridge, 1971.

87. Cf. Andrew Tudor, 'The Dynamics of Stratification Systems', *International Journal of Comparative Sociology*, X (September/December, 1969), pp. 211–33; and Roland Robertson, 'Toward the

Identification of the Major Axes of Sociological Analysis', in John Rex (ed.), *Approaches to Sociology*, London, 1974, ch. 5.

88. Gananath Obeyesekere, 'Theodicy, Sin and Salvation in a Sociology of Buddhism', in E. R. Leach (ed.), *Dialectic in Practical Religion*, Cambridge, 1968, pp. 7–40.

89. Ibid., p. 11.

90. Ibid.

91. Weber, *The Sociology of Religion*, op. cit., pp. 143–4. Cf. Turner, op. cit.

92. Weber, *The Sociology of Religion*, op. cit., p. 139.

93. Ibid., pp. 100–1.

94. Parsons, 'Introduction' to Weber, *The Sociology of Religion*, op. cit., p. xlvii. See also Parsons' editorial note at p. 89 in Weber, *The Theory of Social and Economic Organization*, op. cit. In addition see Parsons, *Essays in Sociological Theory*, Glencoe, 1954, pp. 208 ff.; and Parsons, *The Structure of Social Action*, op. cit., pp. 481 ff., 636 and 680.

95. Parsons in Weber, *Theory of Social and Economic Organization*, op. cit., p. 26.

96. Reinhard Bendix, *Max Weber: An Intellectual Portrait*, London, 1960, p. 273 (emphasis added).

97. That conventional critical interpretation of action theory is now much less viable. See, for example, Talcott Parsons and Gerald M. Platt, *The American University*, Cambridge, Mass., 1973, esp. pp. 423–47. See also Bellah, *Beyond Belief*, op. cit., ch. 15.

98. See Eisenstadt, 'The Implications of Weber's Sociology of Religion . . . , op. cit. See also Bert F. Hoselitz, 'Economic Development and Change in Social Values and Thought Patterns', in George K. Zollschan and Walter Hirsch (eds.), *Explorations in Social Change*, London, 1964, ch. 26.

99. The notion of *code* as applied sociologically is a tricky one. What we have in mind here is something akin to Simmel's use of *form*, a conceptual and methodological tool which Simmel used as an extension and modification of Kant's *a priori* categories.

100. Parsons, in Weber, *The Sociology of Religion*, p. xlv.

101. Cf. Robin Horton and Ruth Finnegan (eds.), *Modes of Thought*, London, 1973.

102. Mary Douglas, *Natural Symbols*, New York, 1973.

103. Bendix, op. cit., p. 269.

104. Weber did sometimes veer in such directions. See Weber, *The Sociology of Religion*, op. cit., p. 19.

105. And yet Weber's work on salvational paths and directions might be recast in that direction.

106. Conversion and cultural change in Africa is discussed in chapter 6.

107. Parsons, *The Structure of Social Action*, op. cit., p. 667.

108. On the difference between Weber and Durkheim in the explanation of religious beliefs see W. G. Runciman, 'The Explanation of "Religious" Beliefs', *European Journal of Sociology*, X (1969), pp. 149–91.

109. This complex issue is bound-up with Weber's insistence upon sociology dealing in explanation in both causal and meaningful (or intelligible) modes. However, those modes are to be seen not merely at the second-order level of sociological analysis but as part of first-order empirical reality. How? and Why? are not, of course, exhaustive of the dimensions of meaning. Philosophical discussion would be needed to go any further into this issue. For a recent survey see Thomas E. Hill, *The Concept of Meaning*, New York, 1971. Weber, unlike Durkheim, displayed little interest in symbolization. Cf. Raymond Firth, *Symbols*, London, 1973; Bellah, *Beyond Belief*, loc. cit.; J. O'Malley, *Sociology of Meaning*, London, 1973; and David Goddard, 'Max Weber and the Objectivity of Social Science', *History and Theory*, XII, 1 (1973), pp. 1–22.

110. Bendix, op. cit., pp. 270–1.

111. Weber, *The Protestant Ethic and the Spirit of Capitalism*, op. cit., p. 182.

112. 'One particular result of the methodical training of the total personality pattern is that the social and ethical quality of actions falls into secondary importance, while the religious effort expended upon oneself becomes of primary importance,' Weber, *The Sociology of Religion*, op. cit., p. 156.

113. Jean-Paul Sartre, *The Problem of Method* (trans. Hazel F. Barnes), London, 1963, pp. 15–16. MacRae (op. cit.) makes a similar point in an essay published after the present argument was completed.

114. Ernest Becker, *The Birth and Death of Meaning*, Glencoe, 1962.

115. Parsons, *The Structure of Social Action*, op. cit., p. 674.

116. See Bellah, *Beyond Belief*, op. cit., ch. 9. See also Robert N. Bellah, *The Broken Covenant*, op. cit.; and Parsons and Platt, op. cit., pp. 20 ff.

117. The literature on such themes is growing at an enormous rate. See Douglas, *Natural Symbols*, op. cit.; also Robert J. Lifton, *Boundaries*, New York, 1970. In particular see Baum's crucial notion of *diachronic solidarity*: Rainer C. Baum, 'The System of Solidarities',

Indian Journal of Social Research, XVI (1975), pp. 306–353. Cf. Leon H. Mayhew, *Society*, New York, 1971.

118. See Allan Janik and Stephen Toulmin, *Wittgenstein's Vienna*, New York, 1973, esp. ch. 2.

119. Hans Gerth and C. Wright Mills, *Character and Social Structure*, London, 1954, pp. 274–305. Cf. Peter McHugh et al. (eds.), *On the Beginning of Social Inquiry*, London and Boston, 1974, ch. 2.

Chapter Four

Inner-Worldly Mysticism: Before and After Weber

It would hardly be an exaggeration to say that Kant limited the rights of theoretical knowledge in order to be able to ascribe to practical knowledge infinitely more rights than had ever been ascribed to it.

Nicholas Lobkowicz

[Max Weber] pointed out the limits of empirical science in order to protect the *'existential'* freedom of the individual from the encroachments of the cogent. . . . Weber's determined separation of the sceintifically knowable from what belongs to the realm of personal evaluation aims at more than the contrast between the rational and the irrational which leaves the latter without light and responsibility. On the contrary, Weber's whole energies were directed at narrowing the sphere of the irrational. In a gigantic effort he attempted to gather all the light which reason provides and to focus it on the secret sources of our choices and decisions. Thus he pointed to the true freedom while engaging his whole strength in the service of the un-ending rational analysis.

Ernst Manasse

The practice of detachment for the sake of meditation need not be more than a stage in the training of the mystic; it does not imply that mysticism is quietism. One need not suppose that such detachment, or meditational practices in general, have an adverse effect on the other activities a person engages in. But the opposite need not be true either – that meditation improves one's performance in other respects (a piece of advertisement sometimes invoked in contemporary commercials in support of the practice of meditation). Of course, sitting quiet is always healthy in a society based upon strife. . . . But at a deeper level, all such questions can only be dealt with at a later stage of the exploration of mysticism. . . . (T)he view that mysticism is connected with passivity and/or irresponsibility is pure prejudice.

Frits Staal

As we have intimated, social scientists have only in the past few years begun on a wide scale to plumb the depths of Max Weber's extremely complex corpus of writings. As this enterprise proceeds one of the most compelling issues becomes that of the intellectual background of Weber's thought. Again, until quite recently thinking about this problem has been remarkably narrow and unimaginative. Aside from the much worked-over issue of Weber's relationship to Marxist thought, precious little has been done to probe the intellectual traditions and specific intellectuals who influenced his thought. At this time a few sociologists are indeed beginning to broaden our thinking in this respect. On the other hand, we have the impression that many think that Weber developed most of his concepts and his *Problemstellungen* from scratch. Thus within the sociology of religion many still apparently believe that motifs like theodicy, asceticism, mysticism, church, sect, disenchant-ment, inner-worldliness, other-worldliness, and so on, were either created or 're-created' by Max Weber — in the sense that he picked-up theological and philosophical terms and more or less totally recast and interconnected them at the conceptual level. While we would not deny for a moment the great originality of Weber both in terms of theoretical ideas and empirical generalizations, the fact remains that the vast majority of the concepts which he used and the *Problemstellungen* that he worked in reference to were absolutely central to German thought as the latter developed from the mid-eighteenth century onwards. Indeed that is in a sense too restricted a way of stating the point, in that — as we shall intermittently indicate in what follows — much older ideas, deriving particularly from ancient Greece, Rome and from sixteenth-century Lutheran contexts are to be found in Weber's work. This should not be surprising. It would be readily granted that each thinker has his precursors, that no man actually follows Comte's cerebral-hygiene maxim, and that only a miniscule number of intellectuals achieve what has been called an epistemological rupture. However, much appears to have been lost of relevance both to our understanding of Max Weber as a social scientist and, more important, our understanding of the modern world by the tendency to accord Weber the accolade of more-or-less total originality.

It is perhaps inevitable that any successful attempt to show the degree to which a man or woman was dependent upon his or her predecessors will lead to a diminution of his or her stature, especially when the stature is of the enormity of a man such as Max Weber. On the other hand, this may only be of short-run significance. Thus it may well be that after the dust has settled following exploration of the ways in which an intellectual was dependent upon his predecessors, the substance of his originality will be better understood. As things stand at present, little is explicitly known about the origins and background of Weber's work on culture and religion.

It must be emphasized, however, that only in part is it our particular concern to point-up the degree to which previous generations of German intellectuals had concerned themselves with problems similar to those which preoccupied Weber in his sociology, particularly in his sociology of religion. The more important thrust of the present discussion is to show how deeply embedded in a major – some would say *the* major – philosophical tradition has been the general theme of the problem of the relationships between contemplation and the empirical world.[1]* It is precisely around that issue that the *general* discussion of mysticism has largely revolved since at least the eighteenth century – while it can also be said that that problem was of absolutely central concern to much of ancient Greek philosophy and to the Neoplatonic philosophers. Cast in that light the discussion of mysticism has to be seen as not merely a sociology-of-religion problem, but also a problem, *inter alia*, of major concern to the sociology of politics and to the epistemology and methodology of science. Perhaps nothing better illustrates the argument that epistemology is necessarily bound-up with substantive images of phenomena than the theme of mysticism – for the latter has to do both with the terms under which knowledge is obtained and with the ways in which individuals and groups orient themselves to the larger collectivities of which they are social members. The relevance of mysticism to the perennial theme – particularly but not only in the German context – of the relationship between reason and reality; or, in different mode, to the relationship between subject and object, can from that standpoint be readily appreciated.

The emphasis which has here been put upon German intellectual thought should not be taken to mean that ours is solely an inquiry into 'the German perspective'. The recent revival in the study of German social thought, notably the revival of interest in Weber, Hegel, Marx and, to a lesser extent, Nietzsche and Simmel, plus the almost uninterrupted interest in Kant on the part of non-German scholars (as well as of course among German intellectuals) tempts us to believe that there is something of particular relevance to the understanding of the modern condition generally that can be gleaned from that tradition. Two closely related themes seem to be related to the revitalization of interest in the German tradition – notably in the U.S.A. – namely, the problem of the relationship between individual and society, and the question of the meaningfulness of life. In the German context these two themes have always, or nearly always, been extremely prominent. The connection between the two was sharply and dramatically manifested in the Protestant Reformation period, when the Lutheran reformation presented the problem of religiousness – and the more general theme of individual salvation – in terms of the rival claims of society and the individual. There is much to suggest – as we shall explore more fully in the next chapter – that the Lutheran *Problemstellung* has returned to haunt us, while it clearly has never left the German context. The Calvinist way of posing and solving the individual/society dilemma has of course seen an important explicit revival in recent years, centered upon the work of Bellah (in his theme of civil religion as a form of societal covenant), but the view permeating a number of the discussions in this book is that processes of individuation and societalization have gone too far to be able to speak facilely in Calvinist terms of covenantal relationships between individual and society. And in that connection it is of more than passing interest to note that it is to the more individualistic-mystical elements in the Anglo-Saxon tradition that Bellah himself draws attention – exemplified by his praise for the relevance of Blake as against the English and Scottish utilitarians.[2] In sum, one of the major reasons for being positively interested in the German tradition is that it has consistently addressed the problem of the relationship between individual identity and societal authority in the mode of their claims to meaningful legitimacy.

Hegel and Before

Hegel insisted that one of the unique – and, for him, advantageous – features of Lutheranism was that in the latter's sacrament of the Holy Communion (involving the conception of trans-substantiation) that which is external is absorbed. In contrast, in Catholicism externality is left as such, the subject thus having to accept that which is external on an entirely passive basis. In the Lutheran case 'the presence of God is of a purely spiritual sort, directly connected with the faith of the subject'. (For Hegel, in the reformed-church conception God is 'lowered to the prose of Enlightenment . . . and expresses a merely moral relationship'.) The notion of *unio mystica* – which Weber was later to employ on more than one occasion – may, said Hegel, indicate a union of the infinite Divine and the finite human such that it 'dissipates the human into the Divine'.[3] Summarizing Hegel's negative attitude toward the latter possibility, Fackenheim argues: 'Were this the case, Holy Communion would be an otherworldly experience which fled from rather than transfigured the world. . . . Such an otherworldly mysticism would be *confined* to the mystical experience; it would not be the climax of a cycle of cultic life. Rather than postmoral it would be amoral if not antimoral.'[4] Thus Hegel implied that Lutheran sacramental mysticism constituted a form of inner-worldly mysticism that could be regarded as the basis for both man's separation from as well as his union with God.

Hegel's attitude toward mysticism sets the scene for consideration of the ways in which that topic has typically appeared as a *Problemstellungen* in German thought. Mysticism can be seen as a bridge between – on the one hand – the finite, the particular and the subjective, and – on the other hand – the infinite, the universal and the objective. That is not to say that the mature Hegel embraced mysticism. Far from it, for if there was a mystical phase in Hegel's thought it was early and short-lived – notwithstanding the quite widespread tendency to attribute mysticism to the whole of Hegel's *œuvre*. While to some extent an understandable reaction, the latter view has failed to recognize that for Hegel the problem was to overcome, to transcend the subject/object dilemma. Thus what was important to him about different forms of mysticism was the degree to which they articulated a definite delineation of the finite from the infinite, the particular from the universal, the subject from the object. His position on that score comes out very clearly in his double-headed treatment of the idea of alienation. On the one hand, alienation consisted in the separation of object from subject; while, on the other hand, it consisted in the obliteration of that separation through an act of surrender on the part of subject in relation to object. Schacht has put Hegel's position on alienation very succinctly:

Alienation . . . is a condition which occurs when a certain change in a person's self-conception takes place. It is neither something one does nor the intended result of a deliberate action. One *finds* that the condition has come to exist. Alienation$_2$, on the other hand, is . . . something deliberate. It involves a conscious relinquishment or surrender with the intention of securing a desired end: namely unity with the social substance.[5]

It must quickly be emphasized that in his exposition Schacht is speaking specifically of Hegel's position in respect of the relationship between individuals in their particularity and the 'social substance', the latter being for Hegel that which is universal in the realm of interpersonal interaction among the people of the society in question. This way of thinking was employed by Hegel after his early more religious phase.

Around the very beginning of the nineteenth century he began to think that it was not religion but philosophy that had the capacity to re-establish the harmony that had been broken in mankind, strongly emphasizing at the same time that man's nature must be treated in terms of both its individuality and its unity with infinite life.

Weber was later to eschew ideas that the antimonies of which Hegel spoke so much could be overcome — at least not on a collective basis. Thus even though he was to retain some similar concerns about the dangers of other-worldliness, much of Weber's life's work was concerned with working-out a system in which a balance could be maintained between the individual and society — hence the oft-stated and accurate interpretation that he remains one of the most important theorists of the liberal state. However, unlike the vast majority of political liberals in relatively modern times Weber remained throughout his work very much concerned with the quality of life at the level of meaning of individual lives (but not explicitly, of course, in prescriptive mode). Hence the centrality of the notion of salvation in his work. In a major sense Weber attempted on a realistic, sociological basis to update and revitalize the Kantian mode of thought that had been rejected by Hegel, the Young Hegelians, and Marx and Engels.

Kant had gone to great pains to keep separate some of the main antimonies that Hegel sought dialectically to synthesize. Indeed, it was very largely in terms of reacting against Kant that Hegel worked. In general Hegel's project consisted in an attempt to reconcile synthetically the split between reason and reality. In particular, it was the wish to overcome the Kantian split between intellect and passion that sparked the Hegelian enterprise. (Other notable figures such as Fichte, Schiller and Schelling did, of course, play an important part in mediating Kantian problems to Hegel.) That split had been a *leitmotif* of Kant's work. The phenomenal realm of nature was determinate — made so by Kant's view that the human mind (the transcendental ego) imposed order upon nature — while the realm of the noumenal was the realm of freedom. For Kant the problems of theodicy were not soluble (they came to be regarded as soluble by Hegel and then, in different terms, by Marx) and the need for God as a necessary fiction was ineradicable from the human condition. Progress was to be seen on the Kantian view in terms of the increase in individual freedom and the growth of specific forms of reason and rationality. In contrast, for Hegel the main problem was to work out a system in which individual freedom merged with human progress, and the real was made rational and the rational real. Weber's image of the modern world is primarily one of the victory of *instrumental* rationality in dominant institutional sectors, while *substantive* rationality is seemingly to be found primarily at the level of individual systems of ideation. Weber, like Simmel, was apparently very concerned that the 'spirit' should not be socialized – although Simmel's thinking on this is much more clear than Weber's. (This arises in large part from the fact that whereas Simmel had very definite ideas about the concept 'individual' and the processes of individuation, Weber hardly even began to develop a concept of individuality in his writings.)

We will not, however, be able to appreciate the Weberian attitude toward mysticism without stepping more definitely back beyond Hegel to consider the problem of contemplation in German thought. 'Contemplation' has been one of the most frequently employed terms in the history of German social thought (that resting in significant part on its salience for ancient Greek philosophy) and from the time of Marx it has been one of the most value-laden of all terms of discourse about sociocultural life. One of Marx's major concerns – perhaps one might say his major concern – was to expel the contemplative attitude by substituting for it his notion of the unity of theory and practice, to substitute in effect inner-worldly, theory-informed practice and practice-informed theory for contemplativist philsophy. (Philosophers, Marx said, have taught us how to understand the world, the problem now is to change it.) Ever since Marx, the term 'contemplation' has been used as a leading term of abuse in the Marxian lexicon – abuse which has been directed particularly at Max Weber. (Although some of the most vociferous employment of the term has been exhibited by Lukacs in relation to his former teacher and that most epistemologically Kantian of all sociologists, Georg Simmel.)[6]

The links between Kantian epistemology and the long tradition of German mysticism are clearly indicated by a crucial statement of the Dominican mystic, Meister Eckhart (1260–1327):

Every time that the powers of the soul come into contact with created things, they receive the *created* images and likenesses from the created images and absorb them. In this way arises the soul's knowledge of created things. Created things cannot come nearer to the soul than this, and the soul can only approach created things by the voluntary reception of images. And it is through the presence of the image that the soul approaches the created world: for *the image is a Thing, which the soul creates* with her own powers. Does the soul want to know the nature of a stone – a horse – a man? She forms an image.[7]

This is hardly Kantian language, but the fundamental principle of Kant's idealistic-subjectivist epistemology is nevertheless here caught in most of its nuances. In her extensive – if now slightly out-of-date – exploration of mysticism in historical perspective, Evelyn Underhill rightly contrasts Eckhart's statement with Humean epistemology where direct sense impressions of the external world are paramount. The empiricist, skeptical stance is almost by definition much more active – more ascetic and less contemplative – than the Kantian. (As Gellner has cogently remarked, empiricists have been much more willing to put their ideas to work – to empirical, operational test – as exampled in the modern period by the activism of behavioral scientists, and the 'passivity' of idealists.)[8] We must, however, not deny the religious grounding of empiricist epistemology. Although the details have been subjected to much recent dispute, we have got to know much since Merton's pioneering work about the link between Puritan religion and the development of modern science. A connection which contrasts greatly with the case of mysticism is provided by the argument that Francis Bacon 'adapted to empirical science the procedure for obtaining mastery over nature proposed for the illuminated Magus in Renaissance magic'.[9] In Bacon's view the redemption of man was conceived in terms of a reintegration involving the faculties of mind and the unity of nature.

The continuity between mysticism – particularly German mysticism of the fourteenth to sixteenth centuries – and Kant's philosophy has been noted on more than one occasion. Perhaps Simmel has highlighted the cognitive – as opposed to the empirical-historical – continuities best of all. He argued that two main attempts have been made to grasp the totality of all beings and to make intelligible the idea that the inquirer 'is somehow affected by this totality and responds to it intellectually'.[10] One of these, says Simmel, is the way of mysticism (and he selects Eckhart as typical), the other is the way of Kant. 'In the most diverse forms, the following theme runs through the religious mysticism and the philosophical speculation of all times: The deepest submersion into ourselves, overcoming all diversity, leads us at the same time into the absolute unity of things.' In Kant's case, however, the emphasis was not upon finding the object of the philosophical project in existence conceived as a whole or immediately experienced, but rather 'in existence insofar as existence has become a science'. What, in other words, does not conform to the conditions of science, says Simmel in interpreting Kant, is not 'real'.[11]

Interestingly, the way in which Simmel · links mysticism and philosophy in effect denied one of the tenets that was to become basic to much of what Weber was to utter about mysticism. Said Simmel: 'the cognitive representations of things are not poured into us like nuts into a sack, that as knowers we are not passive recipients of sense impressions like the indifferent wax tablet that is given form from the outside by the impression of the stamp'.[12] The idea that contemplation is *not* a passive posture has indeed been claimed by a deviant tradition that extends in the relatively modern period from Kant through Simmel to Karl Mannheim. However, Weber was in a sense correct to speak of mystics, particularly those of the East, as passive vessels. But only in a sense; for the facts of the matter are, as we now clearly know through more recent research and analysis, that mysticism varies greatly in a cross-cultural respect in its degree of activism-passivism – similarly it varies in the degree to which it involves a conception of God or of gods. Many of the more elaborate and active – in the sense of requiring special techniques and practices – types of mysticism are to be found in the East. Weber, of course, did tend to treat Oriental mysticism as more or less entirely passive, and to that extent he clearly erred.

It is very important at this juncture to point out that within Christianity, certainly since the medieval period, individualistic mysticism has largely been regarded as deviant and irrational. Indeed our quotation from Eckhart may be taken as an indicator of his concern to reconcile individualistic mysticism with Christianity.[13] In the view expressed in our quotation (bringing an *a priori* to bear upon ultimate reality) it is clear that Eckhart was conscious of the need to reconcile his mysticism with the Christian emphasis upon faith and traditional, doctrinal imagery. Further, we should note also the lengths to which Eckhart went to emphasize the positive, moral implications of his form of mysticism – implications that centered upon his claim that 'what we have gathered in contemplation we give out in love'.[14] It was the question of love in relation to mysticism that was to puzzle and plague Max Weber – but which also preoccupied others in the relatively modern period, notably Hegel. To contend that mainstream Christianity has for a number of centuries been opposed to individualistic mysticism does of course run into the problem of the mystical elements in Luther's religious system and the subsequent history of Lutheranism. (Other reservations about this generalization are touched in chapter 6.) But it is of more than passing significance that many explorations and surveys of mysticism do not even mention Luther. This probably arises from the fact that mysticism has very often been thought of, by those interested in the issue as an autonomous area of study, as by definition being other-worldly. A long German tradition has, however, taken a very different view, two of the major representatives of that tradition being Hegel and Weber. Thus the emphasis upon salvation and the religious 'servicing' of the self which has been typical of Lutheranism, particularly in its indigenous German form, does not fit easily into many conceptions of mysticism; particularly those which, in emphasizing the cognitive aspect of the mystical orientation, speak of mysticism being alien to religion, or beyond both science and religion – the latter being Simmel's view.

The relatively uniquely-German attempt to confine mysticism within the world – inner-worldly mysticism – has had the consquence of posing the subject/object dilemma in a particularly acute manner. The attempt to keep mysticism – a mysticism which is on some views not even worthy of the name – within the confines of the secular, societal framework is precisely that which provided the background against which so many sociocultural, epistemological and ontological problems were tackled by German intellectuals in the eighteenth, nineteenth and early twentieth centuries. The attenuated mysticism of Luther brought mysticism into the world and thus created the basis for direct concern with its societal consequences – primarily in terms of its ethical consequences for the operation of societies, and its contemplative significance in epistemological terms. These were matters that Hegel clearly recognized.

Hegel and After

Let us return now to the period of Hegel, in particular to the period of his so-called 'early theological writings', remembering that the problems which he wished to tackle in large part revolved around the antimonies which he found in Kant's work.[15] In one of these early writings Hegel's attempt to reconcile intellect and feeling centered upon the idea of love, which from his standpoint obliterated oppositions. Still holding to the view that religion – as opposed to his subsequent concern with philosophy as the major vehicle of resolution of antimonies – was the pivot of his system, Hegel spoke in terms that can best be described as that of mystical union of the restricted self with pervasive, infinite life. If we can call Hegel a mystic with any viability at all it is in this early period, when we would characterize thus on grounds very similar to those in which we would characterize a thoroughgoing vitalist as a mystic.[16] This, we emphasize, is not to characterize Hegel *per se* as a vitalist – only to claim significant overlap with vitalism, particularly in his early work where 'life' is more important than 'spirit'. As Underhill has said, the first great principle of vitalism is: 'cease to identify your intellect and yourself', a conception held against the background of a belief in entelechy and the place of the 'hidden steersman' in driving 'the phenomenal world on and up'.[17]

Of particular relevance to our present concerns is the fact that in his early period Hegel utilized the theme of church and sect, within the context of his focus upon relationships between the individual and the society (which focus was to shade into the functional significance of the state in conditions of rapid and extensive social differentiation and pluralization).[18] We can indeed see in Hegel's comments upon the church-sect theme some of the basic parameters that came to preoccupy Weber, including the idea of the routinization of charisma. That was not exactly the terminology which Hegel used — for he spoke instead of the triumph of 'ecclesiastical statutes' over an initial sense of religious freedom. More important, we see in Hegel's early work a strong interest in such issues as the degree of rationality of different forms of religion; the relationship between religion and freedom; and the significance of asceticism in mediating the relationship between church and state, as functioning as a mode of social control.

Hegel's discussions of sects were closely bound to these general themes. Particular opprobrium was reserved for what Hegel called the positive form of sect, this being largely defined in terms of 'non-reasoned commitment to the doctrine of a religious group — commitment, that is, to what was posited. A 'philosophical sect', on the other hand, was one that did involve an emphasis upon reasoned commitment. In general terms, Hegel's criteria in this respect depend upon his emphasis on the positive form of sect, this being largely defined in terms of non-reasoned immediate contingency and the facticity of superficial, empirical encounter.[19]

Thus Hegel depicted the church-sect motif in terms of the encapsulation of Christianity in a vicious circle of accommodations: sects try to break out of the compromises of the church, but quickly are enmeshed in those same ecclesiastical compromises — and so the process continues. Hegel's own prescription for this dilemma was rooted in his attempt to overcome what he saw as the major limitations of Kantian thought; and in his early work he adopted a position characterizable as a 'Pantheism of Love' — an attempt to overcome Kantian contrasts between morality and impulse, reason and passion, duty and inclination.[20] Our argument here is that the sect-church dilemma is importantly linked to the subjectivity-objectivity dilemma. In that view sectarianism constitutes a form of socially organized subjectivity, while churchism constitutes a form of socially organized objectivity. These characterizations fit the more modern tendency to say that whereas one joins a sect, one is in contrast born into a church.

As far as the relationship between sect, church and mysticism is concerned, we undoubtedly see in Hegel's early work an attempt to bridge the sect-church dilemma in terms of a form of collective mysticism. Many analysts do, as we have remarked, contend that Hegel maintained an essentially mystical view of the dialectical resolution of subjectivity and objectivity throughout his work – although there is no doubt that the romantic, pantheistic elements in his early thinking gave way to that uniquely Hegelian conjunction of *Realpolitik* and spiritualistic idealism in his theory of the state, embodying in his later work that which he called 'absolute spirit'. We must consistently remember that it was Hegel's ongoing project to discover the Absolute in the world. As Fackenheim aptly says:

To be sure, this Absolute, when present as such, heals the fragmentation of the actual world *in which* it is present, for those *to whom* it is present, which is why its presence in and for thought may be called a mysticism of Reason. But unlike so many mysticisms, this mysticism is no flight from the actual world, which takes that world as mere sham and illusion. According to Hegel, it is much rather such a flight which is a sham, compared to which steadfast existence in the actual world, even if taken as ultimately fragmented, has substance and reality. The Absolute, if accessible to thought at all, is accessible only to a thought which *remains with* the world of sense, not to a thought which shuns it in 'monkish fashion'.[21]

Thus we see in this aspect of Hegel's philosophy a particularly clear statement of the possibility of inner-worldly mysticism, a possibility indicated strongly through the development of German mysticism since the thirteenth century, finding a religious expression in Reformation Lutheranism.[22] In terms of our approach to Max Weber the more general and significant point is that in the course of his life's quest Hegel had cause to make many suggestions – particularly in *Phenomenology of the Spirit* – about what generically we may call modes of existence.[23] What Weber later came to call radical types of salvation stand securely in that tradition, although obviously the emphasis is different.

In the first half of the nineteenth-century others – some from anti-Hegelian standpoints, others from less hostile positions – were to pursue the general idea of modes of existence. In that connection two people stand-out, namely Schopenhauer and Kierkegaard. It is these two, who, along with the Young Hegelian schools laid the basis for the ways in which Marx and then Nietzsche addressed directly the nature of empirical life. Kierkegaard interested himself in modes of existence in terms of his quest for an appropriate religious mode of living – hence his great importance in the development of existentialism as a normative philosophy. Schopenhauer, too, took the world as it is, as his departure point, but found it so wanting – so inherently objectionable – that he proposed only what was in his view the most adequate method of denying it. The Young Hegelians of the left-wing helped to precipitate the Marxist strand of thought which was to eschew both the spiritism of Hegel and the kinds of thought which stood in the tradition of theodicy. The latter style of thought had been initiated in philosophical form by Liebniz and as a topic had been the subject of attention by Kant, who insisted that theodical problems – the problems of the meaning of life, but in more technical form the problems arising from the disparity between the idea of an omnipotent God and the perception of life as replete with suffering – were not soluble in the sense of their being settled by pure reason. (In a sense we may see Weber's discussions of theodicy, including his types of radical, religious salvation as an application of the mode of practical reason – the latter being in turn the major mode of his orientation to the problem of rationalization.)

We only group Kierkegaard, Schopenhauer and the left Hegelians together for the purpose of specifying the shift from spirit to life in its materiality. On other grounds they have, of course, little or nothing in common. Both Kierkegaard and Schopenhauer specifically focussed on modes of existence, Kierkegaard producing an elaborate scheme, categorizable into public, aesthetic, ethical and religious forms.[24] In the present context, however, Schopenhauer is of more interest. In many ways he was the first of the German irrationalists. Bendix places the interest of Schopenhauer in broader perspective when he says that Weber's emphasis upon interests in human life exemplifies the latter's 'indebtedness to the antirationalist tradition that Hans Barth has traced from Bacon's theory of idols through Helvetius' analysis of prejudices to Marx's theory of ideology, on the one hand, and on the other to Schopenhauer's and Nietzsche's efforts to uncover man's will and affect behind every manifestation of thought and reason'.[25] But our interest here is largely in the contribution of Schopenhauer in conceptual and empirical terms. For he pointed to the mode of existence which Weber was later to use under the heading of *other-worldly asceticism*. In his extremely pessimistic attitude toward life Schopenhauer saw aesthetic contemplation on a this-worldly basis as one possible escape from the Will, but, on the other hand, he regarded it as merely a temporary form of escape. It was only through renouncing the Will to live completely that secure escape was possible. In this view Schopenhauer was very much influenced by the Hindu philosophy of Maya and by Buddhism. It is a moot point whether his mode of escape should be regarded as mystical, as ascetic or a combination of both. In the main, denial of the Will of the phenomenal world seems to involve a straightforwardly ascetic stance; but Schopenhauer does address the possibility that escape from – in a different sense penetration of – the phenomenal world may lead to a psychic circumstance that is not simply a state of nothingness. As Coppleston puts it: 'Hence there is presumably the possibility of a state being achieved through a self-renunciation which does not amount to nothingness. It could hardly be a state of knowledge, for the subject-object relationship is phenomenal. But it might resemble the incommunicable experience to which mystics refer in obscure terms.'[26] The emphasis upon ineffability in discussions of mysticism is currently being challenged in some quarters, but that point aside this observation on Schopenhauer points clearly to the slippage between asceticism and mysticism, particularly in the so-called other-worldly contexts.

But, even more important, we can see in Schopenhauer's work that considerable strides were taken into a comparative frame of reference in respect of the general problem-area of modes of existence and types of salvation. In particular Schopenhauer opened up a line of inquiry into the idea of salvation from the world on a cross-cultural basis. Not that we can clearly point to Weber having been directly influenced by this aspect of Schopenhauer's work. But we do know with certainty that Weber was familiar with Schopenhauer from early in his academic career; while it is generally acknowledged that Schopenhauer was influential in stimulating an interest among German scholars in Oriental patterns of thought.

The idea that life could be approached – or better denied – in terms informed by familiarity with Eastern religion and philosophy was of course eschewed by Marx, while subsequently Nietzsche was to castigate Schopenhauer directly on this point. In one way or another the alleged escapism – that is, other-worldliness – of Eastern civilizations was strongly rejected by Marx, Nietzsche and then Weber.[27]

Marx's contribution to the intellectual odyssey of mysticism and adjacent themes were very diffuse and not demanding of much attention here. His materialistic, this-worldly immanentism was predicated upon the rejection of many of the kinds of concern that are relevant to the study of mysticism and adjacent themes. From very early in his intellectual career Marx was eager to characterize Hegel's general stance as a mystical one: 'Hegel's aim is to give the political constitution a relationship to the abstract idea, to fit it in as part of the life history of the idea – an obvious mystification.' As McLellan notes, that conception was adopted from Feuerbach, who maintained that mystification arose from depiction of the wrong relationship between subject and predicate: 'The true subject – man and his relation to other men and to nature – was mystified by being turned into the mere predicate of the idea.'[28] This kind of approach to, or use of, 'mysticism' is significant in that it expands the notion to the point of encompassing all forms of what might be called 'de-concretization', of assimilating concrete phenomena to 'other realities'. In that mode the terms 'mystical' and 'mysticism' became increasingly available for pejorative deployment – along with their brethren 'contemplative' and 'contemplationism'. (The latter pair have come to enjoy in Marxian circles a connotative mixture of ideational passivity, irrationality and indulgent pondering of 'the eternal verities.') However, one of the core components of most characterizations of mysticism is retained in the marxian usage – namely, the obliteration or suspension of empirical contingency; which specifically entails the severe diminution of subject-object contingency.

Finally, in our brief survey of the background to Weber's thinking about mysticism we must mention, if only fleetingly, the work of Nietzsche. Probably the most appropriate light in which to view the impact of Nietzsche upon Weber is with respect to Weber's own concern to develop an ethic of responsibility. As we shall see in a moment, that concern informed much of that which Weber wrote on the subject of mysticism. In a very loose sense Nietzsche's conception of the Dionysian stance parallels some of the issues which Weber raised in connection with mysticism, for in both cases there is an emphasis upon release from worldly contingency; while, on the other hand, the Apollian mode emphasizes the adherence to norms and values – this having a significant resemblance to Weber's use of the term asceticism. However, we would not claim much in respect of direct conceptual impact upon Weber.[29] Rather it is the problem of selecting from, synthesizing or transcending traditional dichotomies that is relevant here. (One cannot ignore Mitzman's claim that there was a tension in Weber's writing between charisma and rationalized disenchantment; the former constituting, argues Mitzman, a combination of mysticism and Nietzschean 'worldly heroism'.[30] Other aspects of Neitzsche's work which can be linked to Weber include the idea of meaningful suffering, the relativity and diversity of ideational systems, and the problem of the relationship between science and life-meaning.)[31]

Regardless of the degree to which Weber was influenced in specific respects by particular individuals, it is clear that his work must be understood in terms of its location in a national-intellectual tradition which tended to focus on particular sets of problems more than others and to subscribe to particular categorical guidelines in so doing. For example, our emphasis on the importance of a Hegelian legacy derives in part from Hegel having utilized the church-sect distinction for the specific purpose of coming to terms with individual-society problems, from a perspective which insisted on the essential link between religion and central-societal politics. Not in the sense of fusing religion and politics – except of course at the level of 'metaphysicizing' the state – for Hegel insisted on the separation of religion (in the conventional sense of particular religious faiths) and the state; but rather in seeing the meaning aspects of religion as intimately linked to the meaningfulness of being a member of a sociohistorical entity. Hegel was one of the first modern analysts to recognize fully the respects in which the circumstances of modern differentiated and pluralized societies acutely underscore the problems of the meaningfulness of life and death.

With such matters Weber was preoccupied throughout most of his adult life. The fact that on nearly all respected interpretations it is agreed that he tried to steer a path between the totalistic positions of revolutionary socialism and romantic conservatism makes not one jot of difference to the proposition that Weber saw little point in discussing matters of *Realpolitik* without attending to necessarily impinging problems of life-meaning. By the same token, the synchronic and diachronic ramifications of religious orientations had to be at the heart of the analysis of religion. Many modern social scientists have been misled into thinking that because Weber tried to keep certain aspects of life apart from each other at the level of political-philosophical prescription, that justifies our analytically studying, say, religion and politics as relatively segregated aspects of societal realities. The point is that Weber's (ambiguous) prescriptions on such matters as fact and value, science and ultimate meaning, and so on, were set out in the face of their perceived empirical interconnectedness, an interconnectedness which at times seems to have led Weber to sociological despair with respect to how life in modern societies could be ordered at both personal and large-scale levels.

As we have seen, concern with the reconcilability of opposites has formed one of the most salient threads of German social thought, even though the specifically Hegelian approach received decreasing attention as the nineteenth century unfolded. In any case, it is almost certainly impossible to appreciate Max Weber's sociology without fully recognizing not only the salience of this theme, but also its relationship to Lutherianism. Not only is it necessary to understand Lutheranism as a general backdrop to many of the intellectual issues which Weber inherited from previous German thinkers, but in the present context it is of great importance to grasp the problem of the relationship between 'religion and the world' as that problem was made manifest in Lutheran Germany. In even broader vein, we must over again remind ourselves that the religion/world motif is closely related to the individual/society problematic. In the German context they both loosely parallel the sect/church and subjectivity/objectivity polarities.

Under the weight of the great attention given to Weber's interest in Calvinism, and its historical association with entrepreneurial capitalism, we have undoubtedly tended to overlook the degree to which the array of problems which Weber confronted were of a basically Lutheran type. As Nelson has noted, Weber approaches 'Religion' and 'World' as 'an heir of Luther', a position which he compares to Parsons' 'inextricable association with the American Calvinists, who regard the world, with all its shortcomings, as the only relam in which to execute God's will'.[32] To speak of Weber as an heir of Luther and to leave the matter at that is, however, very misleading. For Weber frequently expressed hostility to Lutheranism, and it is best to speak of Weber being an inheritor, like many German intellectuals, of *'the' Lutheran Problemstellung* concerning the relationship between religion and world. In that respect we should note in sociology-of-knowledge vein that the 'religion-and-the-world' perspective in the modern sociology of religion rests considerably on Weber's mediation of a Lutheran epistemology and ontology. Of course, the general theme of the boundaries and relations between religion and society, between the sacred and the secular, are in a larger sense part and parcel of the wider Christian tradition – but 'the Lutheran view' is one which has been more dominant than other Chrisitan views among sociologists. That does not, it almost goes without saying, mean that a large number of modern sociologists of religion consciously subscribe to German Lutheran ideas, nor that they are saturated with substantive Lutheran perspectives. On the other hand, the easy, undialectical acceptance among many American sociologists of the idea that religiosity is primarily a private, internal matter – a stance strongly facilitated by methodologies which commit the individualist fallacy – testifies further to the amorphous impact of traditional Lutheranism. (By way of contrast we should note that there is a strong, minority Calvinist thrust – best seen in the Bellah-Parsons advocacy of civil religion, at the center of which lies crucial remnants of Calvinist notions of covenantal theocracy and the synchronization of intra-individual and inter-individual orderliness.) Perhaps the best way to summarize Weber's sociology of religion in reference to such considerations is to say that he focused on a Luther-based *Problemstellung* under a self-imposed challenge from a diluted and sociologically restructured Calvinist perspective. That suggestion must of course be regarded within the context of the eighteenth- and nineteenth-century contributions which have already been mentioned.

The recent revival of interest in mysticism among sociologists, notably in the American context, displays a sense of surprise that should be contrasted with Weber's frequent emphasis upon the mystical element in Lutheranism and, even more important, upon the fluid nature of the relationship between asceticism and mysticism in larger perspective. Again, there is an interesting offshoot of the reception of Weber in America. Under Parsons' influence, but of course assisted by more diffuse mythic expressions, the belief in 'instrumental activism', the 'work ethic', and so on, became part of the conventional wisdom – as characterizations of highly salient American cultural motifs. That particular view has been closely intertwined with a rejection of mysticism. The unpenetrable 'ultimate reality' which figures so largely in Parsons' recent theorizing is closely aligned with Weber's attempts to reject metaphysical questions and his existentialist-like, living-with-the-unknowable perspective on society. In that respect it is worthy of note that in his emphasis upon the senselessness of direct seeking of 'the ultimate situation' Weber's great admirer and friend, Karl Jaspers, focused on almost exactly the components of ultimacy which have been so much the concern of modern action theorists: death, suffering, struggle and guilt.

The general tenor of Weber's comments upon Lutheranism in general and Lutheran mysticism in particular jells with views which have been stated adamantly by those of many different theoretical and ideological persuasions.[33] German Lutheranism's frequent emphasis upon faith and the idea of Christian liberty as residing in the self – as an 'inner value' – diverted attention from the conditions of 'the world', the world beyond the religious life of the individual. It is in such terms that we see the simultaneous rejection and acceptance of Lutheranism by Weber. The rejection is overt and specific to the doctrinal statements and behavioral proclivities of much of German Lutheranism; while the acceptance is simply a positive recognition of the problem of how the individual *qua* individual could most viably cope with external social reality, and how the latter was sustained for the individual. As Marcuse has cogently argued, 'German culture is inseperable from its origin in Protestantism. There arose a realm of beauty, freedom, and morality, which was not to be shaken by external realities and struggles; it was detached from the miserable social world and anchored in the "soul" of the individual.'[34] And even though Weber's own life does not exactly conform to Marcuse's claim that the German 'educated' classes thus were rendered impotent to apply themselves to the shaping of their society, there is, to our mind, a shading in Weber's work which suggests that he was often more preoccupied with the idea of things, rather than the things themselves, with transcending reality in the direction of ideas. (This is, of course, a not infrequently perceived characteristic of intellectuals. Weber's own tendency to focus – most times in negative format – on contemplation as a common feature of mysticism has a strong bearing on this point.) Such considerations are essential in attempting to understand Weber's writings on mysticism.

Mitzman is persuasive in saying that Weber's comments at the 1910 inaugural meeting of the German Sociological Association set the tone for much of Weber's subsequent work in the sociology of religion. This meeting, it should be said, occurred at the beginning of a period in which Weber became closely acquainted with the mystical notions of Stefan George, Georg Lukacs, Ernst Bloch, and a number of East European (especially Russian) students.[35]

Probably the most striking aspect of Weber's 1910 statements consists in the focus upon forms of mysticism which emphasize personal brotherliness. Such foci are particularly striking in their exclusion of both individualistic, Lutheran mysticism and the collectivist, ritual-governed, mysticism of the Roman Catholic kind. The latter exclusion was, of course, a feature of Weber's work as a whole. (It would be wrong to say that Weber never exhibited strong interest in Catholicism *per se*; but the mystical component in Catholicism did not attract much Weberian attention.) On the other hand, his interest in what he called 'the oriental Christian church' was marked by a concentration upon precisely the latter's concern with brotherly love – a tendency exampled in the 1910 discussions by his reference to the classical mysticism of the Greek Orthodox Church. Such foci stand in contrast to Troeltsch's concentration upon the *individualistic* character of Christian mysticism, which Troeltsch apparently saw as an individuated reconciliation of sectarianism and churchism. Weber's ambivalence with respect to mysticism is to be seen in the attractiveness of a brotherhood founded on mystical principles, on the one hand, and the acosmistic implications of such fellowship on the other. In his essay 'Between Two Ethics' (1916), Weber couched this problem with reference both to the Russian sources of mystical pacifism and the Russian threat to German society which would be encouraged by the spread of mystical pacifism within Germany.

It is not at all easy to locate systematically the concept of mysticism within the general body of Weber's work, although the view that 'Weber thought of mysticism as little more than a superstition from the Neolithic Age' is clearly an exaggeration.[36] For apart from his 1910 comments on Greek Orthodox, primitive Christian and modern Russian forms of mysticism based on what Weber called acosmic love, he was obviously intrigued by the nature of the Quaker form of mysticism. (Quite apart from his obvious concern with mysticism in non-Occidental religions, to which we shall intermittently refer in subsequent pages.) There is, to be sure, a strong tendency in Weber to associate the mystical with the traditional, with behind-the-times circumstances; a stance which, one suspects, was in turn closely bound to Weber's negative orientation to religious ritual. Ritual was for Weber the major blockage to processes of rationalization, and it is from that angle – the angle of witnessing Weber's lack of appreciation of the socio-cultural and psychic significance of ritual – that we might profitably view his neglect of the more structured, sacramental forms of mysticism. These Weber seemed to identify too closely with magic. We might also note that historically Christianity has been unique among the world religions in its *emphasis upon* paradox and mystery – features which, to be sure, were attenuated within some major branches of the Protestant Reformation.

The general thrust of Weber's studies of religion is clearly centered upon the implications of different religious forms for social organization and for relationships between individuals and collectivities (including, of course, societal collectivities). (By this we do not mean that had he been more 'Calvinist' than 'Lutheran' he would have thereby failed to attend to such matters. But had he been a 'Calvinist' in his sociological-analytic mode he would, we contend, have looked at these matters in a significantly different light.) This is certainly the case with the two schemata which most concern us in the present context; namely, the church-sect theme and the types of religious salvation. The major problem is to comprehend the status of mysticism as it appears, on the one hand, as injected into the church-sect theme, and on the other hand, as a central component of the typology of salvational forms. In one sense the problem is attenuated by underlining the fact that the conceptual binding of mysticism with the church-sect theme came at a stage of his work when Weber was just becoming interested in mysticism, whereas the discussions of mysticism as a counter to asceticism within the context of the inner-worldly/other-worldly distinction were central to Weber's later comparative studies. Thus mysticism was deployed in two superficially separate analytic modes. The first of the two modes of deployment has an affinity with the Troeltschian perspective as a 'third way'; constituting an avoidance — better, transcendence — of the dilemma of the ascetic principles of disciplined insulation from 'the world' versus disciplined adaptation to 'the world'. Both sectarianism and churchism imply through their doctrinal emphases particular forms of social organization, while on Weber's view religious mysticism leads only indirectly to particular organizational forms. The latter are, in effect, unintended products of the pursuit of *unio mystica*.

Mysticism was for Weber generally characterized by its contemplativeness and, relatedly, by its *acosmicism*, the latter term referring to an indifference to consequences in the human cosmos of the pursuit of ultimate ends. (Although, from time to time, Weber does allude to more activist types of mysticism.) The ethic of brotherly love is a contingent matter, because the mystical quest for salvation 'fosters an attitude of humility and self-surrender as a result of its minimization of activity in the world, and its affirmation of the necessity of passing through the world incognito . . . as the only proven method for demonstrating salvation'.[37] It is interesting to note that in conjunction with this comment Weber spoke specifically of the experience of intellectualism as always bearing within itself this possibility; that is, of the 'acosmistic and non-specific experience of love', an argument which Weber further shaded into a consideration of the intimate link between eroticism and mysticism.

Thus although he was for a short while intrigued by the viability of religious mysticism in the modern world, Weber tended to comment negatively on the fit between religious mysticism and modern, hyperationalized circumstances. Troeltsch, it should be said, hinted that twentieth-century mysticism would be related increasingly to ideas drawn from the spheres of art and science. It is in that light that we should probably view Weber's feeling that religious mysticism is unstable in Western, inner-worldly contexts. (Recent students of mysticism have tended to differentiate between types of mysticism, including certain secular forms.) On the other hand, Weber's interest in the sociology of mysticism was apparently retained until the last years of his life, an interest marked by much ambivalence, both with respect to his own personal attitudes and his more 'neutrally' sociological analyses of religion in different kinds of society. He spoke of mysticism as the prostitution of the soul, yet he remained intrigued by the possibility of what one can only call mystically-flavored charismatic breakouts from the containment of rational-legalism. He castigated romantic, self-indulgent intellectualism, yet clearly showed an abiding tendency to seek the node of freedom in terms that resemble certain tenets of existentialism. But overall his judgement on mysticism seems to have been that it was out-of-tune with modern societies and that when mysticism reared its head something was going awry – a perspective which ought to be taken seriously by those modern sociologists of religion who have decided to devote a lot of (seemingly positive) attention to new forms of mysticism.

The kernel of Weber's argument in the latter respect is to be found in his statement that 'the mystic who flees the world is more dependent upon the world than is the ascetic. . . . If he is to live consistently according to his theory, he must maintain his life only by means of what nature or men voluntarily donate to him.'[38] In the Occidental world 'even religions of an explicitly mystical type regularly became transformed into an active pursuit of virtue. . . . There occurred along the way an inner selection of motivations which placed the primary preference upon some type of active conduct, generally a type pointing toward asceticism. . . .'[39] The only historical exceptions to this tendency were a few quietist sects. For Weber, the most conspicuous of the latter was as we have already remarked, the Society of Friends – where, as Mitzman persuasively puts it, Weber saw a meeting point between, on the one hand, mysticism and acosmic love, and, on the other hand, an emphasis upon mutual responsibility and ethical rationalism. It is a pity that Weber did not analyze the Quakers at length, for it would seem that that movement represents a major example of the rationalization of mysticism. Indeed the latter concept highlights again one of the major lacunae in his work. For Weber's general sense of sociocultural evolution did not encompass the changes which occurred in types of religion which had, as it were, been 'left behind' in the evolutionary process. Hence the seriousness of his failing to attend systematically along such lines to Catholicism. What, in other words, happened to Catholicism in terms of rationalization after Protestantism had mounted its inner-worldly ascetic drive? The Roman church was, after all, according to Weber – and undoubtedly he was correct – one of the two 'greatest powers of religious rationalism in history' (the other being Confucianism). But in any case his own optimism about the ascetic drift of inner-worldly mysticism has to be regarded skeptically, particularly since he gave no convincing argument in substantiation. To that matter we will return.

Mysticism was thus particularly problematic to Weber because of its tendency toward acosmicism, its indifference to the condition of 'the world'. Moreover, by virtue of its historic association in many, but by no means all, circumstances with sacramental ritualism, mysticism bore the trademarks for Weber of traditionalism and resistance to rationalization. Perhaps, as we have suggested, the brotherliness of some forms of mysticism did attract Weber. As did the undeniable fact that there is a mystical element in intellectualism; for the acts of social diagnosis and prognosis are themselves ways of circumventing the alienation of the individual's context from himself or herself – which is an important ingredient of the mystical orientation, at least in the West. Rather characteristically, Weber remained ambivalent about such matters, but on the whole tried to maintain an anti-mystical stance.

Weber's discussions of mysticism, particularly when we consider them against the backdrop of German intellectual history and within the context of early twentieth-century German thought, point the way to our need to bring the sociology of religion more directly to bear on the discontents of modern societies. The outer side of mysticism, as Weber always reminds us, is the withdrawal of affect from the wider societal system. It is unfortunately a hallmark of much of modern sociology notably in America and Britain that it tends to consider sociocultural phenomena on a fragmented, self-contained basis. One would thus not realize from reading the growing number of studies of modern mysticism that the latter could have much bearing upon such matters as the nature of the modern state, the character of political authority in modern societies, and so on. Moreover, the formal separation of 'church' and 'state' has blinded American sociologists to what in Weber's view was an indissoluble link between political authority as a meaning complex and the life-world of the individual. (The 'civil-religionists' obviously represent an important reaction against this.) There has of course, always been a tendency for those in the Anglo-American orbit to vindicate the separation, the differentiation, of the individual (and his or her 'quest for meaning') from central political structures (and the latter's concern with guaranteeing the parameters of 'ordinary living'). Such a differentiation is in the conventional view, indeed the Weberian view, the hallmark of modernity. And yet in perusing Weber's work (and, indeed, the work of Durkheim and Marx) we see that the meaningfulness of life is incontestably bound-up with – although not entirely contingent upon – the ways in which life is politically facilitated. In this respect it is probably to Hegel that we owe – or ought to owe – the greatest debt for his analyses of alienation. (Rousseau stands out as a controversial candidate, a problem which gets some attention in the next chapter.) The differentiation which we see in modern Western societies is, however, only an 'attempt' at a solution to a dilemma – the dilemma of where does political authority end and personal identity begin? For political authority has or is claimed by authorities to have meaning (however problematic); while identity (which is conventionally related to a sense of meaningful coherence) is in one crucial perspective directly related to the attempt to exercise 'authority' at the level of the individual;[40] the problem of the relationship between the two being a major concern of *inter alia*, Hegel, Simmel and Durkheim. Modern mystical tendencies are, on that view, seen clearly in 'the quest for identity'.

Probably the most significant of the difficulties which we encounter in utilizing Weber's work in reference to modern matters hinges on the 'Religion and the World' perspective. For that perspective was, as far as it is possible to tell, the analytic foundation of Weber's emphasis upon salvation. No matter that Weber's most acute interest was in innerworldly asceticism (in contrast to the most world-negating religious orientation, namely other-worldly mysticism), the fact remains that the word 'salvation' carries heavy connotations of *release from* the world. (Weber in fact says in his study of Indian religion that there is an important respect in which religious asceticism is not salvation-oriented at all.) Thus we have to note that Weber's whole typology of religious orientations tends toward predication of the idea of a tension between a sphere of religion and a worldly sphere, between the noumenal and the phenomenal. The idea that inner-worldliness should be seen as an evolutionary successor to other-worldliness assists in recognizing that in an important sense inner-worldliness as a religious orientation is intrinsically less salvational than other-worldliness. On the other hand, in fairness to Weber it must be emphasized that his four basic types of religious orientation were – as Parsons shows – 'radical solutions on a personal basis'. In other words, the need for salvation is a response to an acutely experienced discrepancy between worldly interests and 'the nature of an order thought to be intrinsically capable of providing an answer in terms of truly "ultimate" meaning. . . .'[41] But even though we have to give due acknowledgment to the radical nature of Weber's conception of salvation, the fact remains that in his specific discussions of concrete religious forms of faith Weber uses the inner-/other-worldly and ascetism/mysticism schema so freely as to venture into areas where the notion of *radical* solution is clearly not tenable.

Hegel, in effect, had created philosophically a synthesis of sectarian subjectification and churchly objectification in his early work. In a sense we may interpret Troeltsch's position in the same analytic spirit – mysticism being an individualistic attempt to circumvent socially structured subjectivist/sectarian-versus-objectivist/churchly contingencies at the level of the self. However, Troeltsch's conception heralds more than implicitly a basically secularized form of mysticism.[42] Weber's stance may be related to that of Simmel. In Simmel's terms the mysticism of the early twentieth century – particularly the mysticism of young German intellectuals – constituted an attempt to make religion synonymous with life, whereas for Simmel religion was only one of a number of possible modes of ordering life-as-experienced.[43] For Simmel diffuse mysticism was a fruitless, and 'dangerous', attempt to break out of the anthropological givenness of the contingencies of, and the ideational vehicles for, ordering life.[44] Weber, as has sometimes been noted, seemed to agree with Simmel's contention that objective form has the last word; and both Weber and Simmel made much of what they saw as the anti-form character of mysticism. Simmel held strongly to the neo-Kantian view that each 'world' – for example, religion, philosophy, art – had its own set of *a priori* modes of apprehension and associated forms of cognition. Diffuse mysticism constituted, therefore, a confusion of the spheres of life. There are shades of this kind of thinking in Weber's work of the 1910–20 period.

It is not without interest in the present context that what Simmel regarded as the essentially mystical nature of the attempt to make religion synonymous with life has been in part sociologically 'validated' in the 'invisible religion' perspective. The most conspicuous representative of that stance has been Luckmann, who bases his contention that modern religion is coterminous with the sociocultural (or trans-biological) condition; on the lack of fit between, on the one hand, religion in objective form (the sacred, institutional 'umbrella') and, on the other hand, subjective religious experience.[45] The latter dissonance is sharply reduced by making 'lived life' religious – a position which does not necessarily politicize religion. In turn the Parsonian perspective, which resonates with an upgraded mixture of Calvinist theocratism and Durkheimian 'moralism', should not be confused with mysticism; in that it demands that the inscrutability of 'ultimate reality' be fully accepted, and this-worldly affairs conducted with due respect for, but not fused with, that ultimate domain. It should be said, however, that even though the civil religion advocates are fundamentally insisting upon a religiously-sanctioned secular order there are tinges, notably in Bellah's work, of mysticism. The multiplex nature of the modern religious condition which Bellah describes does have an affinity with Simmel's characterization of mysticism's project: 'Religion would function as a medium for the direct expression of life. It would be analogous not to a single melody within the symphony of life, but to the tonality within which the whole work is performed.'[46] In different vein we can also see mystical elements in the idea of life as, to use Baudelaire's phrase, 'a forest of symbols' – the latter being one way of characterizing Bellah's commitment to the position of symbolic realism.

A Reconstruction of Weber's Stance

In returning to the two different analytic modes in terms of which Weber deployed the concept of mysticism, we must recognize the need to modify the definitions which he used in the typology of salvational tacks. In line with much that Weber wrote, and indeed our present knowledge of different forms of mysticism, the basic requirement is to conceptualize inner-worldly and other-worldly directions of salvation such that the first is contingently more conducive to asceticism and the second more conducive to mysticism. From a Weberian standpoint this is very necessary, in that Weber clearly saw inner-worldly asceticism as the polar opposite of other-worldly mysticism.

There has been a strong tendency in interpretations and expositions of Weber's work to give equal   dimensional weight to asceticism-mysticism and innerness-otherness, so yielding four 'conceptually equal' types by cross-tabulation. But the more expositionally faithful and, even more important, empirically accurate approach is to regard inner-worldly mysticism as a variation upon a more fundamental form of inner-worldly asceticism and other-worldly asceticism as a variation upon a more fundamental form of other-worldly mysticism. We argue that inner-worldly mysticism arises as a method of self-actualization in a context where the leading emphasis is upon acting in 'this world'. In contrast, historically speaking we regard asceticism as having arisen in other-worldly contexts – most notably the Indian one – as a method of coping with minimal worldly necessities.

In such a perspective it is the inner-worldly/other-worldly dimension which takes analytic precedence – that is, it is the more crucial variable. The inner-worldly orientation may then be defined as the view that the everyday world is to be regarded normatively as an unavoidable set of empirical contingencies; while, on the other hand, the other-worldly orientation can be characterized as the view that the everyday surface world is to be normatively regarded – and relatively speaking – as an avoidable set of empirical contingencies. Given the felt-need for salvation, the first of these, the inner-worldly, tends toward asceticism; while the second, the other-worldly, tends toward mysticism. But asceticism comes to acquire a complement of mysticism in the first case; while in the second case mysticism acquires a complement of asceticism.

Asceticism is used here in reference to an orientation involving commitment to a form of self-discipline in the pursuit of a set of ultimate values; while mysticism is defined as an orientation involving belief in and valuation of the consummatibility of human subjects. These definitions, it must be emphasized, are of the *in vacuo* type. That is they make no empirical sense unless located within the frame of the inner-worldly/other-worldly variation, which constitutes the basic terms in which dualistic cosmologies of the 'higher religions' type may be understood. The asceticism/mysticism distinction may then be regarded as the definining orientations of individual salvation, given either an inner-worldly or an other-worldly orientation (and remembering also that here we stress the tendency for inner-worldliness to yield initially asceticism, and other-worldliness to yield mysticism).

We arrive then at the following conceptualizations. *Inner-worldly asceticism* involves a normative commitment to self-discipline, in order that the value-commitment of accepting positively the contingent nature of this world in relation to ultimate reality may be guaranteed. *Other-worldly mysticism* involves a commitment to consummation of the self through its absorption into an other-worldly realm, so denying as far as possible the contingencies of this world. *Inner-worldly mysticism* is a form of self-actualization conceived with respect for worldly contingencies, in terms of the relationship between this world and another realm of ultimate reality. *Other-worldly asceticism* involves commitment to the necessity for self-discipline as a mode of minimization of the impact of worldly contingencies for the sake of obliterating the salience of the latter relative to the other-worldly realm.

It would seem that each of these four types of modes of existence – or, more narrowly, in Weberian terms types of salvation – carry with them specific strains toward acquiring complementation. And in attempting to specify such mechanisms of change we can indeed draw quite directly from Weber's comments on asceticism and mysticism. In the present context, then, we are seeking to show how in the most general terms asceticism acquires mysticism, and how mysticism acquires asceticism. More specifically, we need to show how inner-worldly asceticism comes to acquire a complement of inner-worldly mysticism, and how other-worldly mysticism comes to acquire a complement of other-worldly asceticism.

In the simplest terms the religious ascetic needs mysticism to the extent that there must be some contact of ego with another-worldly realm.[47] The Calvinist conception of the inscrutability of God, in combination with the possibility of not being of the elect, is probably the furthest that doctrine has gone in principle in eliminating all traces of this. But, as Weber intimated, there is even within such a doctrine the strong probability of there arising confusion between working for the glory of *God* (asceticism) and *self*-glorification, the latter having been evidently a strong tendency among Calvinist Saints, most notably perhaps in the Cromwellian period in seventeenth century England. In contrast, the mystic requires asceticism in that discipline of some kind is necessary in order that mystical states may be generated at all. To be sure there are cases of 'carefree' access to the mystical condition, but even those require a kind of negative asceticism, in that they need procedures for closing-off pre-mystical constraints. But in any case the maintenance of a mystical orientation certainly does require ascetic conduct, closing-off particular empirical contingencies of the everyday world.

In terms of long-term change in systems of action the perspective sketched thus far can fruitfully be given further analytic weight through injection of Weber's notion of rationalization. Addressing relatively modern circumstances in which there is a relatively high degree of individuation – that is, differentiation of individuals from social and cultural circumstances – as well as differentiation of social from cultural realms, we can in ideal-typical form regard combinations of asceticism and mysticism in both inner-worldly and other-worldly contexts as aspects of rationalization processes. A combination of asceticism and mysticism involves making more situationally consistent from the actor's point of view the demands of acting in accord with the needs of society, on the one hand, and acting in accord with the needs of self, on the other hand.

Speaking specifically of Western, inner-worldly contexts the development of a mystical complement to asceticism involves making good some of the 'deficiencies' of asceticism. Mysticism counterbalances three particular characteristics of asceticism. First, it offsets the ascetic's tendency to execute in society something which he has no time to understand – that is, the ascetic does not from the point of view of the mystic really care about the nature of God. Second, mysticism counterbalances the ascetic tendency to manifest a 'happy stupidity' with respect to the meaning of the world; for the ascetic being a man of inner-worldly action fails to cope, from the mystic's point of view, with the problem of ultimate reality. Third, the mystical orientation provides a counter-point to the asceticist tendency in working for the glory of God to confuse this with self-glory – mysticism facilitating the differentiation of working *for* God from relating *to* God. The latter is a specialty of the mystic.

Thus in an inner-worldly context the injection of mysticism provides solutions under conditions of pervasive individuation to deficiencies of ascetism; such that when a situation of inner-worldly *ascetic mysticism* is reached the three main antimonies implied in the previous paragraph can be integrated. Broadly speaking, the circumstance of inner-worldly ascetic mysticism provides for both immanent active participation in the world and transcendent reflection upon the world (in even broader terms for the differentiated integration of practice and theory).

Our concern is with the Occidental world, but the present phase of discussion demands that we indicate the way in which asceticism may ideal-typically come to complement mysticism in an other-worldly context. In the latter asceticism provides counter-balances of the following nature. It offsets mystical tendencies to live-off the products of a 'bad' world; to be obsessed with the nature of ultimate reality; and to be obsessed with union with – and in a sense, therefore, alienation from – ultimate, other-worldly reality. Almost needless to say, the mode of complementation of mysticism by asceticism in an other-worldly context – *mystical asceticism* – is very different from that involved in the inner-worldly case of ascetic mysticism; and thus its structuring of a potential differentiated integration of theory and praxis is also dissimilar. In any case the extent of individuation is much less in such contexts – one of the major factors inhibiting such being the sustaining of a mystical other-worldliness through *collectivist forms of ritual*. Also of key importance is that whereas in the inner-worldly context mysticism emphasizes *self-realization* in relation to an activist asceticism, in the other-worldly context asceticism emphasizes discipline for the procuring of conditions necessary for the pursuit of *ego-dissolution*.

Even though we have drawn on Weber's sketches of mysticism and asceticism in order to arrive at the theses just stated, the fact remains that Weber did not give much direct attention to the fate of different types of religious orientation under conditions of rationalization. His general view was that instrumental rationality had gained autonomy *vis-à-vis* its religious base in inner-worldly asceticism – although he clearly saw the possibility of individuated mysticism as arising among certain middle class categories (especially intellectuals) as a response to the triumph of instrumental rationality. But there is little or no attention paid in Weber's work to the functions of mysticism in conditions of rationalization. In speaking thus, we particularly have in mind the significance of the concern with self-realization which has been such a strong feature of modern America – the attempt to discover the noumenal in the self, as in numerous imported Eastern religious orientations, the so-called charismatic movement and to an extent the resurgence of glossalalia. Such tendencies as the latter are, of course, forms of definitely-religious mysticism. But many secular varieties of psychotherapy and programs for self-consummation have a strong mystical flavoring, by the criterion which has been offered above. That is not to say that all forms of modern therapy and guides to personal living are mystical. Far from it. Many are purely utilitarian, in the sense that they address the extrinsic, material benefits which will flow from the strengthening of the ego, the acquisition of new interactional abilities, quasi-scientific knowledge, and so on. But even these developments involve in many cases the stripping of id/superego concerns and the enchancement of ego/ego-ideal matters; which in itself may in the longer term make for a high degree of disposability to concern with the mystical possibilities of the self. However, the more important point here is that enlargement and pursuit of 'the real self' – along the lines suggested by some of the more elaborate self-enrichment and expansion-of-consciousness movements – may constitute an aspect of the rationalization of action complexes. It has to do in large part with *the development of self-sufficiency in the face of perception of the increasing 'self-sufficiency' of other domains*, notably the domain of social-structure (a point which will be taken up again shortly). We are speaking, then, of a mode of adaptation to the cultural, social and biological realms of human existence. The search for self-sufficiency relates to rationalization in that, and insofar as, it is a mechanism for dealing with self under conditions of extensive differentiation and individuation. (In a very loose sense the mystical search for self-sufficiency and self-enhancement is utilitarian, in that it is concerned with the maximization of gratification – but we would prefer to reserve the term 'utilitarian' for cases of extrinsic reward-seeking.)

In fact Weber did briefly note something of the kind about which we have just been talking when, in the course of discussing the 'systematization' of an ethic of 'good works', he slips quickly from the idea that 'religious good works with a social orientation become mere instruments of *self-perfection*' to pointing out that ethical religions were preceded (in the traditional Indian context) by the planning of 'religious consecration'.[48] That involved ecstasy as an instrument of self-deification. Weber's main argument is that a 'particular result of the methodical training of the total personality pattern is that the social and ethical quality of action falls into secondary importance, while the religious effort expended upon oneself becomes of primary importance'.[49]

Superficially it would seem that some modern, inner-worldly mystical tendencies approximate the situation which Weber attributed to the German fourteenth-century mystic, Tauler (whom, according to Erikson, Luther admired, but felt unable to follow): 'A mystic of the type of Tauler completes his day's work, and then seeks contemplative union with his god in the evening, going forth to his usual work the next morning . . . in the correct inner state.'[50] Erikson describes this as the condition of passive identity – a system which 'retreats far behind the gnostic position. . . . It is the return to a state of symbiosis with the matrix, a state of floating unity fed by a spiritual navel cord'.[51] However, even though thorough empirical study would almost certainly show that there are some significant traces of this kind of relatively passive mysticism, the notion of inner-worldly ascetic mysticism being proposed here indicates a much more activist, *engagé* modality. In other words, in the modern kind of *ascetic mysticism* the emphasis is much more positive, both with respect to the significance of worldly activity and the active quest for personal realization. This is in part due to the greater secularity of the modern condition, in which meaning has to be *actively* sought and utilized. It is also in part undoubtedly due to there being a relative surfeit of material, biological, social, cultural, and temporal resources. Such factors assist in distinguishing between modern Western mysticism and traditional Eastern mysticism, for, as Weber noted, in the Orient mysticism has frequently been the primary preserve of élites, whereas Western mysticism, particularly of the kind which we are addressing here, has been and is very 'democratic' and egalitarian. In the modern world, then, *relative surplus* provides a general condition for the nurturing of mysticism – indeed mysticism becomes virtually a consumable product in a context of mass institutionalization.

As we have remarked, there is in the work of Weber and that of Troeltsch a somewhat puzzling relationship between the church-sect theme and the asceticism-mysticism motif. In that connection it would seem that mystical 'options' parallel the 'options' available to the religious ascetic. The latter has at one extreme the sectarian option of coping with the world by purification in relation to that world, while at the other extreme he has the furthest churchly option of participating in the moral or religio-ethical organization of the world. The mystic in seeking to avoid worldly contingencies can range in *his* 'strategy' from seeking mystical, contemplative transcendence to the position of vitalizing the world.

In a sense, the latter (vitalization) involves enchanting or re-enchanting the world. A good example of a self-conscious intellectual endeavor of this kind is provided by the attempt of a number of German idealists and romanticists of the late eighteenth century and early nineteenth century to revive German speculative mysticism. (Here again we confront the problem of the degree to which Hegel subscribed to mystical ideas.) There was in that period a discernible set of notions of a virtually millennial character centered, as Lobkowicz puts it, on the idea that 'God needs man to reach his ultimate completion, and by uniting with God, man comes to stand so close to the First Cause that he almost becomes a *causa sui*.' Lobkowicz argues that if one lays aside the phrase 'by the help of God' one can quickly reach Hegel: 'God only is God if he knows himself; furthermore his knowing himself is his self-consciousness in man and man's knowledge of God which leads to man's knowledge of himself *in God*.'[52] On the other hand, it could equally well be said that Hegel draws on mystical ideas in order to facilitate a process of the secularization of Christianity. This suggestion can be brought into sharper relief by additionally proposing that there are both mystical and ascetic secularization routes – the Marxian and the Liberal.[53] The Marxist route has its origins – ideas of Marx effecting an 'epistemological rupture' not withstanding – in the ideas concerning enchantment or re-enchantment of the empirical world through absorption of spirit into human life – life thereafter being sustained by the work of men and women in relation to the laws of life. (The great pejorative sensitivity about 'mysticism' and 'mystification' in the Marxian tradition can thus be partly explained as being a kind of recognition of vitalistic-mystical origins – that is, *a concern not to regress along the secularization trajectory*.) The Liberal route has its origins in notions concerning autodetermination at the level of individuals, via the operation of increasing cognitive rationality.

The strategy of mystical transcendence is clearly, almost tautologically, individualistic, and it is that kind of mysticism which Troeltsch clearly had in mind in postulating his trio of religious 'organizations' (church, sect, mysticism). The fact that an anti-organizational form figured in Troeltsch's array is of course problematic. On the other hand, he did refer to what he called the 'parallelism of spontaneous religious personalities' – a clear pointer toward the limited form in which individualistic mysticism might to a degree be organizationally institutionalized. (Weber's interest in the Quakers seems to have been guided by such a consideration.) And yet Troeltsch did underestimate the importance of mystical fellowship. Weber's expression of interest in the acosmic brotherhood of East European forms of mystical fellowship shows an appreciation of some of the limitations of seeing mysticism in solely individual forms. Wach argued that because mystical experience is ultimately ineffable (ineffability being one of the most commonly noted of the attributes of mysticism) there are left 'mainly two forms of sociality in which the mystic will participate: human companionship in what concerns all daily life and mutual support in the protest directed against traditional religious forms and institutions'.[54]

At the other extreme of the range of mysticism, any attempt to vitalize the world requires that there be frequent inter-individual validations – an ongoing culture of mysticism – to the effect that the world is indeed full of mystery. In that connection Wach's emphasis upon the protest nature of one major form of mysticism is important. Although he does not explicitly address such tendencies in speaking of mysticism, it can safely be said that the so-called Free Spirits of the Reformation period fit the protest form of mysticism very well. The significantly collective dimension of that form of mysticism is elicited through emphasizing the tendency for mysticism to be combined with rationalism in the Reformation period. As Bainton puts it, 'the combination was possible through a division of spheres. Reason might operate to demonstrate the inadequacy of rival systems, including even those reared by reason itself, and then the diving board was ready for the mystic leap. . . . Mysticism and rationalism could combine partly by a demarcation of sphere and partly through a coincidence of interest. The rationalist aversion to theological niceties could be undergirded by the mystic's indifference to credal refinements.'[55] (Bainton, moreover, unintentionally provides a major clue to Weber's ambivalence about mysticism: Rationalism and mysticism combined 'mainly because man is incurably religious and if the rationalist undercuts the traditional faith he has nothing left to live by unless he can establish a direct contact with the eternal'.)[56] There are, surely, significant echoes of the combination of rationalism and mysticism in some very recent protest movements.

An issue which is closely related to any discussion of mysticism (and contiguous matters) is that of the balance between immanence and transcendence. In one sense immanence and transcendence respectively parallel the 'vitalistic' and individualistic, transcending modes of mysticism of which we have already spoken: in the first case the world is seen as infused with spirit, with mystery; in the second case spirit lies beyond, or 'over', the world. Christianity in its historic development tended to stress the simultaneity of immanence and transcendence. ('He is transcendent, and therefore cannot be attained or comprehended or experienced as He is in Himself by any created faculty; yet He is immanent in creation by His power, His presence, and His essence, for without this power and presence no creature could exist.')[57] Although the balance between the two has been at the heart of many disputes, most notably in the Reformation period, it would seem that transcendence has historically been conceived as a mode of ultimate reality 'standing over' a secular world. The degree to which the latter is infused with the powers and actions of the former has been a major basis for doctrinal dispute and of sociocultural variation.

Moltmann argues that the traditional relationship between immanence and transcendence has been reversed. Citing Hegel in order to pinpoint Romanticism as a major historical locus of change in this respect, he argues that 'the unhappy consciousness of the beautiful soul' (Hegel's phrase) has 'fled from the constricting, alienating and meaningless reality of phenomena into the dream world of the beyond, into the unhindered realm of play where imaginary possibilities abound. Yet, it is precisely this flight which has . . . abandoned the social and political dimensions to human powers.'[58]

Moltmann's argument expressed in more straightforwardly sociological terms is that the economically-oriented aspects of modern social structures – and we suggest political aspects as well – have acquired a fixity and stability that is seemingly unresponsive to individual-human volition. That social-structural domain constitutes a realm of stabilized immanence in that it is perceived to be something unto itself – no longer, in this perspective, guided by or symbiotically linked to a transcendence, nor energically conditioned by creative, imaginative action. Put in sociological terms, Moltmann is speaking of a crucial phase in the differentiation of the individual from the social-structural domain in response to the autonomization and rigidification of the latter. Thus, 'The Augustinian inversion that we "need" the world in order to enjoy God has become much more apposite.'[59]

Moltmann continues:

In modern immanence . . . 'transcendence' has lost its job, as it were. . . . The 'realm of necessity' serves as the ground upon which the realms of play, culture and transcendence are constructed. Indeed, the more stable immanence becomes the more unstable and open can transcendence be understood. Whereas transcendence had to be thought of earlier as a stabilizing factor of order – as 'the highest star of being' (Nietzsche) – in a stabilized world, transcendence can be thought of precisely in its boundless openness, as the inexhaustible fascination of new possibilities and fantasies.[60]

For all its effectiveness in conveying some key features of modern societies, and particularly the ground upon which mystical orientations are based, Moltmann's characterization does not assist in analytically solving a problem which has become increasingly salient among a number of social scientists. If we can agree that traditionally in the West it is culture which has functioned as the mediator of the sense of transcendence, as manifesting a 'lift' over individual subjectivity and social-structural objectivity (and also, of course providing *models for* transcendence), we have to ask what is the function of culture in a situation where transcendence is experienced at the level of selves? One argument is that the latter – the multiplicity of subjective expressions of experience – increasingly is constitutive of culture. (That, indeed, might well be the corollary of Moltmann's position.) The subjectivization-of-culture argument is, however, deficient in two major respects. First, it suggests that culture varies at random in relation to social structure; second, it implies that social structure – particularly in its economic and politico-administrative aspects – literally does operate on its own, unguided by any generalized beliefs, values and symbols. Both indications are sociologically implausible. In the first case, it is surely true that subjective transcendence will be constrained by the nature of that which is being transcended (which is to take very seriously the implications of the 'Augustinian inversion'); in the second case, it is impossible to conceive of institutionalized social relationships being conducted without the facility of shared, trans-situational beliefs, values and symbols. Thus we have to distinguish between the latter (which constitutes objective culture) and subjectivist ideation. The latter can, following Simmel, be divided into protoculture and subjective culture.[61] Protoculture consists in ideas developed to cope with particular 'chunks' of experience, and has therefore a primarily instrumental character. Subjective culture, on the other hand is culture in the mode of cultivation of objective culture – its development – on the part of, and in reference to, individuals.

A major clue to an understanding of the modern circumstance is provided through recalling that in the nineteenth century there was a tendency to highlight the significance of culture via its alienative character. Culture was sometimes defined as a form of alienation – something having a large degree of autonomy and disjunctiveness in relation to the social-institutional and experiential life of individuals, from whence derives the ideal/actual distinction. Thus we may conceive of the seeming autonomization of culture as a first step toward the sense that transcendence had to be accomplished by man and woman – not 'automatically' funneled through a closely intertwined mixture of ideational and social-institutional domains. In that perspective not merely social-institutional reality but also objective cultural reality has taken on the character of an immanence without an overarching, suspending transcendence. What some have diagnosed as a situation of free-floating proliferation of cultural innovations appears in the interpretation offered here as in part a form of alienation from culture, as play upon and reaction to the more solid, more slowly evolving ideational forms which still function as an 'umbrella' and more tacitly constitute the coding of everyday interaction – including the coding of the way in which mystical tendencies manifest themselves. (Some of these issues are discussed further in chapter 6, with special reference to what is called microcultural analysis.)

Of course, there remains the problem of the public-cultural ramifications of mystical ideation. Here the issue is the conditions under which subjectivistically-generated ideations (protoculture) become part of (objective) culture – become, for example, beliefs that can be subsequently institutionalized and widespreadly cultivated. That is too large and tangential a question in the present context. Suffice to say that we now need analytic tools which will enable us to speak of the institutionalization in the societal, social-structural realm of beliefs, values and symbols which have been manufactured and laundered in the subjective realm of identity embellishment; as well as the analytic lenses for coming to terms with culture modification via subjectivist generation.

Such considerations relate to the theme of inner-worldly, ascetic mysticism as follows. The immanent fixity and autonomy accorded to the economic and political sectors of the social-structural realm, appearing to 'manage' (efficiently or not) without transcendent cultural constraints, leave individuals *qua* individuals ever more conscious of their mortality, particularly in the context of a modern-historical emphasis upon instrumental activism. The latter has increasingly, since the Reformation of which it is a secularized outcome, implied that both society and self have become objects of attempts to pursue 'perfection'. One of Weber's major worries was that there was an incompatibility between the pursuit of society's welfare and the pursuit of individual salvation. The fact that societies have indefinite life-spans, while individuals have relatively little time in which to realize themselves, throws this worry into sharp relief.[62]

Before Weber, Simmel had spoken dramatically of a sharpening cleavage between the needs of society and the needs of individuals. Simmel's view was that in modern circumstances, where societies were highly societalized and individuals highly individuated, society 'demanded' that individuals contribute to the completeness of society while, on the other hand, individuals sought to complete *themselves*.[63] Thus society demands individual specialization, while individuals demand wholeness. Weber's standpoint – particularly as it can be distilled from his essay 'Science as a Vocation' – seems to have been that whereas for society the ethical contributions of science are relevant (primarily because there is time to attend to the consequences of taking different courses of action), for individuals – relatively speaking – that is not so (in large part because of relative scarcity of time). Thus for Weber combining rational-ethical contributions to society with contributions to self-perfection in the name of ethical demands was not possible.

Ascetic mysticism *can*, however, be seen as bridging the hiatus between societal and self demands in conditions of extensive societalization and individuation. Following the specifications provided above (pp. 128 ff.) ascetic mysticism is compatible with an activist stance *vis-à-vis* 'perfection' of society *and* 'perfection' of self. It allows generalizable contributions to societal 'perfection' to be combined with – and symbolically tied to – protected and privileged, particularistic and diffuse, contributions to 'self-perfection' of a rational and rationalizable nature. Such compatibilities and combinations are made possible by a reinterpretation of standardized contributions to society in a way so as to permit, indeed to a large extent encourage, freely chosen objectives pivoted upon the notion of self-realization.

Such then is the ideal-typical picture that emerges from our attempt to reconstruct and elaborate Weber's views on types of salvation – an interest which Weber inherited from nineteenth-century German concern with modes of existence, and which in long-term historical perspective goes back to the Greek concern with ways of life. Indeed, in a very important sense our discussion of the combination of mysticism and asceticism in the modern world relates quite directly to the ancient Greek preoccupation with the relationship between the realm of necessity and the realms of human fulfillment, a focus which was to be continued in philosophy through to the crucial contributions of Kant, Hegel and Marx. We have, however, tried – following Weber's lead – to conceive of this general problem-area in realistic, empirically-sensitive sociological terms; even though our specific empirical references have been very few in number.

At this concluding juncture two warnings are necessary. First: we have been speaking of mysticism as a particular orientation to life, but have not thereby intended to say anything specifically about mystical experiences *per se*. Whether individuals have 'genuine' mystical experiences on a widespread basis in modern societies is a different kind of problem from that with which we are concerned here. On the other hand, the fact that talk of mystical experience has become more widespread in recent years, particularly in America, can fruitfully be seen in the context of the more generalized concern with consciousness-raising and altering states of consciousness. Thus concern with mystical experience, heightening consciousness and altering states of consciousness is here regarded primarily as constituting a set of indicators of the presence of mystical orientations as sociologically defined. We must, on the other hand, be wary – as has already been emphasized – of regarding the indicators of mystical orientations in too inclusive a manner. For many of the orientations – or, in different mode, many of the styles of individual and group psychotherapy – that have been popularized in recent years have been focused on the issue of enabling individuals to be more successful in terms of their contributions to and instrumental gains from the 'material' aspects of the social-structural domain. In contrast, our ideal-typical depiction of inner-worldly mysticism pivots upon self-realization in a relatively autonomous sense, *but* an autonomy conceived in the mode of differentiated parity with (ascetic) participation in social affairs, particularly those concerning the economic and/or politico-administrative aspects of society. In another respect, we might say that mysticism has to do with life, whereas asceticism has to do with society – a combination that in principle overcomes an antimony which we can quite clearly discern in the works of the two major German sociologists of the classic period, namely Simmel and Weber.

The second main warning has to do with the issue of secularization. Much of our discussion has centered upon distinctively religious definitions of asceticism and mysticism, particularly as they derive with modification from Max Weber. On the other hand, we have more than hinted at the idea of these becoming secularized. Here it is necessary to emphasize that there is an important respect in which the combination of asceticism and mysticism itself allows for – can indeed constitute – a form of secularization. The key point here is the fact that although we have defined our major concepts and their relationships with each other in primarily religious terms (in the relatively exclusive sense of the latter phrase) that does not mean that we are thereby committed to seeing all modern societies in this perspective. Thus much of the asceticism and mysticism of the modern world is indeed highly secular. For example discussions and controversies about the conduct of social life have in recent years tended to focus on morality as seen in purely secular terms, while although sometimes being influenced by religious conceptions many, but by no means all, of the modern emphases upon self-realization, altered states of consciousness and the like have been seen in secular – often indeed scientific-secular – terms.

One of the main tasks of this chapter has been to locate mysticism within a definite sociological problem-area. It is clear that in German philosophy and sociology a major general tendency has been to treat mysticism with respect to its negative bearing upon active participation in social affairs. In attempting to distil a viable, coherent and isolable cluster of problems we can in summary reinvoke the notion which was generated in discussion of Hegel, namely that religious sectarianism has to do with socially organized subjectivity and that churchism has to do with socially organized objectivity – the former emphasizing the subjectivity of *man's* attitude toward 'the world', the latter laying stress upon the shaping of 'the world' in its objectivity. In turn – although we have not claimed direct influence of Hegel – Troeltsch and Weber utilized the distinction between church and sect in empirical investigation. Troeltsch saw mysticism as a 'third way' – a form of religious orientation marked by its individualistic nature, in the sense of being concerned with the particular religious needs of individuals *qua* individuals. Weber, on the other hand, did not directly link mysticism to church-and-sect. Mysticism found its place in the Weberian scheme in the typology of salvation modalities.

Troeltsch was concerned exclusively with Christianity, while Weber widened his interests in religion in a global-historical direction. The fate of the Troeltschian array of church, sect and mysticism has primarily been its use in establishing typological facilities for the study of religious collectivities. Thus we find from the work of Becker onwards a concern with the cult as a form of quasi-collectivity.[64] And there has ensued a protracted debate about the relationship between the loosely organized cult founded on religious individuation and more definitely collective forms of religion. In the process of elaborating these matters many analysts have lost sight of the doctrinal history of mysticism, the latter's orientational underpinnings and ramifications, and, indeed, the significance of religious individuation *per se*. Thus for some sociologists of religion 'mystical' has been transformed into 'cultic' – with a serious loss of sociological information, not to speak of subsequent confusion. The fact that now there is a shift away from concern with collectivities *qua* social organizations to using the church-sect motif in terms of 'responses to the world' is both significant and ironic – in that, broadly speaking, that is where the intial Weber-Troeltsch approach was situated; while Weber's later deployment of salvational orientations took precisely the direction of being concerned with religious orientations to 'the world' on an historical, comparative basis.[65]

A persistent theme in the history of Western thought has been the relationship between contemplation and worldly activism (and one can find parallels in other civilizational contexts). These are summary terms disguising a number of antinomies which Hegel and Marx were in the nineteenth century to try to overcome. Weber, on the other hand, maintained a deep concern to preserve the realm of absolutes – of existential freedom – from the encroachment of instrumental rationality; while he was equally concerned – in the interests of societal stability – to sustain ethics of responsible participation in societal affairs. In his conception of absolute spirit Hegel had developed the idea that the problem of the particularities of societies in relation to societal universality could be overcome in terms of a social agency (the state), which would function as a form of societal self-reflexion. That was an idea which was to be pursued with different emphases and for different purposes by people such as the English Hegelians, Lenin (the vanguard and the dictatorship of the proletariat), and Mannheim (the intellectual élite). In contrast another tradition, two of whose most notable members were Simmel and Weber, took the path of individualism: it was at the level of the individual that human self-reflexiveness primarily lay – and hence freedom.[66] The position of the latter tradition was undoubtedly in part a philosophical-evaluative one, but it was also – particularly in Simmel's case – based upon sociological interpretations concerning increasing individuation and the concomitant differentiation of society as a form of life, and individualism as a form of life.

Such cleavages can be summarized in terms of the distinction between inner-worldly asceticism and inner-worldly mysticism. The church-sect motif may be seen as having to do with an asceticism axis of societal functioning. It concerns how and in what terms the social world should be participated in. The mysticism motif (ranging from individualistic, 'sub-social' mysticism to collective, super-social mysticism) has to do with the issue of how the social world should be interpreted relative to life as a whole, including the nature of ultimate reality.

The trend of the present discussion has been to emphasize the relevance of the combination of asceticism and individualistic mysticism in analyzing trends in modern Western societies, particularly the U.S.A. Processes of individuation have intermittently figured prominently, a consideration which at this concluding stage leads to our pointing-up the significance of the denominational type of religious organization in having played a crucial role in the Anglo-American complex. The emphases in religious denominationalism have included pluralistic acceptance of other religious positions and individualism – characteristics which, it has cogently been claimed, played an important function in the development of liberal political and social participation in some Western societies, notably the U.S.A. and Britain. In such terms denominationalism – as a kind of mid-point on the church-sect axis of social participation – has been a seed-bed for the development of both individual contributions to society and to self.[67]

NOTES

1. Cf. the brilliant discussion by Hannah Arendt, *The Human Condition*, Chicago, 1958. See also Nicholas Lobkowicz, *Theory and Practice: History of a Concept from Aristotle to Marx*, Notre Dame, Indiana, 1967.
2. Bellah, *The Broken Covenant*, op. cit., p. 124.

3. Emil L. Fackenheim, *The Religious Dimension in Hegel's Thought*, Boston, 1970 (paper edition), p. 148.

4. Ibid.

5. Richard Schacht, *Alienation*, p. 44. Schacht's interpretation influences much of what follows.

6. Cf. Lukács' recanting introduction to the 1967 edition of his *History and Class Consciousness* (trans. R. Livingstone), London, 1968. Also, Lukács, 'Max Weber and German Sociology' (trans. Anthony Cutler), *Economy and Society* I, 4 (November, 1972), pp. 386–98.

7. Quoted in Evelyn Underhill, *Mysticism*, London, 1961 (first published 1911), p. 6.

8. Gellner, op. cit., *passim*.

9. M. H. Abrams, *Natural Supernaturalism: Tradition and Revolution in Romantic Literature*, New York, 1971, p. 490.

10. Georg Simmel, 'The Nature of Philosophy' (trans. R. H. Weingartner), in Simmel et al., *Essays on Sociology, Philosophy and Aesthetics* (ed. Kurt H. Wolff), New York, 1959, p. 287.

11. Ibid., p. 288.

12. Ibid., p. 290.

13. For very sharp criticisms of Christian-based discussions of mysticism, see Frits Staal, *Exploring Mysticism*, Berkeley and Los Angeles, 1975. See also Agehananda Bharati, *The Light at the Center*, Santa Barbara, 1976. It must be emphasized that we are not in this essay discussing the 'proper way' to study mysticism. We are almost entirely concerned with its general sociological significance, and our definitional approach is therefore dictated by sociological concerns. Studies which have informed this discussion are too many in number to list here. Some of them are referred to directly or indirectly in Roland Robertson, 'On the Analysis of Mysticism: Pre-Weberian, Weberian and Post-Weberian Perspectives', *Sociological Analysis*, 36, 3 (Fall, 1975), pp. 241–66 which reproduces a few paragraphs from the present chapter.

14. Quoted in Rudolph Otto, *Mysticism East and West* (trans. B. L. Bracey and R. C. Payne), New York, 1932, p. 225.

15. See in particular G. W. F. Hegel, *Early Theological Writings* (trans. T. M. Knox), Chicago, 1948.

16. For a brief, but instructive discussion of mysticism in relation to vitalism, see Underhill, op. cit., ch. 2.

17. Ibid., p. 32.

18. Much of our thinking about this aspect of Hegel has been influenced by Shlomo Avineri, *Hegel's Theory of the Modern State*, London, 1972.

19. Hegel, op. cit., pp. 67–179.
20. Richard Kroner, 'Hegel's Philosophical Development', ibid., p. 11.
21. Fackenheim, op. cit., p. 79.
22. Cf. Steven E. Ozment, *Mysticism and Dissent: Religious Ideology and Social Protest in the Sixteenth Century*, New Haven, 1973.
23. This perspective is admirably highlighted by Richard Schacht, *Hegel and After: Studies in Continental Philosophy Between Kant and Sartre*, Pittsburgh, 1975, esp. chs. 3 and 4.
24. See ibid., chs. 6 and 7. See also Becker, *The Denial of Death*, op. cit., esp. chs. 5 and 8.
25. In Reinhard Bendix and Guenther Roth, *Scholarship and Partisanship: Essays on Max Weber*, Berkeley, Los Angeles, London, 1971, p. 268.
26. Frederick Copleston, *A History of Philosophy*, Vol. 7, *Schopenhauer to Nietzsche*, 1965 (paper edition), p. 52.
27. For other aspects of the negative attitude in nineteenth-century thought toward the East see Turner, *Weber and Islam*, op. cit.; and Perry Anderson, *Lineages of the Absolutist State*, London, 1974.
28. David C. McLellan, *The Young Hegelians and Karl Marx*, New York, 1969, p. 105.
29. Agreeing in this with MacRae, op. cit.
30. Arthur Mitzman, *The Iron Cage: An Historical Interpretation of Max Weber*, New York, 1970.
31. For a provocative and relevant recent study of Nietzsche, see Tracey Strong, *Friedrich Nietzsche and the Politics of Transfiguration*, Berkeley, 1975.
32. Benjamin Nelson, Review article on Max Weber, *The Sociology of Religion, American Sociological Review*, 30, 4 (August, 1965), p. 598. Cf. B. H. Gerrish, *Grace and Reason: A Study in the Theology of Luther*, Oxford, 1962.
33. See the contributions of Edwin Latzel (pp. 177–209) and Ernst Manasse (pp. 369–92) in Paul Arthur Schlipp (ed.), *The Philosophy of Karl Jaspers*, La Salle, Illinois, 1957. See also Karl Jaspers, *Leonardo, Descartes, Max Weber* (trans. R. Manheim), New York, 1964.
34. Herbert Marcuse, *Reason and Revolution*, New York, 1941, pp. 14–15.
35. See Robertson, 'On the Analysis of Mysticism', op. cit., which responds directly to the 1910 meeting. See also the responses of Theodore Steeman (181–204), William Garrett (205–33) and Benjamin Nelson (229–40) – all in *Sociological Analysis*, 36, 3 (Fall, 1975). For a partial record of the proceedings of the 1910 meeting see

'Max Weber on Church, Sect and Mysticism' (trans. J. L. Gittleman), *Sociological Analysis*, 34, 2 (Summer, 1973), pp. 140–9. See also Bendix and Roth, op. cit., esp. ch. 1.

36. Gert H. Mueller, 'Asceticism and Mysticism', *International Yearbook for the Sociology of Religion*, VIII (1973), p. 72. In spite of its idiosyncrasies, this is a most valuable essay, particularly in its criticisms of Weber and its emphasis upon the ways in which inner-worldly mysticism made such an impact in the Reformation and post-Reformation periods.

37. Weber, *Sociology of Religion*, op. cit., p. 226.

38. Ibid., p. 172.

39. Ibid., p. 177.

40. See Roland Robertson and Burkart Holzner (eds.) *Identity and Authority*, Oxford, forthcoming.

41. Parsons, 'Introduction' to Weber, *Sociology of Religion*, op. cit., p. xlix.

42. On Troeltsch and mysticism: Theodore M. Steeman, 'Church, Sect Mysticism: Periodological Aspects of Troeltsch's Types', *Sociological Analysis*, loc. cit.; and William R. Garrett, 'Maligned Mysticism: The Maledicted Career of Troeltsch's Third Type', ibid.

43. Simmel, *Sociology of Religion*, op. cit.

44. Georg Simmel, *On the Concept of Culture and Other Essays* (trans. K. Peter Etzkorn), New York 1968, chs. 1 and 2.

45. Luckmann, *The Invisible Religion*, op. cit.

46. Simmel, *The Conflict in Modern Culture*, op. cit., p.

47. Much of the following few pages constitutes a re-assembling of Weber, *Sociology of Religion*, op. cit., chs. 10 and 11. In this exercise I am indebted to Rainer Baum.

48. Ibid., pp. 156–7. This may be the best point to emphasize the tremendous impact in German social theory of the idea of self-realization. (In 1859 John Stuart Mill said that 'few persons, out of Germany even comprehend' such notions. John Stuart Mill, *Utilitarianism, Liberty and Representative Government*, London, 1910, p. 115.) The idea is encountered very frequently in Simmel, and it certainly figures prominently in Weber. For Marx see Gianfranco Poggi, *Images of Society*, Stanford, London, 1972, p. 238. The presence of the idea in the 'mature' (as well as the young) Marx is evident. See Karl Marx, *The Grundrisse* (ed. and trans. David McLellan), New York, 1971.

49. Weber, *Sociology of Religion*, op. cit., p. 157.

50. Ibid., p. 176.

51. Erik Erikson, *Young Man Luther*, New York, 1958, p. 189.
52. Lobkowicz, op. cit., p. 173.
53. An idea orally consolidated by Victor Lidz.
54. Joachim Wach, *Sociology of Religion*, Chicago, 1944, p. 164.
55. Roland Bainton, *The Reformation of the Sixteenth Century*, London, 1963, p. 236.
56. Ibid.
57. David Knowles, *The English Mystical Tradition*, New York, 1961, p. 5.
58. Jurgen Moltmann, *Religion, Revolution and the Future* (trans. M. D. Meeks), New York, 1969, p. 185.
59. Ibid., p. 186.
60. Ibid. Such views have much in common with John Marx, 'The Ideological Construction of Post-Modern Identity Models in Contemporary Cultural Movements', in Robertson and Holzner, *Identity and Authority*, op. cit. See also Rieff, *The Triumph of the Therapeutic*, op. cit., esp. pp. 26 ff.
61. See Weingartner, *Experience and Culture*, op. cit.; and *Georg Simmel on Individuality and Social Forms* (ed. David Levine), Chicago, 1971, esp. chs. 16, 23, and 24.
62. See especially Weber, 'Science as a Vocation', op. cit.
63. See especially Simmel, *Sociology of Religion*, op. cit.
64. Howard Becker, *Systematic Sociology . . . of Leopold von Wiess*, New York, 1932.
65. Bryan R. Wilson, *Magic and the Millennium*, New York, 1973.
66. The degree of self-consciousness about Hegel in Weber's work remains problematic. But it would seem that he was indeed very conscious of it. (The influence of Hegel on Simmel is manifestly obvious.) Light is cast on this by, *inter alia*; Anthony Giddens, *Capitalism and Modern Social Theory*, London, 1971, p. 173; Bruun, op. cit., passim; and Bendix and Roth, op. cit.
67. Cf. J. F. Maclear, 'The Making of the Lay Tradition', *Journal of Religion*, 33 (1953), pp. 113–36; David Martin, 'The Denomination', *British Journal of Sociology*, XII, 1 (1962), pp. 1–14; David Martin, *Pacifism*, London, 1965.

Chapter Five

Individuation, Societalization and the Civil Religion Problem

I see the most capacious and far-reaching collision between society and individual, not in the aspect of particular interests but in the general form of the individual life. Society aspires to totality and organic unity, each of its members constituting but a component part. The individual as part of society has to fulfil special functions. . . . ; he is expected to modify his skills so that he will become the best-qualified performer of these functions. But this role is opposed to man's bent toward unity and totality as expressions of his own individuality. He strives for his own perfection rather than for a model of society; he wants to develop his faculties in their totality without concern for the special requirements demanded of him in the interest of society. This is truly the essential meaning of the individualistic demands of liberty over against social restrictions. . . .

Georg Simmel

The term individualism embraces the utmost heterogeneity of meanings . . . (A) thorough, historically-oriented conceptual analysis would at the present time be of the highest value to scholarship.

Max Weber

One of the most controversial matters of recent intellectual concern, particularly in America, has been the theme of civil religion. Although the debate has indeed been mainly conducted in reference to American society, following the presentation of Bellah's essay 'Civil Religion in America' (1967), the issue has much more general significance. In one respect such a suggestion needs no substantiation beyond pointing to the centrality of the notion of civil religion in French social thought from the mid-eighteenth century onwards, and in turn the impact which Rousseau's thoughts on civil religion have had in other parts of the world. In another respect, however, the general significance of the civil-religion debate needs much elaboration. We refer to a theme which was in fact at the heart of Rousseau's original exposition, but which has been detached from it in the historical development of sociology – namely the structure of the relationship between individual and society.

Durkheim and Simmel on Individualism

There is much to suggest that individuals *qua* individuals are becoming more detached from national societies – in particular from what has traditionally been called the state. On the other hand, the diffuseness of the relationship between individual and state has apparently increased during the present century – in respect of the range and scope of activities and behaviors coming into the domain of political facilitation and political demand. The upshot is a complex mixture of relationships of independence and dependence.[1]* It is rather well-established by now that the development of the modern state and the development of what Durkheim called the cult of the individual are associated phenomenon. Durkheim's own thesis concerning the mutual amplification of what we may call the 'stateness' of society, on the one hand, and of the individuality of the individual, on the other hand, is the most well-known and adamant presentation of the argument.[2] Another view concerned with the same problem, but which has received less attention, is that of Simmel. He too clearly recognized the mutual contingency of societalization and individuation; but in contrast to Durkheim, Simmel did not regard the two processes as being solely founded in societal developments. This arose in large part from Simmel's view that life was a more fundamental category than society, and that it was individuals who were the constituents and vehicles of life. Moreover, for Simmel 'society' was a form – a kind of *a priori* – 'imposed upon' the flux of life experience.[3]

For Durkheim, since stateness and individualism were both products of the evolution of society it was natural for them to develop in harmonious interdependence, each needing the other; and it was from that perspective that Durkheim came to advance prescriptions concerning the ways in which the relationship between state and individual should be maintained. If the state was impaired individualism would be at risk, and *vice versa*. For Simmel, in contrast, it was individuals who had created both the form 'society' and particular conceptions of individualism Society was 'made possible' through the

* Notes for this chapter begin on p. 181.

individual experience of being both an individual and being involved in relationships with other individuals. This experience of being partly an individual and partly more (or, perhaps, less) than an individual had, according to Simmel, its ideal-perfect form when individuals could both be individuals *per se* and at the same time not jar with the functioning of the conception of society. That, however, it must be emphasized, was for Simmel not an immediately realistic state of affairs – it was only the perfected extension of the observation that no matter what the individual is or does society always accords him some kind of role, if only the role of the deviant. Thus when he moved from the level of philosophical discussion of what makes society possible to consider concrete historical circumstances Simmel found much tension between conceptions of the individual and conceptions of society.

En passant, it should be noted that both Durkheim and Simmel were Kantians, but of very different kinds. Durkheim believed that categories (comparable to Simmel's forms) were socially produced (including the categories society and individual) whereas Simmel believed that forms (including those of society, relation and individual) were cognitive modes of imposing order on the flux of life. Thus Simmel wanted to free the transcendental ego from society. Durkheim in contrast inserted it in society, in terms of collective representations and the *conscience collective*.[4] Both Durkheim and Simmel agreed that at least as far as the modern period was concerned (in their cases the nineteenth and very early part of the twentieth century) society and the individual developed, enlarged themselves, in tandem. But they came to virtually opposite conclusions as to the implications of this circumstance. The difference arose over the question of mutuality versus incompatibility. For Durkheim individualism and societal stateness amplified each other in a complementary manner; for Simmel both were developing toward completion of themselves, and thus at odds. Durkheim thought that individualism was granted and protected by the state, and that the latter grew largely in response to the needs of individuals, although Durkheim's insistence on the moral significance of society led him to provide reasons for the strength of the state other than simply its direct assistance to individuals *per se*. Simmel's insistence on the freedom, cognitive and moral, of the individual similarly led him to have relatively independent reasons for being concerned with potential encroachment upon the individual, particularly in his case a split between the societal aspect of the individual and the 'spiritual' part. But Simmel also saw societalization and individuation as having sprung from similar sources.

Specifically, Simmel focused the interrelated emphases upon the division of labor and the notion of uniqueness – both being part of a broader trend toward individualization. The secular trend of increasing individualization was one which encompassed all cultural, social and psychic entities. The division of labor – so conspicuous a material fact of Western life since the late eighteenth century – was clearly encouraging of specialness, of uniqueness, while uniqueness itself was a cultural idea, sown and crystallized in the motifs of romanticism, which encouraged the division of labor. In such a respect individualization had as much relevance to large-scale social forms as it did to small-scale ones, as well as to indviduals themselves. Hence a corollary of Simmel's analysis is that the emphasis upon the unique individual, and associated notions like that of self-realization, is intimately bound-up historically with the individualization of national groups. Simmel was not of course the first to note the connection – although his analytic perspicacity in these matters deserves special notice.[5] In the odysseys of ascribing individuality to persons and to collective actors we frequently find historical periods of significant conjunction – for example, Renaissance Europe was a crucial seed period for the development of both modern conceptions of the individual and of the rise of nation-state absolutism.[6] Such conjunctions have been noted from time to time.[7] But it is probably not until the late eighteenth century and the early nineteenth century that we find intellectuals adumbrating principles directly relevant to Simmel's stance. In that period one of the most conspicuous of such thinkers was Herder, who held to the view that national-societal development should be conceived in terms of collective self-realization and that in international perspective the world as a whole could be conceived along the lines of all nations contributing in their own unique, self-realizing ways to the overall development of the global system. (That conjunction of a division-of-labor scheme and an emphasis upon unique self-realization finds a modern echo in the Parsonian conception of international evolution.)[8]

Simmel's view that there was an impending 'collision' between society and individual was based upon the idea that while the division-of-labor and the attendant notion of uniqueness encouraged individuals to pursue completeness in their individuality, the very same processes also encouraged societies to pursue a completeness which was contingent upon individuals being incomplete. Societally speaking, individuals had to play special, societally needed roles that ran against the grain of the push toward completeness at the individual level. In this view Simmel was undoubtedly influenced by the emphasis which Marxists of the nineteenth century had strongly placed upon the alienating effects of the division of labor, although he viewed socialism's emphasis upon, as he saw it, equality without liberty as not adequately reflecting the real, strong empirical trends in individual-society relationships. However, Simmel did speak directly to the issue of the development of a new form or relationship between individual and society which would be more symmetrical and mutually enhancive. We will dwell on that prospect later.

It is on the question of the division of labor that Simmel and Durkheim seem to diverge very significantly. Durkheim tended to see the division of labor as a circumstance that led to the mutual, reciprocal enhancing of individuals – that individuals completed themselves in division-of-labor relationships, and that the state had a part to play in shaping the division of labor in such a way as to be promotive of such. Simmel, on the other hand, saw the division of labor as having recently accelerated uniqueness, but at the same time being part of a trend toward fragmentation of the individual. (For Simmel there were, on the other hand, social trends that tended to make individuals more individualistic, in that the complexity of relationships and the distance between individuals in modern urban settings made individuals stand-out against, gestalt-wise, their backgrounds. One of the consequences of this was to make the individual seem more mysterious.) It is, however, in their respective attitudes toward the future resolution of individual-society problems that our present interests lie. We have mentioned that Simmel hoped for a less conflictful relationship in the future – to which we add the comment that Simmel hoped for what may be called a 'Lutheran' compromise between individual and society, with the two synchronized in such a way as to guarantee individual freedom to pursue his or her own spiritual welfare.[9] Durkheim, on the other hand, seems to have moved toward a civil-religion solution.[10] In other words, in order to shore-up the individual-society connection Durkheim advocated a mode of moral-religious binding of the individual to the societal collectivity.

There is no doubt that these formulations in themselves reflect important differences between two sociocultural modalities of treating the individual-society connection. In other words, Simmel and Durkheim respectively represented different ways of coding the connection between individual and society – one in German terms, the other in French (a point which we will elaborate shortly). We cannot ignore the phenomenon of there being variations cross-societally in the folk epistemological and ontological foundations of individual-society connections. Undoubtedly within the social sciences and philosophy too little attention has been paid to *in situ* perceptions of individual-group relationships – and much arid talk at the analytic level about the rival merits of methodological, ontological and epistemological forms of individualism and collectivism could have been avoided by addressing the issue of how in real, sociocultural circumstances individuals 'move' from the individual to the collectivity level and *vice versa*.[11] That, surely, constitutes the genuinely sociological problematic; not the problem of how logically pure, rational scientists should think. The classical sociologists and many of their predecessors were clearly conscious of that problem, even though they frequently reflected or refracted character-istics of their own particular sociocultural contexts.

One of Durkheim's most important, and controversial, arguments was that a major task of the state is to free individuls *per se* from 'partial societies' – such as families, religious collectivities and labor and professional associations. Modern individualism thus, on Durkheim's argument, depends very much upon preventing the absorption of individuals into what in that perspective are regarded as secondary or mediatory groups. It is in modern circumstance through the state, according to Durkheim, that individuals have a moral existence, an existence at all. Conversely, from Durkheim's standpoint the modern state in large part owes its existence to the process of individuation; and it is this double perspective on the individual/society relationship that is the hallmark of Durkheim's stance – that from a Durkheimian's point of view marks it off from both individualistic conceptions of societies *and* what Durkheim himself called mystical conceptions of the Hegelian kind. Mention of Hegel makes it necessary to reiterate his great significance in drawing attention to the problem in modern societies of the degree of compatability between the specific nature of the authority society exercises over individuals, on the one hand, and the specific nature of the conception of individualism, on the other hand.

Durkheim's and Simmel's arguments were presented at a time – the very early part of the twentieth century – when the development of the state (at least in the Western world) was undergoing a rapid expansion of its frame of reference and operation. That was the period when in a number of societies the state's relationship with the individual in matters of economics, education and social welfare was intensified on a scale not previously experienced. There was set in motion a process whereby the state expanded through political and bureaucratic changes that had the effect of proliferating the criteria in terms of which individuals could be classified, could classify each other and classify themselves. This proliferation of classificatory criteria must surely be regarded as one among a number of bases upon which has arisen the modern sense of individuals having identity problems. So numerous and fine-grained are the modern forms of classification and identification which issue from governmental sources that individuals increasingly feel that specific aspects of their sense of identity are beyond their control. By the same token, demands to be treated more fairly and adequately on the part of individuals, or particular categories of individuals, lead to the proliferation of more rules and regulations. The extent to which identity in its ethnic and nation-of-origin modalities has been bound-up with state action in the modern U.S.A. provides an excellent constituency of examples.

Durkheim's arguments were focused primarily upon the link between the expansion of personal freedom and the fact of central government being the major source for such expansion. That formulation shades into the proposition that industrialized societies – of all kinds – rely significantly more upon 'institutionalized anxiety' than direct occupational role-performance. Baum subsumes such ideas under a general conception of the link between Durkheim's individuation and Weber's bureaucratization. Bureaucratization he defines as a growth in the power of societies – 'increased efficacy of society as a cooperative system'. Individuation, on the other hand, has to do with 'growth in the quest for a sense of personal autonomy'. The crucial link between the two is that 'no complex and functionally differentiated social system could conceivably rely primarily on coercion in mobilizing and steering motives for role performance. Even if coercive center control were informationally possible, the administration of coercive compliance would require allocating socio-political resources to internal integration and control functions to such an extent that no upgrading in overall collective performance *vis-à-vis* environments would register at all.'[12]

The Individual, a Societal Member?

Generally speaking, modern sociologists have tended to think of the individual as only a societal member – or at least to think in terms of the ways in which individuals are socialized into society. To that extent much has been lost to modern sociology of what was valuable in the old social contract debates of the seventeenth and eighteenth centuries.[13] (It is, on the other hand, of the greatest importance to take note of the degree to which in the modern period the phrase 'social contract' has seemingly returned to everyday discourse; while one of the most publicized of recent social-scientific debates resonates with social-contract themes – namely the confrontation between the positions of Rawls and Nozick with respect to the viable foundations of modern societies.) Sociologists have tended to take the society too much for granted. In recent years the scattered attempts to undo that predicate within the sociological community have in the main merely criticized the empirical centrality of the national-societal focus, and have thereby ignored two critical matters. On the one hand, the denial of the salience of state apparati in the modern world flies in the face of the continuing strengthening of the state, which a number of political scientists have analyzed in terms of 'the new corporatism'; while the question of the degree to which individuals are indeed only societal beings has been left unattended. It is also somewhat ironic that the analytic retreat from the society as a conceptual entity has occurred before many sociologists had gotten around to developing the study of national societies, nationalism and international relations.

The recently announced denial of the significance of the national-society category amounts for some only to a claim that what is called in everyday discourse a society – such as America – is really only a complex mixture of ethnic, regional and transnational groupings. For others of a civilizational persuasion the shift away from the national-societal focus constitutes a realistic and cogent demand that we take carefully into account wide-ranging and long-term social and cultural phenomena in our discussions; and do not, for example, automatically attribute uniqueness to a trend which has recently become evident within a particular society, without careful consideration of its possible connection historically to phenomena not transparently in evidence in that society in the modern circumstance. To a considerable extent this latter, civilizational perspective informs our arguments here. Such a perspective directs our attention to transcending analytically the particularities of the modern relationship between individual and national society in order to understand that relationship.

Sociology arose – not coincidentally – at the same time that the modern national society was developing. It is generally thought that protosociology developed in the Enlightenment period, that its self-conscious claim to independent existence was the work of men writing during the nineteenth century, and that its full potential and its liabilities have been displayed in the twentieth century. Similarly in the case of the rise of the modern national society we may speak of three phases. The major problems of societies in the Enlightenment period (with the quite extensive break-up of the absolute state), culminating in the American and the French Revolutions, pivoted upon the viability of the idea of national societies being governed by principles of participation. The nineteenth-century phase was marked by political and economic struggles over the details of citizenly participation. The present century has been characterized by attempts to cope with extensive participation and state obligation, with a rather recent sense that the limits of such have to be thought anew.

The fact of modern sociology having arisen in tandem with the development of the modern national society invites consideration of the extent to which sociologists may have tended to overlook some inherent problems of national-societal functioning. Much of mainstream political sociology has consisted in the analysis of processes of citizenship *inclusion*, with relatively little attention being paid to the problem of the ways in which individuals allocate their commitments to the respective demands of society and self relative to life-concerns in highly modern circumstances. To be sure there has been considerable discussion of the rivalry between commitment to the wider, inclusive national society and quasi-groups within and beyond the societal framework; but that kind of discussion has been lacking in concern with the problem of societal membership *per se*. To some extent foci sparked by the thesis of increasing privatization and its implications also approach the kind of questions with which we are here concerned. However, such perspectives frequently lack attention to *the nature* of privatization and the ways in which such is or is not sustained in relation to the wider-societal setting. What is needed, then, is a mode of discussion which attends to the relationship between commitment to 'society' and commitment to 'self'. In particular, we need to focus upon the meaning aspects of these forms of commitment.

What we are here particularly interested in are the ways in which concern with self has been cast in terms that pose a problem for societal functioning. In the conceptual format of the previous chapter either of the forms of other-worldliness – mystical or ascetic – clearly must be seen as problematic relative to an 'active society', where there is ongoing concern with the maintenance or promotion of secular 'perfection'. Clearly, in speaking, as we do, almost exclusively of Western societies the use of the term 'other-worldly' is relativistic; that is, the notion of other-worldliness is a relative not an absolute one. Thus Catholicism at certain periods and some forms of well-insulated sectarianism qualify as relatively other-worldly.

When we talk of the idea of 'selfish' religious commitment we of course focus most directly upon the idea of individualistic concern with salvation outside of the frame of societal functioning, where in extreme form worldly involvement is regarded as sinful by individuals in a highly autonomous manner. But in the history of the Christian West there have of course been – particularly prior to the Reformation – various forms of collectivist religious commitment which were in intent and/or consequence disruptive, or potentially so, of the 'official' societal order. The Reformation witnessed the break-up in a number of societies of the close alignment of Church and state and thereafter the Catholic Church came to be regarded in many contexts as the primary locus of religious diversion from or challenge to societal commitment. Thus in predominantly Protestant societies concern with the anti-societal nature or consequences of religious commitment frequently focused from the Enlightenment onwards upon the Church-mediation of anti-societyness, while in other societies the concern was more with individualistic forms of religious commitment being anti- or at least a-societal.

The idea of individual religious commitment being a rival basis of loyalty in relation to the state was strongly challenged during the seventeenth century when Calvinistic Protestantism was a vital factor in diminishing royal absolutism in Switzerland, the Dutch Netherlands, Scotland, and particularly, in England. As revolutionaries 'the saints' themselves did of course demonstrate just how much the state could be undermined by religious groups strongly imbued with a concern with immortality; but the other side of the story is that the Calvinist saints provided a relatively new model for political participation, one which had a deep impact in subsequent periods (not to speak of their direct influence in the development of American society). One of the strongest arguments of the latter kind is that of Walzer:

It was the Calvinists who first switched the emphasis of political thought from the prince to the saint (or the band of saints) and then constructed a theoretical justification for independent political action. What Calvinists said of saints, other men would later say of the citizen: the same sense of civic virtue, of discipline and duty, lies behind the two names. Saint and citizen together suggest a new integration of private men (or rather, of *chosen* groups of private men, of proven holiness and virtue) into the political order, an integration based upon a novel view of politics as a kind of conscientious and continuous labor. This is surely the most significant outcome of the Calvinist theory of worldly activity, preceding in time any infusion of religious worldliness into the economic order. The diligent activism of the saints – Genevan, Huguenot, Dutch, Scottish and Puritan – marked the transformation of politics into work and revealed for the first time the extraordinary conscience that directed the work.[14]

The importance of such developments must, however, not be misconstrued, for the Calvinistic model did not, as Walzer readily concedes, endure 'as an integral and creative force'. Rather, its major historical impact was in laying the foundations for a new form of self-discipline. Walzer argues that 'Lockeian liberals found it possible to dispense with religious, even with ideological, controls in human society and thought enthusiasm and battle-readiness unattractive'.[15] Thus on this view the historical importance of Calvinism resides in its synergic characteristics — that is, in erecting a model that facilitated individuals conceiving of their making a simultaneous, positive contribution to the self *and* society. That the contribution to self was supposed to be made on the basis of self-denial matters little in the present context — for in the strong version of the Calvinist view denial of everyday self*ish* desires constituted the basis for the new freedom. Thus freedom from temptations of a selfish kind became in itself the mode of self-satisfaction. Such conceptions have been operative in a number of contexts outside of the sphere of direct Calvinist influence, not least in modern Communist societies.

The Civil Religion Debate, Bellah Style

Bellah's 1967 article on the civil religion of America has led to considerable debate and controversy.[16] The debate has focused mainly on the questions: Is there really an American civil religion? If so, what are its contents and vehicles? And if not, why is American civil religion not possible in modern circumstances? It is evident, however, that there has been little attention paid to the theoretical underpinnings of the idea of civil religion — even though that notion has been quite prominent in social thought, most explicitly in France, for over two hundred years. Much of the recent concentration upon surface and purely-American aspects of the idea of civil religion is attributable to the original Bellah exposition — which simply asserted, with only slight empirical embellishment, that the U.S.A. has historically (but also problematically) manifested a tradition of civil religiosity. But it would seem unlikely that a few pages of sociological polemic (a characterization not here cast in the pejorative mode) could have created sustained scholarly attention over a period of about ten years unless there were some very important analytic issues at stake. Of course, one does have to entertain the proposition that the civil religion debate constitutes a blind alley from the standpoint of the theoretically sensitive sociologist. It might, for example, be argued that what kept the controversy alive was its coinciding with the American Bicentennial – that once the debate lasted up to, say, 1973 it was bound to continue until, say, 1978. But the fact that the debate has indeed really been going on since at least as early as the middle of the eighteenth century (and some would argue the debate is as old as ancient Greek philosophy) lends much support to the proposition that something very important may be at stake, extending well beyond the confines of the question: Does America have a civil religion?

That the idea of civil religion is of great *theoretical*-sociological significance has been clearly recognized only in the modern period by Talcott Parsons, who has – without much elaboaration or the provision of a rationale – incorporated it conceptually in one of his most recent comprehensive statements on the theory of action.[17] In the latter, 'civil religion' appears as a subsystem of the social-system segment of the total action system, where its import is highlighted definitionally by the use of the phrase 'constitutive values'. Civil religion does, then, for Parsons refer to the most basic operative values in systems (notably societal systems) of social interaction. Clusters of intrinsically significant values become operative through processes of institutionalization from the stock of cultural items. Parsons' incorporation of the concept of civil religion is relevant to the present discussion in one major respect. It shows how Bellah's ideas about civil religion have already acquired generalized analytic status without comprehensive dissection of the theoretical issues implied in the civil religion debate. (Parsons obviously makes the idea of civil religion central to 'the problem of order', as we shall see in more detail.) That contention imposes an immediate obligation to sketch the themes that Bellah has raised.

In his 1967 article Bellah argued that 'few have realized that there actually exists alongside of and rather clearly differentiated from the churches an elaborate and well-institutionalized civil religion in America'.[18] This 'religious dimension . . . has its own seriousness and integrity and requires the same care in understanding that any other religion does'.[19] From the earliest years of the American republic there has existed a collection of symbols, beliefs and rituals relating to sacred things and institutionalized in the national collectivity. 'This religion . . . while not antithetical to, and indeed sharing much in common with, Christianity, was neither sectarian nor in any specific sense Christian. . . . There was an implicit but quite clear division of function between the civil religion and Christianity.'[20] Speaking in a vein which he has subsequently come to characterize as *hermeneutical*, Bellah spoke concretely of three 'times of trial' which have both provided explicit demonstration of civil-religion motifs and exerted pressure on existing civil religion, in the sense of constituting a crisis for the latter. These were specified as the revolution-independence period; the Civil War; and a third time of trial that is still with us.[21] The latter, which has mainly been the bone of contention in the New Civil Religion Debate, centers upon what Bellah called in 1967 'the problem of responsible action in a revolutionary world, a world seeking to attain many of the things, material and spiritual, that we have already attained'.[22] The third time of trial was, in Bellah's view, manifested dramatically and tragically in the Indo-Chinese conflict which was raging at the time of his first contribution to the civil religion theme. In a subsequent statement (1974), Bellah understandably saw the crisis in civil religion deepening even more rapidly in the context of the Watergate experience.[23]

What can be gleaned from Bellah's original statement and some of his replies to his critics leads to the conclusion that Bellah undoubtedly regards all societies as in fact having and needing a civil religion of some kind.[24] (This proposition has been made particularly problematic by the argument that Judaism and Islam have over most of their history been civil religions. Does civil religion have only societal reference? Or can a religion in and of itself be a civil religion?)[25] Given the emphasis upon the themes of origin, purpose and destiny in Bellah's discussions of the American case, we can also derive the suggestion that civil religion has to do with ideations centered upon what might be called the ultimate grounds of societal existence and functioning – a characterization which was backed from the outset by Bellah's own insistence upon the notion that civil religion relates (ideal-typically) to American society in transcendent mode.[26]

In responding to criticisms of the 1967 article Bellah has presented a number of elaborations. First, he has denied emphatically that civil religion refers to a common denominator among the principal faith clusters. Second, he has tried to refute the idea that civil and *transcivil* religions potentially give rise to conflicting loyalties. Third, he has rejected the proposition that his thesis involves 'a misplaced sacredness, a blurring of the necessary boundary between church and state'.[27] (According to Bellah, his critics 'either lacked a comparative dimension, believing American patriotic piety to be a peculiarly American aberration, or they placed it in a very negative comparative context in which the chief other member was Nazi Germany'.)[28] Fourth, Bellah has argued that 'the very currency of the notion of civil religion is the earnest of its reality. It is now part of the description of the place in which we live and that at a certain level is that'.[29]

Bellah's first three responses indicate that he is clearly concerned with *the sociological problem of order*. Suffice to say at this juncture that in speaking of the problem of order we do not thereby commit ourselves to agreeing with the precise manner in which that motif has been used by Parsons as the departure point for much of his sociological theorizing. Rather, the tack adopted here is to consider the problem of order in the perspectives of both whole (national) societies *and* the individuals who 'belong' to such societies. Proposing that the problem of order has to be pitched at *both* societal and individual levels is, we believe, well in line with the central problems tackled by the founding fathers of modern sociology.

The term 'order', then, relates here to *three* specific matters – order at the societal level; order at the level of the individual; and *order in the relationship between individual and society*. No matter that the founding fathers certainly did not see the individual-society relationship in exactly the same ways – nor that Parsons may have exaggerated the extent to which 'his' founding father were ongoingly preoccupied with the problems of societal order – there can surely be no serious refutation of the proposition that orderliness in the most general sense (covering not simply sociocultural aggregates, but also individuals *qua* individuals and the relationships between the latter and large-scale, complex entities) was at the very core of the work of Durkheim, Marx, Simmel and Weber.

In fact in turning to the historical development of American civil religion Bellah has himself more explicitly addressed the problem of order. New England, Calvinistic Puritanism is seen as having embodied the interlocking principles of *covenant* and *conversion*; a balance between, on the one hand, a collectivist emphasis upon man's fundamental sociality and collective responsibility to God, and, on the other hand, internal, experiential commitment. The collective principle was, according to Bellah, 'derived from the classical conception of the *polis* as responsible for the education and the virtue of its citizens, from the Old Testament notion of the Covenant between God and a people held collectively responsible for its actions, and from the New Testament notion of a community based on charity or love and expressed in brotherly affection and fellow membership in one common body'.[30] The conversion principle involved 'a strong sense of the dignity and responsibility of the individual and especially stressed voluntaristic individual action. But Calvinist "individualism" only made sense within the collective context. Individual action outside the bounds of religious and moral norms was seen in Augustinian terms as the very archetype of sin.'[31]

However, from an early stage conflict arose with respect to the balance between collectivism and individualism; leading-up to the situation toward the end of the eighteenth century, when upon the occasion of the establishment of the Republic individualism prevailed over collectivism, in the sense that there was more emphasis upon an external convenant between associating individuals than upon one internal to those individuals. In other words, Bellah argues that from the beginning of the Republic external law and restraint were given much more emphasis than internal commitment on the part of individual citizens: obedience stressed more than love. Evidently Bellah is convinced that since the late eighteenth century American civil religion has been primarily focused upon the external covenant (a civil religion which he says – as of 1975 – has now become 'an empty and broken shell').

What is of particular interest in the present context is that Bellah in his most extended commentary on the theme of civil religion approaches the latter almost exclusively in terms of the relationship between the individual and the national society. In language which he does not himself employ, we may say that Bellah is concerned with the balance of emphasis upon individual identity and societal authority. To be sure, it is central also to Bellah's own overall thesis that the term 'covenant' conveys a relationship between the society and God; but the fact of the matter is that the central component of his exploration of 'American Civil Religion in a Time of Trial' (the sub-title of *The Broken Covenant*) is the individual-society relationship. In the dissection of the vicissitudes of that relationship in the American context, civil religion appears primarily as a foundation of, a reference point for, and a legitimation of particular forms of connection between individuals and society. These seem, in Bellah's view, to be the main social functions of civil religion (when indeed it is functioning at all). The broader perspective on civil religion – concerning its interpretive, judgmental significance relative to history, other societies, and 'ultimate reality' – can in any case also be seen to be bound-up with questions of the nature and conditions of the allegiance of individuals to the national society, and the legitimate expectations which a national society has of its members.

In attempting to distil the essence of the modern civil-religion *Problemstellung* we face in the work of Bellah, and some of those who have joined him in debate, the irony that although a number of versions of social-contract and covenantal thinking are raised, there is hardly any focus upon that strand of social-contract theorizing which initially focused (at least in modern history) the civil-religion issue. After having acknowledged the significance of Rousseau (man of Calvinistic Geneva and Catholic France) in invoking the conception of civil religion in the middle of the eighteenth century, Bellah leaves the tradition of civil-religion thinking *per se*, apart from some pertinent references to that motif in his assessment of Durkheim's sociology.[32] Clues to that omission lie in Binder's argument that 'in a sense, the tension in contemporary democratic theory is the result of the attempt to justify seventeenth century British constitutional reforms in terms of late eighteenth century French democratic theory'.[30] That prospectus squeezes out of the reckoning a line of thought of a more philosophical-anthropological nature, beginning with Rousseau; and passing through such thinkers as Kant, Hegel, and Marx — and which mainly because of the Germanness of the latter group has relevance to the work of German sociologists of the period 1890–1920. (Parsons has tantalizingly expressed regret at having failed to attend to a French eighteen- and nineteenth-century tradition of social theorizing; and in so doing specifically mentions Rousseau, a theme to which we will shortly return.)[34]

Binder has argued that the juxtaposition of seventeenth-century British constitutional reforms and late eighteenth-century French democratic theory 'is the consequence of the appearance of the peculiarly modern problem of the relationship between the individual and the state'. His argument proceeds thus:

It may be surprising that the problem of the relationship between the individual and the state is described as a peculiarly modern problem, for is not this problem one of the 'great issues'? Yet in mediaeval times, whether in Europe or in the Islamic East, the individual was properly a religious and not a political category of concern. Subjective identity, too, was not political identity as nationalism holds that it must be. The unity of individual and communal political spheres was a characteristic of only the most perfect theocratic societies, the ancient Hebrew, the early Islamic, and perhaps the Greek city-state. The social and economic changes which led the rising bourgeousie to demand the reaffirmation of the independent sphere of the individual also undermined the exclusive social basis of the state.[35]

As Binder further argues, the political changes were interpreted by Marx as rendering the state the superstructural instrument of the bourgeoisie. What is even more significant, says Binder, is 'that the state should represent the interests of anyone but itself. There may always be an analytically definable ruling class, but when that class is no longer a functionally specific oligarchy and acknowledged as such by common sense observation, then surely a profound change has occurred.' Binder brings his arguments to a climax, by arguing that:

. . . once it is understood that the state is not the exclusive prerogative of a clearly defined group, an entirely new set of questions is opened. The real purport of these political changes is not simply whose interests are to be represented by the state. . . . The far more significant issue running through the whole of modern political thought is the proper relationship of individual and collectivity. . . . The social dualism which, it is held, was a constant feature of Western civilization, was not a political problem until social class was no longer the basis of political functional specification. Once this change took place, it became necessary to reconcile the political and the non-political roles of the individual. . . . The major form which the intellectual reconciliation of the diverse roles, political and non-political, of the individual took was nationalism.[36]

In an important but diffuse sense the 'nationalism solution' is one that is deeply embedded in much of the sociological tradition. Many writers since the end of the eighteenth century, including of course such directly influential figures as Durkheim, have in one way or another subscribed to the view that the national society must be the major point of empirical and analytic reference. This has meant that the 'problem of societal order' – but not of *national*-societal order – has received a considerable amount of attention. More specifically, the problem of the ways in which commitment *to the society* on the part of individuals is maintained has framed the ways in which numerous sociological themes have been declared and treated. It is almost certainly that frame of reference which led to there being controversies centered upon the proposition that mainline sociology of the twentieth century, notably in the hands of Parsons and his associates, had erected 'an oversocialized conception of man' (where, perhaps, the more accurate depiction would have been '*over-societalized*'). For once given the (national) societal paradigm it is inevitable that shortfall in commitment to the 'sacredness' of the society will be conceived negatively, as problematic both for the society and the individual, but particularly for the former. In that image there are indeed echoes of Rousseau's famous – and controversial – proposition that man has to be forced to be free. Bellah's emphasis upon conversion (defined in effect in terms of release from sinful, antisocietal forces) as the 'internal' aspect of the societal covenant and the associated interpretation of the Puritan emphasis upon conversion (to the collectivity and its covenant with God) as a form of liberation relates problematically to the Rousseauesque vision. On the one hand, there is similarity to the extent that much emphasis is put upon the need for sociopolitical involvement in the fate of the society, with individualism – in terms traditional to the

French intellectual tradition – being regarded as anti- or pre-social. On the other hand, individualism is applauded to the extent that it is, in the Bellah view, from within the individual (relative to super-societal concerns) that the commitment to the society should derive. Running through such perspectives is the idea that freedom in any given society must of necessity be societally given – that individual freedom is institutionalized by 'the society' and only makes operative sense when exercised as a member of that society. This conception – finding its most crystallized and emphatic expression in the work of such sociologists as Durkheim, Parsons and Bellah – therefore sees as highly problematic situations in which there is no generalized commitment to the society, built upon the basis of a societally-grounded individualism. It is in that form, for example, that Parsons' early emphasis upon normative voluntarism makes most retrospective sense, and contrasts with both the Lockean conception of there being a natural identity of interests among humans gathered together and the Hobbesian view that coercion is the only way of dealing with what would otherwise be a war-of-all-against-all situation.

That such ideas should have made an impact in the American context, with its heavy stress upon individualism and utilitarianism seems at early encounter puzzling – a puzzle thrown into sharp relief by Parsons' simultaneous emphasis upon a Durkheimian conception of how societies are held together and a characterization of the major values of American society being those based upon instrumental activism.[37] However, the increasing emphasis in Parsonian theory during the past ten to fifteen years upon differentiation within action systems in modern societies – notably differentiation of the individual level from cultural and social levels – has constituted a seeming revision of the extreme version of the introjection theorem; and has opened-up the path for conceiving of separate, but yet interdependent, concern with society and self. That perspective actually helps us to see a central problem in the modern civil-religion formulation. For the latter may be seen as an attempt to provide a circumvention of the void opened by the institutionalization of instrumental asceticism in Western societies (whether communist, socialist, capitalist or neo-capitalist) in relation to the Simmel–Weber notion of the need for individual salvation. That institutionalization process has been in many respects a secular one – in that asceticism has become autonomous *vis-à-vis* its historicoreligious grounding. The loss of the religious base has, so to speak, been countered by the Bellah-type civil religion thesis – for the latter in effect seeks to provide instrumental asceticism with a religious base, to put inner-worldly, work-oriented activism within a larger context of religious meaning of societal operation and *raison d'être*. In other words, the modern civil religion thesis denies the thesis of inevitable generalized secularization, but in so doing seems also to deny the empirical status of the Simmel-Weber problem concerning the need for individual salvation (or, more generally, the need for individualistic solutions to mode-of-existence or style-of-living problems).

Types of Individual-Society Relationships

It is clear that in coming to terms with the civil-religion problematic we encounter the need to establish guidelines for interpreting just what is at issue when we find different philosophers and sociologists differentially focusing upon 'individual' and 'society'. The debates which have occurred almost continuously over the last few hundred years in the West about such matters as the social contract, civil religion, individualism, collectivism, and so on have obviously to a large degree been differentially couched in terms of intellectual traditions, observations of intellectuals' own immediate societal context, and with reference to cultural motifs within the societies of particular individuals. Thus although we must surely try always to cope in a direct, purely-cognitive sense with the virtues of particular social-scientific statements, we cannot as sociologists, on the other hand, ignore the substantive epistemologies and ontologies of social theorists as they may possibly derive from their own societal contexts. This actually is not to go dangerously far in suggesting that all sociologists are cognitively victimized by their sociocultural circumstances, for the main point is that up until quite recently analysts when talking about modern problems have tended to use their own societies as the major focal point of their work, even though they may have been interested in contrasting civilizations and/or past historical periods. Thus – with but a few exceptions, such as Montesquieu, Tocqueville, Maine and Marx – we do not often find that sociologists of previous generations were ongoingly concerned to analyze *contemporary* societies other than their own. The two sociologists with whose work we began this chapter – Durkheim and Simmel – were both primarily concerned with and drew their major examples from their own societies. (Even Durkheim's *Elementary Forms* seems to have been undertaken in such a spirit.) A particularly good exemplification of the point we seek to make is that Durkheim (a Frenchman) in attempting to refute the thinking of Spencer (an Englishman) with respect to what were in effect problems of individual-society relationships in *The Division of Labor in Society* made no attempt to assess whether Spencer had said something cogent about *English* society. Rather, Durkheim treated Spencer as if the debate were about all societies, but with tacit concern as to Spencer's relevance to French society.

We need, then, to have clarification of the terms in which particular intellectual traditions have seen and depicted the individual/society issue. In attempting to provide some rough guidelines of that kind it must be emphasized that we are also seeking to generalize about 'real' circumstances in the societies in question – suggesting in effect that the concerns of particular philosophers and sociologists reflect or refract realities of their own societies. It would be impossible for reasons of space to provide here any significant substantiation of that side of the argument (although empirical work has been done which appears to provide evidence in favour of the proposals).[38]

Individual-society relationships may most usefully be typologized in terms of relationships of primacy. That is, we typify societies according to the ways in which ontological and epistemological emphases are balanced with respect to the relationship between individual and societal (or at least, large scale) wholes. The immediate concern is only with those societies which have produced very conspicuous, recent intellectual concern with and contribution to an individual-society problematic. Those societies stand out quite clearly as being: France, Germany, Britain (but primarily England), and the U.S.A.[39] Specifically, the proposal is as follows:

Type 1: Society primary, individual secondary. Exampled by France.
Type 2: Individual primary, society secondary. Exampled by U.S.A.
Type 3: Individual and society accorded distinctive, but problematic parity. Exampled by Germany.
Type 4: Individual and society relatively fused. Exampled by England.

1. France: Here we are talking of a tendency to see society as more real and analytically knowable than individuals. Thus the French took no significant part in the social contract debate until Rousseau (not of course a native of France) advanced a complex collectivist version of contract thinking, emphasizing society over the individual. From that time onward French intellectuals have tended to see 'individualism' and 'individualistic' pejoratively. (Clearly there has been a conception of individualism in a more definitely analytic sense, but that is one which implies the dependency of 'societally suitable' individualism upon the social context itself). The intermittent appearance of the idea of civil religion or something quite like it in the works, *inter alia*, of Rousseau,

Robespierre, Saint-Simon, Comte, Fustel de Coulanges, and Durkheim, and the concern of Tocqueville with the diffuse impact of religion upon societal functioning, relates to this issue very closely, in that civil religion has been seen *mainly* as a form of sociocultural cementing which upholds the significance of the national society relative to history (past and future) and other societies.[40] In the very modern period we see in French intellectual life the great prominence of various forms of structuralism, which downgrades the significance of individuals *per se* in favour of the primacy of the system as a whole. Even within French existentialism, most notably in the work of Sartre, we find a tendency to resist and oppose the more individualistic, self-centered existentialism of the German variety.

The facts that France remained predominantly Catholic during the Reformation period; emphasized collectivism a great deal – notably through the fraternity motif – in its eighteenth-century Revolution; was the home of early scientific socialism and of clear-cut sociology; in a number of respects bypassed the individualistic romanticism that affected England and Germany in the first half of the nineteenth century in favor of collectivist utopianism; and has remained a highly centralized society – each of these characteristics, and others, all point to the primacy of the societal level.

2. America: In many respects intellectual expression in America prior to the immediate post-Revolution period was a theological one. There can be little doubt that in spite of the early talk of synergic convenants between individual and society (relative to God) the dominant mode of emphasis as expressed theologically was individualistic, extended during the eighteenth century to ideas of economic and political individualism. In one way or another the major public and intellectual figures of the early nineteenth century in the main espoused the primacy of the individual – the general trend being toward the national-ideological celebration of individualism, which strongly resisted the collectivist ideas of both European conservative and revolutionary socialism of the mid-nineteenth century.[41] In American social thought from the late nineteenth century various currents adhered to the primacy of the individual – as seen in the individualist bias of pragmatism, the deployment of allegedly Spencerian ideas about the individual, the resistance to Durkheimian and to collectivist Marxist ideas, and so on. One particularly relevant manifestation of the individualistic strain of American thought is Mead's 'translation' of Hegel's suprasocial conception of reflexivity into a virtually behavioristic theory of individual socialization (although it should be said that Mead also presented a less individualistic philosophy of history).[42] A particular complication is of course presented in respect of our present characterization of American thought and society by the work of Talcott Parsons, which in its early phase was a compromise between 'Anglo-German individualism' and 'Franco-German collectivism'. However, the influence of Parsons has more often than not been exaggerated (mainly by his opponents).

In more directly empirical terms the tendency, as Swanson puts it, to operate in associational rather than systemic terms is clear from pre-Republic times, but even clearer from the founding of the Republic; such a tendency to see society as an association of individuals or relatively autonomous units, rather than a system prevailing over the individuals, being largely embodied in the constitution.[43] The Calvinistic origins of America – including the rather rapid demise of Anglicanism – and the accommodation of non-Protestant religious forms to an American pattern have a very strong bearing upon the individualism of American society.

3. Germany: The previous chapter really makes most of the necessary points about German society. Intellectually, from Kant onwards the tendency to emphasize antinomies which, broadly speaking, find their concrete manifestation in a perceived split between the individual and society is very apparent, the attempt to overcome the split between individual subjectivity and societal objectivity being at the core of Hegel's work. As we have seen, subsequently in the nineteenth century there were attempts to overcome antinomies (as in Marx and Nietzsche) or to work out a viable basis for avoiding their impact (Schopenhauer). To be sure there was also a tendency to individualize the societal collectivity, to individualize it in a manner that paralleled the romantic notion of the individual *per se*,[44] and the theme of individuals 'finding themselves' in more or less mystical terms by submersion in the collectivity has been strong in German thought – but so has the opposite theme of particular individuals manifesting in themselves all that is admirable in the society. In view of such characteristics it is not surprising that at the end of the nineteenth century it was in Germany that major steps were taken in intellectual terms to relate the idea, on the one hand, of society as an association of individuals with, on the other hand, the idea of society as a communal whole.[45] As we have seen, the individual-society problem was of central concern to Simmel and Weber (the tension between the two horns of the dilemma being very evident – both empirically and metholologically – in the work of the latter). In the modern period the debate about the problem, not coincidentally, seems to be pursued most avidly among German social scientists.[46]

The relative diversity of German culture should lead to wariness in making generalizations – as indeed in the American case also – but the nature of German Protestantism with its strong Lutheran and Pietist elements is clearly, as we have already seen, of great significance; although we must mention the view that German Protestantism took the form that it did along lines which were constrained by the nature of prevailing social-structural and/or epistemological and ontological circumstances. In any case, the importance of the Lutheran conception of the calling, which involved a bridging of the separation of individual and society in a relatively passive mode cannot be underestimated, and nor can the ideas of individualism at both the levels of the society and the individual *per se* (which as we have seen on the basis of Simmel's commentary, consolidates the idea of a cleavage between two separate realms). Indeed, the latter attribute is manifested in part in the German tendency to seek both very strong central government *and* federalism.

4. England: In this case our contention is that the perception of the individual and society has been a blurred one, or as we put it schematically at an earlier point one of fusion. In the history of modern social and political theory perhaps the major starting point may be seen as Locke, in his notion of the identity of individual interests in relation to the operation of a whole society. In the eighteenth century and first half of the nineteenth century forms of utilitarianism were frequently cast in moral terms (as in the case of John Stuart Mill) or at least in terms which closely related individual gain to the societal good. The English tradition of socialism as it developed from about the 1820s onwards was significant for its attempts to promote individual freedom. Indeed, as has frequently been remarked, socialism in England has traditionally been concerned with the promotion of individual freedom. In effect socialist ideas in nineteenth-century England were superimposed upon an infrastructure of (non-religious) individualism – replacing in part conservative ideas of a Burkean kind which stressed individualism within organicism. Even an adamant proponent of individualism like Spencer eagerly emphasized organicism, and at the same time condemned forms of individualism which were possibly anti-societal.[47]

In all of this the early secularization of English society undoubtedly played a major role, such that the romanticism of the early nineteenth century did not take the form of '*geist*' individualism, which was the hallmark of much of German individualism. The great debates in England about individualism in relation to collectivism in the nineteenth century were often more concerned with intertwining the two than with, as in the German case, reconciling the two relative to cosmic concerns. Undoubtedly in the British case, particuarly in England from the eighteenth century on, class and social-hierarchical distinction has tended to be the major mode of relating to the society. Thus matters of individual identity have been formulated primarily in terms of 'knowing one's place' in an essentially familial conception of society.[48]

These typifications have specific implications for the ways in which each type of society – as delineated in terms of individual-society conceptions – achieves or seeks to achieve collective self-consciousness, which is in large part what the notion of civil religion is about. In the case where society is primary and the individual secondary advocacy of civil religion revolves around the celebration of the society in question and is likely to occur with greatest intensity when the efficacy of the societal entity is at risk. In the case where the individual level takes primacy, advocacy of civil religion is likely when there is difficulty in aggregating sub-societal, particularly individualistic wants and demands 'up to' the level of the society as a whole. The third case, in which society and individual are accorded parity, civil religion is not a 'natural' occurrence. Rather the sense of societal consciousness is likely to occur either through particular types of individuals being taken as manifestations of society or attempts being made to transcend both individuals and society at a higher level (or, perhaps, both of these). In the final case the talk of civil religion is, as in the third, likely to be infrequent. In this case, however, 'civil religion talk' is infrequent because there is little strain toward having such in an explicit sense. The situation as regards individual in relation to society is so involuted that there is little leverage upon the issue of societal self-consciousness. It follows that societal self-consciousness can only come about (in Type 4) in reference to shifts in relationships of the society to other societies – a circumstance that does not need nor precipitate explicit civil-religion concerns; for the societal 'organism' itself performs the focusing of soli-darity function of civil religion, but tends to preclude explicit connect-ing of 'the condition of the society' to 'the nature of the universe'.[49]

Space precludes a rich documentation of each of these theses with respect to France, America, Germany and England. In the immediate context all that we seek is to provide a rationale for the appearance of civil religion concerns in certain types of society and not in others, and indeed for the possibility of there being civil religion in a concrete, empirical sense. In particular our typological discussion seeks to show the reasons for civil-religion concern in France and America. We must, however, note strongly that this chapter is about Western societies, and a more global analysis would require broadening and refinement of the typology.

Religion and the National Society

As we have observed previously, modern concern with civil religion began within the later stages of the social contract debate – a debate which was originally concerned with the analysis of the consolidation of national-societal collectivities as the basic parameters of everyday living. The period of consolidation itself extended from the height of the Reformation in the middle of the sixteenth century to the middle of the seventeenth century. The period of analysis in terms of contract was crystallized by Hobbes; to be followed in the next one hundred years, or so, by Locke, Rousseau, Kant, *et al.* However, concern with civil religion appeared only in Rousseau's work.[50] We surely need to know why Rousseau did this, and the relationship between the idea of civil religion and what we will from hereon call the societal contract.

Highly relevant too is the manner in which the problems brought into focus by the protagonists in the contract debate were treated by other, subsequent thinkers from different perspectives. In that connection the names of Hegel and Marx must surely stand out most prominently. For it was they who most thoroughly followed up many of the issues raised by the contract philosophers and at the same time most completely rejected them, although Rousseau seems to have had a more positive impact in different respects on the thinking of both Hegel and Marx.[51] From both Hegelian and Marxian perspectives Rousseau's conception of civil religion must be regarded as a concession to the alienative disjunction between *state* and *civil society*; and a retreat to thinking in terms of small republics as opposed to large and complex modern societies. (Plato's *Republic* was one of Rousseau's favorite texts.) However, much of Hegel's and Marx's interpretation of Rousseau was conditioned by a natural law interpretation of the latter – an interpretation that made Rousseau into a theorist of atomistic, liberal individualism. In that image Rousseau's conceptions of the general will and the state are seen as emergent from what Hegel called individuals' 'capriciously given express consent . . . .'.[52] In contrast, Hegel was particularly interested in the synchronization, the matching of individual identity with societal authority – which is *not* to say that he conceived of individuals *qua* individuals achieving identity through immersion in or subordination to society (which has been a very frequent interpretation).

Rousseau's complex diagnoses and prognoses entailed a great emphasis upon the elimination of inter-individual and inter-group exploitation and suspicion. His advocacy of civil religion should be seen in the context of his concern to institutionalize respect for basic principles of human conduct and to support the state in its restored 'natural' condition – restored, that is, to its function of administrating law and the establishment of justice. In that connection it is well to recall Rousseau's argument that 'everything is at bottom dependent on political arrangements, and that no matter what position one takes, a people will never be otherwise than what its form of government makes it'.[53]

The spirit of Rousseau's desired state of affairs and his great interest in theodical matters is certainly echoed in much of the Bellah-type advocacy of civil religion in modern America. However, Rousseau's diagnostic insights have not been sufficiently appreciated in this matter – although Durkheim's ideas concerning the relationship between the state and the individual were undoubtedly affected by Rousseau's writings. We can do no better than to quote from the Italian Marxist, Colletti:

> The much-debated chapter on 'civil religion' in the *Contract* . . . , if taken literally . . . , seems to be (as in part, of course, it is) a desperate attempt to reproduce in modern conditions the ancient unity of religion and politics. A more careful examination, however, shows it to be the birthplace of the analysis of the relationship between Christianity and modern 'civil society' (the relationship which – after Marx – Weber, Troeltsch and Lowith synthesized in the concept of 'Christian-bourgeois' society); or which is the same thing, the birthplace of the modern duality of *citoyen* and *bourgeois*.[54]

Colletti cogently links Rousseau's preoccupations to one of the dominant problems of the Enlightenment – namely the part played by the diffusion of Christianity in the fall of the Roman Empire. In the debate centered on that issue we find much that still reverberates with respect to the relationship between religion and politics and the general functioning of national societies. People such as Gibbon and Voltaire argued that Christianity undermined 'civil society' – by virtue of its establishing loyalties and foci of orientation in conflict with loyalty and positive orientation to the societal unit. Rousseau, while accepting the *Problemstellung*, elected to concentrate on the theme of the universality of Christianity. The latter favors human society in general, he said. The 'ideal' society for Christianity is the same as that discussed by natural-law theory. 'Hence . . . we see what we should think of the supposed cosmopolitans who justify their love for their country by their love for the human race, and boast of loving all the world, so that they may have the right of loving no one.'[55] Colletti finds in much of Rousseau's analysis an eighteenth-century basis for Marx's argument:

The difference between the religious man and the citizen is the difference between the shopkeeper and the citizen, between the day labourer and the citizen, between the landowner and the citizen, between the *living individual* and the *citizen*. The contradiction between the religious and political man is the same as that between *bourgeois* and *citoyen*, between the member of the civil society and his *political lion skin*.[56]

Ranged against the Voltaires and the Gibbons, on the one hand, and Rousseau, on the other hand, was of course Montesquieu, who was so important in initiating that trend of which in their different ways Tocqueville and, later, Weber became representatives. That is not to say that each of these three agreed among themselves about the nature of the operative and desirable mode of operation of the religion/society relationship. But clearly each in his own way accepted that there was a problem of the relationship between individual religious pre-occupation and political commitment to the national society. Tocqueville and Weber agreed that in America, in particular, religious pre-occupation and political-societal commitment were equally serviced by the culture and structure of American religion. No matter that Tocqueville may have exaggerated the reservoir of civil morality produced by American religious organizations, nor that Weber possibly over-emphasized the production of democratic sentiment produced by American religious sects. The crucial question is: did they address themselves sufficiently to the relationship between individuals in their religious mode and the central political organs? Did they not fail to take into account the relationship between the individual and the national society in the American context? In Tocqueville's case we may hardly wonder at such an omission since in the 1830s and 1840s the U.S.A. was hardly a national society in the modern sense of the term.

Durkheim stands in the tradition of reaction against the implications of Rousseau's analysis upon which the modern Marxist may seize, in that he takes it as a matter of inviolable empirical reality that modern societies are characterized above all by strong centralized state organs, on the one hand, and the 'cult of the individual', on the other hand.[57]. Durkheim's own proposal that modern French society needed a kind of civil religion is clearly predicated upon the idea that in addition to institutional structures that mediate between the individual and the state there was required a definitely psychocultural form of commitment to the society as a moral entity.[58]

We see, then, that some central figures of the sociological mainstream have indeed confirmed Rousseau's diagnosis of the split between the individual in his 'private' sector and the individual as a member of a national society. Indeed political sociology of the mainstream has tended to welcome positively, and make a virtue out of, what for Rousseau was, an undesirable state of affairs. We may then say again that the idea of a civil religion arises precisely in order to fill the gap opened by a perceived imbalance between the individual and society in its political dimension – a cleavage which for analytical purposes is best described in terms of the relationship between identity and authority. Civil religion may thus be defined as that set of ideations (and, associated structures and practices) that express the nature of the personal identity/societal authority connection, when individual or (at least sub-national) 'identity work' is perceived to make societal functioning ineffective and/or inefficacious.

The tack adopted in response to Rousseau by Hegel, the Young Hegelians and then Marxist thought is still highly relevant to the problems under consideration. The split between man in his civil society and in his political-state aspects lay, of course, at the foundations of Marx's conception of alienation (and much else in Marx's general theory of capitalism) and we can easily see that major writers of the late nineteenth and early twentieth century were acutely conscious of the need to deal with that problematic. Hegel had thought that in the complex conditions of modern pluralistic and differentiated societies the alienative cleavage between private and political man could be overcome precisely by transcending it in the direction of a dialectically, self-reflexive synthesis of subjectivity and objectivity at the level of the state – which would embody absolute spirit. Marx, on the other hand, was even more radical in proposing that the only way the alienative cleavage (providing the basis for opiative civil religion) could be eliminated would be not through spiritualistic, self-reflexive transcendence – but through overthrow of the (economic) conditions that produced the cleavage. That amounted to a materialist, historical 'transcendence'. The critical questions faced by subsequent thinkers have revolved from a sociological point of view around judgements as to the permanence and resilience of the subject-object cleavage at the societal level. There were also some critical questions of a philosophical-anthropological nature, many of them initiated by Kant, not least in his response to Rousseau (some of which inform the present volume).

Change in Forms of Individualism

We remarked in our opening discussion of Durkheim and Simmel that for all the latter's pessimism concerning a clash between individual and society he nevertheless held out hope for a state of affairs in which the individual would stand in a 'better' relationship with society than prevailed in his own time. Simmel's writings on individualism, for all their great suggestiveness, lack coordination and schematic structure. They frequently exhibit considerable tentativeness, and in any case the comments on individualism are scattered across the whole of Simmel's *œuvre*. What seems, however, to have been central to Simmel's discussion of individualism is that there were three main phases in the history of industrial societies (which from Simmel's vantage point, i.e., the period 1890–1918, meant capitalist societies). These three phases were to Simmel characterizable in terms of the relationship between emphasis upon equality and emphasis upon liberty (or freedom), with the process of the division of labor playing a major part as a mechanism of change effecting movement from one phase to another. In addition Simmel tentatively added what for him was a possible future phase. Speaking in the context of the association between subordination and the sense of 'devaluation and oppression', Simmel pointed to the possibility that there would be a growth in the feeling of psychological independence from 'external activity in general and, in particular, of the position which the individual occupies within the sphere of this external activity'. This would involve 'work in behalf of production' becoming 'more and more a mere technique, more and more losing its consequences for the personality and its intimate concerns'.[59] This tentatively stated prognosis (obviously influenced by Marx) raises a number of problems. Suffice to say here that Simmel's image of what he called 'the differentiation of objective and subjective life-elements' bears a resemblance to that which Habermas deals with in the (pejorative) terms of 'the 'stabilization of a nature-like social system *over* the heads of its citizens . . .'.[60] From the standpoints of some contributors to the modern German debate about the nature of individualism and the future of the individual, Simmel's prognosis could indeed be interpreted as pointing towards 'the end of the individual'. However, for the duration we will concentrate upon a modified explication of Simmel's theory of individuation.

We may schematize our exceedingly free interpretation of Simmel thus:

Phase Period	Equality	Freedom	Conception of Division of Labor
1. Late 18th century	Emphasized	Emphasized	Competitive
2. Most of 19th century		Emphasized	Class Stratified
3. Late 19th–20th centuries	Emphasized		Bureaucratized
4. Late 20th century		Emphasized	Technified

The basic idea lying behind this phase model is that each phase generates its own strains toward change, through alternations between emphases upon equality and freedom. Equality of individuals frees them to pursue their own realization – 'the perfection of the soul', in Simmelian terms. On the other hand, freedom of individuals to pursue their own forms of unique realization creates problems of inequality. Such switches in emphasis are provided with an 'accelerator effect' by partly dependent, but mainly independent shifts in the conception of the division of labor in the sphere of work activity. Thus eighteenth-century division of labor was regarded primarily as a matter of fulfilling the needs of competition in a free private-property situation; in the middle of the nineteenth century the class-stratification consequences of division of labor became particularly apparent; by the end of the nineteenth century the organization of socialized individuals in terms of norms of rational-legal authority and super-sub-ordination terms was increasingly evident. Simmel also, as we have seen, saw on his horizon a situation which we here claim has in part already been realized – namely the differentiation of the individual *qua* individual from the work context (this being a broad generalization concerning a discernible trend): such that accommodations have to be made from large-scale social-structural contexts *to* trends at the level of the individual – who is freer to pursue his or her own 'perfection' as a relatively autonomous activity. Again we have to acknowledge these as being controversial suggestions. For example, there are some who clearly deny that this process, even if an empirically discernible one, constitutes a process of individuation – from some standpoints it constitutes 'the end of the individual', as indicated by our recent invocation of Habermas.

In the scenario sketched here the conception is indeed of a relatively 'nature-like social system', which in certain crucial respects appears to work, 'out there', 'on its own'. However, to put it in Weberian terms, asceticism is selectively needed as a mode of contribution to the shaping of and tending to that 'natural' social system – asceticism here being defined in terms of contribution to values regarded as necessary for the functioning of social structures. As was argued in the previous chapter, this Western form of asceticism should be seen in reversal, structurally speaking, of the Eastern case. In other words, the major burden of asceticism of very modern societies becomes – at least in ideal-imperative terms – an élite matter (whereas in the Eastern context asceticism of 'the masses' made provision traditionally for the mysticism of élites).

As far as the equality/freedom balance is concerned, the modern Western world has recently been much characterized by emphasis upon freedom to cultivate one's own destiny, including the proliferation of interests in life-cycle self-consciousness and preparation – even, to a degree, choice about death. On the other hand, in the traditional liberal sense there are shifts away from equality, summed-up in the trend toward a situation of equality of opportunity to achieve equality.[61] It could indeed be said that so-called affirmative action programs in the U.S.A. are part of this tendency, emphasizing liberation from constraint and prejudice rather than equality, and by classical definitions of equality actually often promoting inequality. That point suggests that a more refined version of the phase model presented here would, rather than talking in terms of changing emphases upon equality and freedom, address the issue of changes in cultural definitions of equality and freedom during the past two hundred or so years.

Some Tentative Conclusions

In this and the preceding chapter we have tended frequently to focus problems in terms of Weberian concepts, with much further assistance from Simmel and Durkheim. Continuing that practice we can state that a major issue which has arisen during the present discussion is that modern societies, but particularly those of the neocapitalist sector of the globe, have increasingly since the Reformation undergone relatively simultaneous processes of institutionalization of societal 'salvation', on the one hand, and, of institutionalization of individual salvation, on the other hand – processes which have been in complex respects interwoven, and which received a particular acceleration and crystallization in subsequent periods, most notably in the second half of the eighteenth century.[62] These processes of institutionalization – or, in a different sense, immamentalization – should be regarded as having a very significant degree of secularization fall-out, such that it becomes more appropriate to speak of 'perfection' gradually taking over from 'salvation' (an idea which is more than implicit in the commentaries of Simmel). Under the old Weberian categories this overall two-fold process of institutionalization binds the individual into an apparent contradiction: rational contributions to society are feasible and expected, but to combine such with the rational pursuit of individual self-perfection in the name of ethical demands is not rationally possible.

The thesis advanced in the concluding sections of the previous chapter involved a denial of Weber's position. The notion of inner-worldly, ascetic mysticism was introduced and elaborated in order to solve Weber's dilemma. There is no need to rehearse that dicussion, except to re-emphasize the idea that ascetic mysticism permits a reinterpretation of standardized contributions to society so that individuals can at the same time make – or, as a variation, phase across their life-cycles – contributions in terms of freely and privately chosen goals to their own self-realization and to society. In that prospectus it must again be said that one of the major dilemmas which individuals face in a situation of societal-in-relation-to-self perfection is that of the relative immortality of the society and mortality of the individual. Ascetic mysticism suggests the possibility of operating in such a way as to combine actions relative to both time-spans.

Such contentions relate closely and problematically, as already hinted, to modern discussions of legitimation and motivation in the functioning of modern societies – most notably, perhaps, the profound issues raised by Habermas. We cannot hope to come to terms with Habermas' concerns here. However, a few comments are clearly necessary. Habermas seems to regard a situation of the kind which we have indicated here as involving a subservience of the individual to the social system in its economic and political aspects. Moreover, the modern situation in neocapitalist societies seems in his view to involve a considerable lack of legitimation for the mode of operation of the politico-economic structures and a lack of motivation to contribute to the latter. In a sense all that we have sought to show is that in ideal-typical terms it *is* possible to have in relative parity a situation of contribution to 'the system' and to self, and moreover that the two may be complementary; each, as it were, needing the other. In this sense we have indeed synthesized the general views of Durkheim and Simmel, in terms of Weberian categories. We do not, however, have immediately available the kind of evidence which would be required to document our position adequately. The present discussions are, moreover, intended to do no more than hint conceptually at trends and future possibilities. Much of the weight of the cases advanced here must rest upon not only the feasibility of combining asceticism (in the service of general, societally operative values) and secularized mysticism (self-realization or 'perfection') but also upon the inner-worldliness of the latter. In other words the conception of mysticism in its secularized form which we have adumbrated is intended to have a heavy gloss of reflexivity, an attribute which indeed seems central to German conceptions of individualism.

Moreover, the whole issue of combining and balancing asceticism and mysticism rests upon an assumption of increasing individuation which 'the system' has (increasingly) to take into account. Thus although it is easy to be extremely cynical (and such cynicism is often very justified) about the ways in which neocapitalism 'caters for', indeed often promotes, the self-realization needs and demands of individuals, the fact of the apparent need for the theodical needs of individuals to be taken into account in modern societies cannot easily be denied. What is implied by much of the present chapter, and some of the preceding one, is that the process of individuation has proceeded so far (largely but certainly not entirely with the assistance of the societalization process) that it is not easily resistible by large-scale structural entities. In this process the legal system, notably in the U.S.A., has undoubtedly played a very important part, in enhancing individual rights – and increasingly enhancing obligations of individuals to each other.

We have thus cast 'the civil religion' problem within the context of the relationship between the processes of individuation and societalization. We have also tried to indicate what types of culturally perceived relationships between individual and society are more likely than others to promote 'civil-religion talk'. In a very loose sense of the term 'civil religion' we might well think that such talk would be very widespread in modern societies, given the presumed fact that no matter what the traditional conception of individual/society relationships most modern societies are subject to the mutually amplifying processes of individuation and societalization. But in the perspective of the present discussion such very loose talk about civil religion, or some rough semantic equivalent, would have to be examined to see whether it is most appropriate to use that term. For example, it can surely be no accident that it was German social science which largely gave us the notion of legitimacy (and only in a very oblique sense has there been invocation of the idea of civil religion in Germany), while it was British social theory which gave us the notion of the social contract – a term which has been used extensively in British public life during the 1970s, in rather specific reference to the crisis of commitment in British societies. Thus the main drift of our discussion is in effect to deny the appropriateness of civil-religion talk in certain kinds of society and to suggest that when there is controversy about the individual/society relationship in such cases we should very carefully examine the latter in order to discover what, so to speak, is the equivalent of civil-religion concerns. (We have avoided here the fact that in so-called consociational systems the problem of civil religion is ever-present but virtually by definition impossible to obtain, the paradigmatic Western case being The Netherlands.)

The discussion also suggests that the processes of individuation and societalization have presented to modern societies a 'Lutheran problem'. No matter what the traditional tendencies in particular societies have been with respect to coding the individual/society connection the strength of those processes has posed in striking form the need to treat that connection as both a major personal and a major societal problem. Thus, in very complex fashion, the fact that the modern civil-religion debate has been most conspicuous in the U.S.A. is attributable not simply to traditional coding of the individual/society relationships but also very probably because it is in the U.S.A. that the differentiation of individual life from societal functioning is most acute at the present time. *In principle* – and we must even emphasize the italicization – the combination of mysticism and asceticism in the special senses in which we have used those terms reduces much of the need for legitimation. Thus it may well be that not merely is there a decline in legitimacy in modern societies, there may also be actually a decline in the functional need for it. The simultaneity of servicing self and the wider collectivity, it should be noted, is very apparent in movements which seek to overthrow or replace the present circumstances.[63] Revolutionary movements in the West have moved far away from Engels' insistence upon purely ascetic involvement in 'the movement', for since the mid-1960s such movements have tended increasingly to combine ascetic commitment to the movement with 'mystical' gratification of the self. That, surely, was the major change in Western revolutionary culture of the 1960s.

NOTES

1. These and some other observations in this chapter have been aired in a very different substantive context in Roland Robertson, 'Societal Attributes and International Relations', in Jan Loubser et al. (eds.),

Explorations in General Theory in Social Science, New York, 1976, Vol. II, pp. 713–35.

2. In particular we lean on Emile Durkheim, *Professional Ethics and Civil Morals*, London, 1957. For Durkheim generally and with specific reference to some of the issues discussed here see in particular Poggi, op. cit., chs. 6–9. See also *Emile Durkheim on Morality and Society* (ed. Robert N. Bellah), Chicago, 1973.

3. The main sources for comments on Simmel in this chapter are: Georg Simmel, *Sociology: Über sociale Differenzierung, soziologische und psychologische Untersuchungen*, Leipzig, 1905 (second edn.): Simmel, *Sociology of Religion*, op. cit.; *George Simmel on Individuality and Social Forms*, op. cit.; Kurt H. Wolff (trans. and ed.), *The Sociology of Georg Simmel*, Toronto, 1964, esp. pp. 58–86; and Matthew Lipman, 'Some Aspects of Simmel's Conception of the Individual', in Georg Simmel et al., op. cit., pp. 119–38.

4. See Emile Durkheim, *The Division of Labor in Society* (trans. G. Simpson), New York, 1933; and Durkheim, *The Elementary Forms . . .*, op. cit.

5. Cf. Steven Lukes, *Individualism*, Oxford, 1973, p. 21.

6. See, *inter alia*, Ernest Cassirer, *The Individual and the Cosmos in Renaissance Philosophy* (trans. M. Domandi), New York, 1963. For links between Marx, Engels, Simmel, Lukács, and the idea of Renaissance Man see Roy Pascal, 'Georg Lukács: The Concept of Totality', in G. H. R. Parkinson (ed.), *Georg Lukács: The man, his work and his ideas*, New York, 1970, ch. 5. The rise of absolutism in this period does not require documentation.

7. See Leonard Binder, *The Ideological Revolution in the Middle East*, New York, 1964, p. 159.

8. Talcott Parsons, *The System of Modern Societies*, Englewood Cliffs, 1971. Such views find an echo in Bellah's work on civil religion. Cf. Anthony Smith, *Theories of Nationalism*, London, 1971.

9. Cf. Lipman, op. cit.

10. See Bellah's interpretation of Durkheim, note 2 above.

11. Swanson has done much along these lines, See, in addition to previous references, Guy E. Swanson, 'To Live in Concord with a Society', in Albert Riess (ed.), *Cooley and Sociological Analysis*, Ann Arbor, 1968, pp. 87–150. See also Burkart Holzner and Roland Robertson, 'Identity and Authority: A Problem Analysis', in Robertson and Holzner, op. cit., ch. 2.

12. Rainer C. Baum, 'Authority and Identity: The Case for Evolutionary Invariance', in ibid., ch. 4.

13. For a very useful survey which in part informs some of the thinking here: J. W. Gough, *The Social Contract Debate*, Oxford, 1957.
14. Michael Walzer, *The Revolution of the Saints*, London, 1965, p.2.
15. Ibid., p. 303.
16. Robert N. Bellah, 'Civil Religion in America', in *Beyond Belief*, op. cit., pp. 168–92. There have been numerous replies and collections devoted to this essay. See in particular: Russell E. Richey (ed.), *American Civil Religion*, New York, 1974; and Donald R. Cutler (ed.), *The Religious Situation 1968*, Boston, 1968, pp. 331–94. See also *Sociological Analysis*, 37 (Summer, 1976).
17. Parsons and Platt, op. cit.
18. 'Civil Religion in America', p. 169.
19. Ibid.
20. Ibid.
21. Bellah, *The Broken Covenant*, op. cit.
22. 'Civil Religion in America', p. 184.
23. 'American Civil Religion in the 1970s', in Richey and Jones (eds.), op. cit., ch. 12.
24. Bellah, 'Response', in Cutler (ed.), op. cit.
25. Ibid., p. 391.
26. Bellah, 'Response', op. cit., p. 389.
27. Bellah, 'American Civil Religion in the 1970s', op. cit., p. 257.
28. Ibid.
29. Ibid., p. 256.
30. Bellah, *The Broken Covenant*, op. cit., pp. 17–18.
31. Ibid., p. 18.
32. *Emile Durkheim* . . . (ed. Bellah), op. cit.
33. Binder, op. cit., p. 13.
34. Talcott Parsons, 'Introduction to the Paperback Edition', in Parsons, *The Structure of Social Action*, New York, 1968, p. viii.
35. Binder, loc. cit.
36. Ibid.
37. I owe this point to Robert Bellah in oral communication.
38. See Baum 'Authority and Identity . . .', op. cit.
39. Cf. Lukes, *Individualism*, op. cit.
40. On Tocqueville, see Doris S. Goldstein, *Trial of Faith: Religion and Politics in Tocqueville's Thought*, New York, 1975.
41. See the excellent survey in Yehoshua Arieli, *Individualism and Nationalism in American Ideology*, Baltimore, 1964.
42. George Herbert Mead, *Mind, Self and Society*, Chicago, 1967.
43. Swanson, 'To Live in Concord With a Society', op. cit.

44. One should not get the impression from this and the previous mention of individualizing collectivities that the notion of collective actors was unknown before. The development of national actorness in its economic aspects is dealt with by Immanuel Wallerstein, *The Modern World System*, New York, 1974. In more cultural-sociological mode see the important survey of long-term changes in conceptions of the individual in Marcel Mauss, 'A Category of the Human Spirit' (trans. V. Karady), *The Psychoanalytic Review*, 55, 3 (1968), pp. 457–81.

45. See Lukes, *Individualism*, esp. ch. 2.

46. See, *inter alia*, Dahrendorf, *Theories of Society*, op. cit., esp. chs. 2, 3, 6, and 7; Jurgen Habermas, *Legitimation Crisis* (trans. T. McCarthy), Boston, 1975, esp. pp. 117 ff.; Uwe Schlottmann, *Primäre und Sekundäre Individualität*, Stuttgart, 1968; Baum, 'Authority and Identity . . .', op. cit.

47. See the very helpful J. D. Y. Peel, *Herbert Spencer: The Evolution of a Sociologist*, London, 1971.

48. Cf. Henry Fairlie, 'Transatlantic Letter to England', *Encounter*, XLVI, 1 (January, 1976), pp. 6–21.

49. Alasdair MacIntyre, *Secularization and Moral Change*, London, 1967, p. 29, and *passim*. This slender volume contains some of the most perspicacious comments written on English society in the modern period.

50. See particularly Jean-Jacques Rousseau, 'Of Civil Religion', Book IV, ch. 8, *The Social Contract* (ed. E. Barker), New York, 1960. See also *The Minor Educational Writings of Jean-Jacques Rousseau* (selected and trans. William Boyd), New York, 1962. The interpretation of Rousseau has been particularly influenced by: Ernest Cassirer, 'Kant and Rousseau', in *Rousseau, Kant and Goethe* (trans. J. Gutman et. al.), Princeton, 1945, pp. 1–60; and Lucio Colletti, *From Rousseau to Lenin* (trans. J. Merrington and J. White), New York and London, 1972, pp. 143 ff. See also Gough, op. cit., pp. 166 ff.; and Maurice Cranston and Richard S. Peters (eds.), *Hobbes and Rousseau*, Garden City, New York, 1972.

51. See Colletti, op. cit.

52. Quoted in ibid., p. 188. We are only too painfully aware of the risks involved in eliciting straightforward statements from Rousseau's work. Colletti probably does exaggerate Rousseau's influence on Marx, as is suggested in the introduction to *From Rousseau to Lenin*.

53. Cassirer, op. cit., p. 27.

54. Colletti, op. cit., p. 175.

55. Ibid., p. 178.

56. Ibid., p. 179.

57. See in particular Emile Durkheim, *Montesquieu and Rousseau* (trans. A. Cuvillier), Ann Arbor, Michigan, 1960.

58. Emile Durkheim, *Moral Education* (trans. E. Wilson and H. Schnurer), New York, 1961.

59. *Georg Simmel on Individuality and Social Forms*, op. cit., p. 341.

60. Habermas, *Legitimation Crisis*, op. cit., p. 143.

61. See ibid.

62. It would seem that the notion of societal modernization in the modern period is very closely related to the perfection-of-society ideas discussed here. Cf. J. P. Nettl and Roland Robertson, *International Systems and the Modernization of Societies*, op. cit. For more specific discussion of the tugs between individual and societal welfare see Robertson, 'Societal Attributes and International Relations', op. cit.

63. In using the notion of simultaneity of service to society and self we do *not* mean that it is a matter of symmetry for all individuals. Some will be more ascetic than others; and, as we have noted, asceticism-mysticism is undoubtedly bound up with life-cycle emphases. In more general terms it is very important that we emphasize the tremendous salience of themes of self-realization, self-perfection and eudaimonism in the German intellectual tradition. See W. H. Bruford, *The German Tradition of Self-Cultivation*, Cambridge, 1975.

Chapter Six

Conversion and Cultural Change

Cultural development places the subject even more markedly outside of itself through the formlessness and boundlessness which it imparts to the objective spirit, because of the infinite number of its producers. Everybody can contribute to the supply of objectified cultural contents without any consideration for other contributors. . . . The form of objectivity as such possesses a boundless capacity for fulfillment. This voracious capacity for accumulation is most deeply incompatible with the forms of personal life. The receptive capacity of the self is limited not only by the force and length of life, but also through a certain unity and relative compactness of its form. Therefore, the self selects, with determined limits from among the contents which offer themselves as means for its individual development.

Georg Simmel

Culture is another name for a design of motives directing the self outward, toward those communal purposes in which alone the self can be realized and satisfied. . . . The question is no longer as Dostoevski put it: 'Can civilized men believe?' Rather: Can unbelieving men be civilized?

Philip Rieff

Conversion, Culture and Legitimation

One of the major puzzles of modern societies concerns, as we have seen, the nature and significance of culture and cultural change. In circumstances of a high degree of emphasis upon individual change – in contexts where there is much concern with 'self-realization' – the problem has arisen as to the relationship between, on the one hand, resources devoted to the individual and, on the other hand, the general trajectory of objective cultural change (as well, of course, as the relationship between social-institutional patterns and cultural change). For all of the great emphasis that has been diffusely put upon 'culture' in recent years we seem to have progressed little in coming to terms with that phenomenon in its modern forms. In one way or another the nature of the problem is indicated in the work of the classical sociologists, but particularly in Simmel and Weber. Broadly speaking, the central problem as seen by the latter was the lack of synchronization of individuals and objective culture. (That, of course, contrasts with the analytic amalgam of Durkheim and Freud proposed by Parsons.) Perhaps the general thrust of Simmel's position (in which he was very influenced by Hegel) states the matter best for present purposes. Simmel's statements upon the individual-culture relationship parallel those of his formulations with respect to the individual-society relationship. Thus in Simmel's 'tragic' interpretation the process of individuation frequently clashes with the process of what might be called objective culturation. The clash, as Simmel saw it, arises from the circumstances of the increasing autonomization of each realm. The more that individuals become concerned with the pursuit of their own perfection and realization the more that quest leaves, so to speak, culture to its own objectivity; while the more that culture acquires its object-like status the more difficult it becomes for individuals to realize themselves through the process of cultivation. Thus arises the paradox of an individual having available an increasingly broad range of cultural resources, but yet not being able easily to co-ordinate his or her 'realization' with the course of cultural change. In the more pessimistic vein of Simmel's thinking (pessimism *not* being synonomous with the tragic vision *per se*) so autonomous do the processes of individuation and culturation become that the net effect is the acute, mutual amplification of their respective autonomies: 'Man has become richer and more overloaded . . . cultures which have everything own nothing.'[1]*

It was, perhaps, the diffuse recognition of the differentiation of 'out-there' culture from individual consciousness which formed the intellectual matrix for the simultaneous development in the first quarter of the present century of, on the one hand, the study of cultural change in an objective-trajectorial sense and, on the other hand, the acceleration in the crystallization of highly subjectivist approaches to the study of modern man and woman – manifested in the development, on the one hand, of objectivist cultural sociology and, on the other hand, of existentialism and phenomenology. That same period saw also conscious attempts to bridge the two in the work, of, *inter alia*, Weber, Simmel and, in some ways most important, Dilthey, whose hermeneutic-type endeavors grounded the study of culture in psychology.

* Notes for this chapter begin on p. 217.

This was, of course, also a tremendously important period in respect of attempts among philosophers to provide a non-metaphysical basis for cognition and action – the period of early adumbration of modern pragmatist philosophies and of linguistic and logical positivisms. In the sphere of philosophy we see particularly clearly that the major problematic was centered upon what Gellner calls the legitimation of belief.[2] In a major respect that problem of cognitive legitimacy has its foundation in the issue of how individuals can in a world of seeming diversity and individualism seize a mode of cognitive operation which will steer them in circumstances that have thrown considerable doubt upon received cultural-traditional foundations of truth and validity. In a different respect there was in the first few decades of the present century a flurry of concern with the advancement of philosophical theories which sought either to provide, as Gellner puts it, re-endorsement of received ideas (relativism, evolutionism and 'negative re-endorsement') or bases for selection from ideas and the establishment of new ones. Selector theories (primarily empiricism, materialism and logical-formism) do not flourish, claims Gellner, at the same time that sociology flourishes, primarily because they seek independent criteria of cognitive validity and thus are 'socially blind'. Thus we may, in this perspective, argue that sociology began to decline at the same time as selectionism in philosophy assumed dominance in the inter-war years of the 1920s and 1930s, while the retreat of selectionism – in a sense to be seen in the distrust of 'objective science' – in the 1960s and 1970s paralleled the re-flourishing of the sociological mode in that period. In the latter connection we can clearly see within sociological contexts the revival of relativism (as in neo-phenomenological sociology and in Kuhn-influenced sociology of science); the re-assertion of evolutionism (as in much of Parsonian sociology); and nostalgic concern (as in the highly praised works, for example, of Berger, Bell and Bellah) for a modified restoration of the authoritative-religious past.[3] The latter qualifies as a form of negative re-endorsement in that it in effect says that we have traditionally possessed viable and appropriate modes of legitimation; the problem now is to sift these and fully recognize the worthwhileness of our traditional forms of culture. All would be well if a few obstacles were to be removed.

Broadly speaking, Gellner's two types of cognitive legitimation parallel Rieff's two types of personal therapy, the commitment and the analytic types.[4] Thus the dominance of selectivism in philosophy has been paralleled by analytic, 'non-faithful' therapeutic approaches in psychology. The lead was given of course by Freud in the latter respect, but Pavlov, Watson and Skinner – anti-Freudian as their intentions and impact have been – nevertheless share one orientation with Freud, namely the irrelevance of general meaning questions in the modern world. Sociology and anthropology have been somewhat unique among the behavioral sciences in their interest in such matters, but they too have had phases of 'anti-meaning'.

It is probably relativism which has been most evident in the sociology of the 1960s and 1970s, with the other types of re-endorsement modes and the selector modes offering rather ineffective challenges to them, at least until very recently. It would indeed be more accurate to say that relativism is fundamentally indifferent to problems of legitimation and that the new mid- to late-1970s concern with problems of legitimation constitutes a reaction to that indifference. This may well account within sociology for the return to the classics in the 1970s, for there seems little doubt that, particularly in the German tradition, the classic sociologists were concerned both with the nature of objective cultural change and the problem of how individuals could cope in a situation of cultural (and social-institutional) relativism – and indeed, and certainly not least, the connection between the two themes. The concern in the second half of the 1970s to formulate non-relativistic positions constitutes a resurrection in even more compelling sociocultural circumstances of precisely these themes.

As far as our immediate interests are concerned, it is of great importance to note that intellectual interest in the phenomenon of conversion has flourished at times when concern with the relativity of sociocultural perspectives has appeared to be widespread. Interest in conversion flourished early in the present century (when the psychology of conversion was a topic of great interest) and such matters as identity construction and transformation began to attract much interest in the late 1960s and the early 1970s; there being a discernible tendency, as in the work of Berger, for the phenomenon of identity to be diffusely linked to processes of 'alternation' and conversion.[5] In the terms of some of the general issues which have already been raised, we may see that matters such as conversion and identity are closely related to issues of legitimation, meaning and truth. When, for example, self-conceptions of identity are injected into legitimacy and validity discussions the latter may become, although by no means in a necessarily violent respect, matters of life and death. This, in the sense that identity in its fullest reach defines an individual *in toto*; and thus an argument in which identity is at stake is an extremely serious one. Thus the rise of concern with identity is intimately related to relativism and, in turn, legitimation crises. (It is in such light that Gouldner's worries about the eristic style of disputation and Habermas' advocacy of a theory of communicative competence might be fruitfully placed.)[6]

The thrust of the present discussion consists in sifting and distilling the idea of conversion and themes which bear a family resemblance to it, with an eye to their relationship to culture. The intial motivation to undertake a reconnaissance of 'the conversion area' derived from sensing the seeming irony of there being, on the one hand, widespread concern with such issues as paradigm switches, cognitive revolutions, modernization, identity changes, *Becoming Deviant*, *Becoming Modern*, etc., and, on the other hand, a lack of direct concern with conversion among sociologists of religion.[7] Further consideration leads to the belief that issues which have been dealt with under many rubrics suggesting very significant changes in or of social entities (particularly, but not only, individuals) might well be enhanced by injecting considerations derived from a sociology-of-religion focus on conversion. Traditional categories such as acculturation, assimilation, mobilization, and emigration/immigration suggest themselves in this connection. But it is more recently dwelled-upon phenomena which primarily interest us in their proximity to matters often dealt with – certainly in everyday discourse – in relation to the idea of conversion. We think of such motifs as 'identity voyages', 'consciousness raising', 'trans-sexual journeys', 'life-style changes', 'altered states of consciousness', and so on (as well as more obvious phenomena of religious and ideological change). These kinds of ideas are very much products, at least as we currently employ them, of the 1960s (and we do indeed have to be wary of the undoubted element of fashion involved in the area). Such prognoses are always risky, but it does seem rather safe to suggest that extreme conceptions of the fluidity of identities, life-styles and states of consciousness are already waning, and will continue to wane, *vis-à-vis* their 1960s and early 1970s highpoint. Major clues to the waning, or perhaps it would be more accurate to say modification, are to be seen in the mid-1970s concern with life-cycle issues. The increase in academic discussion and popular readership of theories of development in adult life, stages of personal growth, moral and cognitive development, biological growth and decay, 'growth' into death, and so on, suggest above all a concern with greater fixity in the sphere of individual patterns of living. Or, to put it another way, the concern with predictability in adult life potentially provides a greater sense of natural anchorage at the level of the self. To note the change in emphasis from fluidity to fixity is, we must emphasize, not to take sides in a straightforward scientific sense. We do not, for example, straightforwardly come down on the side of those who say that an identity pattern is established at the end of adolescence and thereafter individuals move through set, predetermined phases of life along tracks established in late adolescence. Nor do we say that there is a definite sequence of crises in the adult life cycle (although there seems to be much evidence that there is such) which act as basic conditioning factors with reference to the kinds of life-orientation – in a narrow sense modes of existence – which individuals have within particular age-ranges.[8] Such decisions are not necessary here. For the direction of present interest is toward the ways in which the experience of modern life is given form. Thus, again somewhat rashly, the general proposition is that the form of experiencing which seemed to involve the idea that the self is 'almost-infinitely' revisable has been provided with a modifying foundation, in the form of a rooting in life-cycle predictability. That does not mean that the sense of revisability of the self crystallized, nay dramatized, in the 1960s has been, or is being, replaced. Rather, it is suggested that the sense of openness and personal flexibility became increasingly challenged through reality tests and the encounter with the fixity, and in a sense the inescapability, of 'hard social and psychological realities' *vis-à-vis* individual aspiration to change. This of course cannot be anything like a complete explanation of the attenuation of the seemingly widespread sense of pure experience, modernism and being-what-one-wants-to-be (with the help of a few easy guides to life-change possibilities). But for present purposes it may suffice.[9]

The situation of personal openness-to-change was clearly – although this is easy to say with the benefit of hindsight – one which could not last in its extreme late 1960s forms. And yet that sense of openness has not disappeared from the Western societies, most clearly the U.S.A., in which it made its dramatic appearance in the 1960s. (Swanson makes a very intriguing argument to the effect that the modern foundations for that period were laid within industrial corporations in the 1940s, when increasing stress was placed upon 'let-it-all-hang-out' methods of participation and involvement in management; a situation summed-up in the idea of management by objectives.)[10] Thus in functional-evolutionary terms it can be argued that a rationalizing step 'had' to be taken toward providing a greater sense of diachronic control of self, in the terms of life-cycle predictability – the latter forming a conditioning baseline for individual choice and, indeed, a kind of protection and boundedness against the openness of purely responding to the social-structural realm and/or of yielding on whim to cultural fashion. Such a shift may be seen also as a further development in the relationship between individuals and objective culture, a development which potentially goes beyond the incompatibility between cultural proliferation and individual cultural 'need' highlighted by Simmel. In terms of the latter's prospectus, the development constitutes a step toward a greater consciousness of and 'room' for the operation of what Simmel called the inner-laws of individual realization, a greater consciousness of the logic of personal unfolding (although we wish here to resist the more emphatic claims as to the life-cycle being seen as a continuing progression). As Simmel put it, the teleology of the individual life is seemingly being grasped (or re-grasped). And so, as in the previous chapter we attempted to draw out Simmel's image of a further, less conflictful stage of relationship between individual and society, we can now see that a similar possibility in the relationship between individual and objective culture is entailed. This would involve a more resilient, individual-centered basis for selection from culture, a reduction in the susceptibility to cultural fluctuation and proliferation indicated in Simmel's more pessimistic moments. We will have occasion to compare Simmel and Freud in that respect.

The Microcultural Perspective

The uniqueness of the interest which Simmel and Weber demonstrated throughout much of their respective *œuvres* in the connection between individual modes of existence and processes of cultural change lies in its concern with what we here call *microculturality*. Both were concerned with the objective course of cultural change (Simmel in terms of formalization, Weber in terms of rationalization) and its relationship to individual modes of existence and changes thereof. But, in particular they were concerned with the vicissitudes of the relationship between individual, small-scale life and culture in its meaningful significance for individuals. (Both were also, of course, concerned with social relationships *per se*.)

    The term 'microcultural' is used, then, to refer specifically to the individual-culture connection. There is, however, a difference between a fully sociological version of this problematic and a 'merely cultural' one. The latter is a more appropriate characterization of Simmel's approach — as is highlighted by the fact that Simmel himself did not consider that he was doing sociology proper when analyzing culture. In comparison, Weber's approach to culture (a term which he used far less frequently than Simmel) was cast much more in sociological terms, by which we mean that Weber nearly always made a definite *social* connection between the individual and culture. (So much so that, as we have intimated, a clear-cut conception of the individual is often lacking in Weber's work.) Thus in its more definitely sociological sense, the concept of microculturality is used in reference to the social-actional and social-psychological aspects of culture, culturation and cultural change. Whereas a macrocultural approach is concerned, on our definition, with objective patterns of culture, culturation and cultural change, the microcultural perspective is concerned with the social and social-psychological dynamics relating to those aspects of cultural phenomena. The macrocultural approach is virtually synonomous with that which is often called culturology – a term quite frequently employed these days by sociologists in pejorative mode, to denote an absence of attention to the social-interactional and logic-of-the-situation aspects of maintenance and/or change at the cultural level.

Weber should probably be given the accolade for having first studied cultural change in such distinctively social and social-psychological terms, although among his predecessors Marx stands out. Weber studied long-term and large-scale cultural change primarily in terms of the social vehicles of such change – classes, status groups, leaders, and so on, a perspective heavily injected by the idea of individual rationalization. In other words, it was the differential-social creation or maintenance of cultural change which particularly interested Weber. And it is always important to note that even when he was seemingly attempting to demonstrate the relatively independent efficacy of beliefs and values he did so not in terms of an immanentist perspective on culture but of one that stressed the interaction of social individuals and ideas. That involved an insistence upon notions of talking in terms of ideal interests and the differential attractiveness of ideational systems, and upon a firm sense of the relationship between individuals-in-situations and the beliefs and values that objectively transcend particular situations. It was the intersection of the situation and the ideas which above all interested Weber and which defined his ontological conception. Weber has been faulted on occasions for the specifics of his actual procedures within the frame of reference adumbrated here. He also sometimes failed to invoke them when the situation seemed to require such, as in his work on Islam. However, as a program Weber's central thesis that culture must be treated in an actional mode is what is at issue here. Again the influence of Marx is in evidence. The major difference between Marx and Weber was that the latter gave more weight to the direct analysis of the ways in which people are attracted to different types of ideas and the ways in which sets of ideas could become so ingrained in particular contexts – from the small-scale to the civilizational levels – that they became what in modern language we would call orientational codes.

In spite, however, of the steps taken by Weber in developing a viable approach to the study of the social aspects of cultural change, there can be little doubt that he neglected in his published work to come to terms adequately with the microdynamics of cultural change. In one respect we might simply say that Weber's neglect of the processes by and in terms of which men and women change their commitments and allegiances did not seem to him to be of much importance. It seems that he was more interested in the social circumstances of such changes – that is, the comprehension of the situations which constrained individuals to turn toward, away from or to maintain commitment or allegiance to a particular perspective. Hence the notion of 'elective affinity'. Not that the latter concept played much part in the general sweep of Weber's empirical studies of cultural change and development, but it is safe to say that he worked most of the time with a diffuse notion of there being a natural fit between individuals-and-groups-in-situations and particular sets of ideas, with particular attention being paid to processes of rationalization relative to social-structuration. The interest in rationalization, however, has much to do with the neglect of attention to conversion-like phenomena – which perhaps from a narrow Weberian standpoint falls within a sphere of irrationalism (a sphere to which conversion seems to have been tacitly consigned by many social scientists). Take one famous case. In his study of Protestantism and capitalism Weber went to considerable lengths to produce a plausible account of the 'logic' of the Calvinist situation, resulting in the conclusion that the internalized doctrine of predestination created a strain toward invoking concrete, worldly signs of salvation. In producing this 'rationalistic' argument Weber overlooked the fact that experience of conversion was frequently regarded by Calvinists and Puritans as a rather adequate sign of being a member of the elect. Generally speaking, we may observe that in spite of the virtues of Weber's overall analytic stance he did not come to terms with processes of cultural change in respect of the ways in which ideas were rejected, adopted, sifted and combined. Thus it is not easy, although not impossible, to see how syncretization would fit into a Weberian scheme. The emphasis upon rationalization within the context of 'big' doctrinal systems gave an overwarranted intellectualist stamp to his inquiries.

For all of Weber's great importance in advancing the study of cultural change — particularly religio-cultural change — there are, then, significant analytic gaps in his approach. One such gap, which has not yet been alluded to, concerns the ways in which the experience of social-structural properties has a bearing upon the manner in which ideas are cast, rejected and accepted. The study of rapid religio-cultural change — as, to take but two examples, in the Reformation and post-Reformation periods and in Africa in the nineteenth and twentieth centuries — seems to demand attention to the crucial issue of why some societies or segments thereof take one particular religious path and other societies or segments thereof another path. It is misleading as one prominent interpreter of the African scene (Peel) suggests to argue that a 'Weberian' approach is appropriate in answering such questions, for Weber was typically interested in the grand sweep of change from one religious doctrinal system to another, and the processes of rationalization which seemed to be, so to speak, on the side of history.[11] But that kind of approach clearly misses such important questions as to why, to continue with our examples, the differentials of the Reformation were what they were — why some societies embraced Protestantism and which kind, and others remained Catholic — and why some African societies have adopted Islam and others one or another form of Christianity. This is the kind of issue which has, at least in part, only been tackled in a neo-Durkheimian mode, with respect to the social-structuring of indigenous epistemologies and ontologies.[12]

At the present time microcultural approaches are very much needed in view of the fact that the general field of study involving the construction, maintenance and transformation of meanings, beliefs, values and so on is pitched at extremes. One very conspicuous extreme is constituted by those ethnomethodological persuasions which focus on underlying factors — variously called basic, interpretive or deep-structural rules. Insofar as anything resembling the modal sociological use of 'culture' is approached, it is in terms of the interaction between these rules and the normative or surface rules. In a nutshell, for this school meaning itself is ever-problematic, and it is the quest for rules that provide ways of making (situational) sense of the world which is the hallmark of much of what is called ethnomethodology. Underlying, universal principles are also at the heart of the Lévi-Straussian structuralist endeavour. The deep-structural extremes thus deny the relevance, indeed in many cases the ontic reality, of culture in the sense of a public ideational resource subject to change in its own right. However, the latter stipulation of the sociological flavor accorded to culture in the present context should not be confused with either the superorganic conception or the conception of culture as template. The superorganic (or immanentist) stance, standing at the furthest extreme in relation to ethnomethodology, has one major merit and one defect. The merit lies simply in the fact that we do know that many systems of recorded beliefs, values and symbols change in patterned form over periods of time. The defect has to do with the claim – implicit or explicit – that this is autonomous at the level of ideation: that culture changes in and of itself without the 'assistance' of individuals and social-structurations – or as, Marx put it, without activity. The attack on the idealist position by Durkheim and Weber was undoubtedly one of the major steps in the history of social science. On the other hand, the superorganic position is undoubtedly correct in addressing the autonomy of culture in the sense that ideational patterns once set in motion manifest their own internal logic and range of uses and outcomes. It is in that element of finiteness of culture – in its patterned element – that there resides a highly significant degree of genuine autonomy. All the same, the finiteness is only revealed in individual and social interpretation and reaction.

Insistence upon the irreducibility of culture informs approaches other than those easily classifiable as superorganic or idealist. Most notable in our immediate purview is the position adopted by Bellah, in his attacks on symbolic reductionism and symbolic consequentialism. The symbolic realism to which he himself subscribes seems to involve a commitment to the ubiquity of a range of symbolic constants in the human condition as such, problems which should be regarded as independent of social-structural and psychological contingencies and exigencies. There is a superficially close relationship between this stance and the culture-as-template position advanced by Geertz. As a composite tendency the Bellah-Geertz view thus sees culture as a 'programming' aspect of human action systems. Taken at face value such a perspective denies the idea that culture is differentially shaped and interpreted – that beliefs, values and symbols should be studied 'at work' or 'on occasion of use', In fact in the work of both Bellah and Geertz, particularly the latter, the culture-as-template position is considerably loosened – as is best exampled in Geertz' distinction between *holding* beliefs and being *held by* beliefs.[13] (There are of course also different ways of holding and different ways of being held by beliefs.) Bellah's position, on the other hand, might in one aspect be regarded as a deep-structural one, a kind of sociological Jungism which maintains that there are archetypical threads running through social life. In another respect Bellah's advocacy of symbolic realism is a call for culture creation on the part of intellectuals.[14]

In what ways does the idea of religious conversion relate to general and historical circumstances of human life? On a narrow view the idea of conversion may well be confined to Christian-based conceptions of diffuse and profound change at the level of individuals *qua* individuals.[15] As we shall see later on, it is not easy to distil a simple working definition of conversion even within the Christian orbit. Nevertheless there is this characteristic which seems to be widespread in the history of Christianity – namely, the focus upon the idea of self-revision relative to God. There has been much disagreement as to whether conversion has primarily to do with inner-psychological change relative to a supernatural agency or with change in sociocultural commitment. Among sociologists the problem seems to have arisen through their reluctance to become involved in discussions of a psychological nature; hence the temptation either to assign discussion of conversion to the psychological level, and thereby ignore the issue of conversion, or to insist upon a purely non-psychological conception of conversion.[16]

A third position involves confining the use of the term conversion to those religious (and political-ideological) groups and individual experiences where the notion of inner, psychic renewal is stressed.[17] That on a number of counts is more realistic and helpful than either of the first two approaches, but it still begs some important issues. One of the most important of these issues arises in connection with etymological considerations. The word 'conversion' in dictionary terms means transformation, or in its most acute sense transformation into an opposite (as in the phrase 'the converse of . . .'). In comparison, the emphasis upon renewal in fundamentalist Protestant doctrines is largely analogous to the very influential eighteenth-century meaning of the term 'revolution'. The modern conception of revolution is, as Arendt argues, 'inextricably bound up with the notion that the course of history suddenly begins anew, that an entirely new story . . . is about to unfold'. This conception 'was unknown prior to the two great revolutions at the end of the eighteenth century'.[18] Indeed the crystallization of the idea of inner-renewal at the individual level occurred, largely under John Wesley's influence, in the same late-eighteenth century period. Thus it would perhaps be more accurate to speak of homologous concepts of revision of selves and societies in that period; the terms revolution and conversion had substantially the same, connected meanings. However, there are variations in emphasis in modern conceptions of revolution that do not involve necessarily the idea of going back and starting history at a higher level, and it would seem reasonable in parallel manner to be willing for analytic purposes to use the term conversion in a somewhat more flexible manner than in reference entirely to an orientation to inner-renewal. We shall see more fully that the conception of individualistic inner-renewal has had very significant consequences for the status and legitimacy of culture in the recent history of Western societies, but to confine conversion entirely to that domain is to sequester it too rigidly and thereby to leave also too isolated transformations of individual 'and group commitment which do not pivot ideas of basic change on such processes as re-birth and purification; both of these two processes being at the heart of the fundamentalist emphasis upon inner-renewal. Thus we are broadly concerned with 'conversion' as a problem-area, with special reference to its intersection with culture, but at the same time acknowledging the paradigmatic significance of the inner-renewal notion of conversion in the modern-historical period. We shall shortly see, however, that in anthropological terms the idea of inner-renewal is in any case embedded in a wider matrix of human foci.

The two most fruitful general angles from which the issue of sociologically situating conversion may be approached would seem to be: first, the salience in human life of the phenomenon of initiation; and, second, the great importance in human societies of what Nelson calls self-images and systems of spiritual direction. Initiation in its most diffuse relevance has to do with procedures for placing individuals in a wider order where they may function effectively in relation to the most fundamental axioms of that order, or sub-orders thereof. Thus initiation in its most extended reference ranges from cosmos-embracing initiation rites in primitive societies – where individual initiation also often involves the re-initiation, or regeneration, of the cosmos and the local society – to some phenomena covered by the modern concept of socialization. Self-images and systems of spiritual direction constitute a general 'catchment theme' which embraces cultural models of and models for selfhood, theories and techniques of spiritual healing and functioning of selves. These two modes of situating the phenomenon of conversion do, as we shall see, overlap empirically and conceptually. Initiation in its phenomenological-anthropological sense focuses, as Eliade cogently argues, upon the idea of starting life over again. Initiation may thus range from 'the obscure desire of every human soul to renew itself periodically, as the cosmos is renewed' to 'moments of total crisis' involving a 'total *renovatio*, a renewal capable of transmuting life'.[19] Our second angle – self images and systems of spiritual direction – is in part an historical and evolutionary outgrowth of the general phenomenon of initiation.

Initiation: Eliade describes the initiation as 'a body of rites and oral teachings whose purpose is to produce a decisive alteration in the religious and social status of the person to be initiated. In philosophical terms, initiation is equivalent to a basic change in existential conditions; the novice emerges from his ordeal endowed with a totally different being from that which he possessed before his initiation; he has become *another*'.[20] Although there have been many different forms of initiation rite, according to variation in sociocultural circumstance, 'the important fact is that all premodern societies (that is, those that lasted in Western Europe to the end of the Middle Ages, and in the rest of the world to the first World War) accord primary importance to the ideology and techniques of initiation'.[21] In the initiation rite 'sacred history', as enshrined in primitive societies in primordial mythology, is 'transmitted intact to succeeding generations'.[22]

In the modern world, says Eliade, 'man sees in the history that precedes him a purely human work and, more especially, believes that he has the power to continue and perfect it indefinitely', whereas in more traditional societies 'everything significant – that is, everything creative and powerful – that has ever happened took place *in the beginning*, in the Time of the myths'.[23] In primitive and traditional initiation rites and images there is a common tendency to involve the initate in a process of regression to what Eliade calls 'a latent mode of being (complementary to the precosmogonic Chaos)'.[24] Modern conceptions of conversion imply the idea of a new start, as expressed in William James' famous notion of the 'twice-born' man or woman.[25] But placed in a larger philosophical and phenomenological context, we see that in many other primitive and traditional situations it is not only a question of a new start simply for the individual but also in a very important respect a question of restarting *society* in relation to cosmic concerns. (In that connection the link between conversion at the individual level and revolution at the societal level, as well as the idea of cultural revolution, must be reiterated, particularly with respect to contemporary revolutionism, which in the West has come to embrace – or, better perhaps, yield to – the notion of transformations of individuals' consciousness.) In the latter case, especially in primitive societies, the intiation rite puts the initiate successively in contact with the cosmogonic chaos and the experience of sacred origin and orderliness. This process involves phases of asceticism and mysticism. It involves emphasis upon asceticism in the sense of pointing-up the character of danger, mysticism in the sense of involving connectedness to purity. (In effect, these two interrelated notions define Lévi-Strauss' 'semiotic' of ritual and myth.) One of the major forms of sociocultural variation in this respect is the function of the mystical phase. In primitive societies where the emphasis in initiation falls very largely upon the puberty rite (or tribal, or age-group initiation), the mystical phase is to all intents and purposes a phase of consummating the involvement of the initiate with the 'mysterious sacredness' of the cosmically-located sociocultural order. But in societies where there is an emphasis upon either of two other closely related initiation rites for entering what Eliade calls confraternities (secret, mystically oriented societies) and mystical vocations, the mystical phase involves the imparting of special knowledge. In the case of the latter forms of initiation in primitive societies the tendency is for special knowledge to be in service of the sociocultural system. But as we move, in an evolutionary sense, away from primitive religion we find that gnostic initiation – for example in both Ancient Greece and traditional India – involved a significant degree of dissociation from the sociocultural system.[26] The Gnostics in Greek speculative thought and espousers of classical Indian philosophy both emphasized the indifference of the transformed individual to the ordinary world (the world of necessity). Primordial myths, in this view, are learned in order to dissociate from their results.

The tremendous importance for the West of the Hellenistic period (which of course was quite heavily imbued with Oriental and Mid-Eastern conceptions of intiation, mystery and rebirth) is well-summarized by Eliade:

For the history of religion, the particular importance of the Greco-Oriental mysteries lies in the fact that they illustrate the need for a personal religious experience engaging man's entire existence, that is, to use Christian terminology, as including his 'salvation' in eternity. Such a personal religious experience could not flourish in the framework of the public cults, whose principal function was to ensure the sanctification of communal life and the continuance of the State. In the great historical civilizations in which the mysteries proliferated, we no longer find the situation characteristic of primitive cultures; there . . . the initiations of youth were at the same time an occasion for the complete regeneration not only of the collectivity but also of the cosmos. In the Hellenistic situation . . . the immense success of the mysteries illustrates the break between the religious elites and the religion of State, a break that Christianity will widen and, at least for a time, make complete.[27]

The solidification and institutionalization of Christianity led to the severe attenuation in the West of the ideas and practices associated with gnosticism and initiation into cosmic mysteries. The focus of regeneration shifted to the sacraments, the Christian-sacramental form of regeneration involving periodic suffusion with spirituality thought to be immanently available through special ritualistic procedures. But that did not involve the conception of the transformation of the whole being which is so common to many evolutionarily-prior forms of initiation. In broad terms, then, the church-administered sacraments provided a severely attenuated form of regeneration of `individuals and congregations which did not directly involve the wider, 'caesar society'. This separation of the purification of individuals from the affairs of the embryonically national society is of great significance in the odyssey of initiation-conversion phenomena, for it accelerated the process whereby institutionalized dilemmas surrounding the relationship between the perfection of self in relation to the perfection of society became virtually institutionalized.

What we are, then, drawing particular attention to is the long-drawn out process whereby in the West individual regeneration becomes increasingly differentiated from the society and how in turn both self and society (both socially and culturally) become separately identifiable objects of regenerative concern; although the degree of the differentiation must not be exaggerated, nor must attempts, as in certain 'millennial moments', to dedifferentiate be overlooked. Bellah's ideal-typical conception of American civil religion involves the central proposition that America in its origins constituted an early-modern form of differentiated, but synchronized individual and societal regeneration, with a special forwardlooking commitment to long-term future perfection of individuals and the society. A major argument in this respect is that in Puritan New England regeneration, the intra-individual change constituted a form of conversion into the covenanted society. On that view the major change which occurred as between classical pre-Reformation Catholicism and post-Reformation American Protestantism was that whereas in the former there were separated emphases upon the maintenance of individual religious purity, through the sacraments, and upon the establishment and maintenance of societies in the form of absolute states, in the latter (the early American) there was closely linked emphasis upon the notions of individual perfection from the basis of regeneration and of societal perfection.

With these most recent remarks we have undoubtedly outstepped the boundaries of that which can viably be included under the heading of initiation. On the other hand, the links between initiation rites as found in primal societies, sacraments in more differentiated societies, and conversion in modern societies are clear in broad anthropological perspective. Initiation 'proper' only remained in Europe by the Middle Ages in vestigal forms, primarily attenuated rites of passage and rituals of induction into occupations, notably in the conception of apprenticeship. The latter prefigures the modern notion of adult (or secondary) socialization, which has in the recent past been the (constraining) analytic pivot of the discussion of individual change during adult life. In this scenario initiation has not merely grown less significant over evolutionary time, it has become increasingly divorced from matters of general cultural significance. However, in a functional sense Protestantistic conceptions of inner-renewal as well as looser conceptions of conversion, involving shifts from one belief system to another, clearly have important implications for culture. As we shall see, the former has been important in Western contexts in building-up resistance to culture on the part of individuals; but has also in particular circumstances been the basis for undoing commitment to one form of culture in readiness for induction to another, links having been frequently noted between fundamentalist conversion experiences and 'coercive persuasion', including 'brainwashing'.

The balance between resistance and disposability in this respect is interesting. On the one hand, the individualistic achievement of a sense of psychic integrity and certainty can constitute a shield against cultural intrusion (and social manipulation); on the other hand, a generalized sense of the realistic possibility – even desirability – of psychic renovation can leave the individual very open to certain forms of persuasion (an other-directedness founded upon a need for inner-directedness). The contrast between the well-established inner-certainty of Jehovah's Witnesses and the persuadibility of Americans in brain-washing conditions demonstrates this point.

In much more general terms the possibility of there being a connection between, on the one hand, initiation rites and, on the other hand, disposability to Christian missionary-conversion attempts should be mentioned – both of them emphasizing ideas of re-birth, or at least *passage* from one state to another. The evidence on that point is, however, very far from clear; deep-probing social-scientific analysis of the major site of African conversion and cultural change only being in its infancy. In this connection it should also be said that in the study of twentieth-century African cultural change ('*the* major instance of the transition to world religions' in modern history)[28] there has been a strong tendency to emphasize the non-radical-break nature of 'conversion' at the individual level. For example, Peel argues in reference to African conversion that people will be attracted to the power seemingly conferred by conversion to a world religion (Islam or Christianity) only if the indigenous religion is not in itself the major identity basis in the autochthonous situation. However, even that idea is not irreconcilable with the notion that emphasis upon a primal form of revisability of self is a central factor in conversion. In that respect the idea of extending personal power, or of enlarging general or specific capacities through conversion, is important. (The ways in which cultural themes are juxtaposed in the process of cultural change, particularly in the African case, is crucial to understanding both microcultural and macrocultural aspects of the problem. Four major possibilities seem to exist: *reconstruction* of the indigenous culture, involving extending the latter to include the 'higher' religious culture; *substitution* of the 'higher' for the primal; *subsumption* of the primal by the 'higher'; and *adhesion*, involving selective, syncretic coordinations of elements both from a world religion and from primal beliefs, values and symbols.)[29]

Before leaving themes sparked by our invocation of the initiation phenomenon we must attend briefly to the question of the almost complete disappearance of rites of passage in modern societies. The phrase, rites of passage, does in fact give an intended twist to our focus upon initiation; for the latter term has facilitated a direct focus on culture and the individual, while the former focuses more directly on what is done to the 'passenger' *vis-à-vis* the wider society. Gluckman has traced the disappearance of rites of passage 'to the fact that the passage to a new role is in our society associated in most cases with a change of the set of interacting persons; the new and the old groups alike know the individual in question in one role only, so the public announcement of a new social quality of the individual . . . will be superfluous'.[30] But the situation in modern societies thus implied takes insufficient account of the differentiation of the social-structural realm from the realm of individual life. Thus in our view the individual through the vehicle of identity has, so to speak, to create his or her own passages. Central to the latter is what Turner calls the phase of *liminality*, the disorganized, non-structured phase between detachment from 'the old' and attachment to 'the new'. The liminal period – between 'desocialization' and 're-socialization' – is, says Turner one of *communitas* when there is revelation 'however fleetingly . . . of a generalized social bond that has ceased to be and has simultaneously yet to be fragmented into a multiplicity of structural ties'.[31] In modern circumstances liminal periods are, of course, more or less uninstitutionalized – at least those which have to do with life-cycle crises. On the other hand, the creation of social spaces or moratoria, not merely in adolescence but also at other adult life-phases, is apparently becoming more evident in modern societies. In this perspective conversion – which in its narrow religious sense occurs most frequently in adolescence – becomes increasingly likely and possible at *other* stages.

Spiritual Direction: In turning to the perspective of self-images and spiritual direction we can begin conveniently by pointing to the East–West contrast which becomes so manifestly evident with the triumph of Christianity in the West (at the same time acknowledging of course that the East–West differential was very much longer in the making than the period of the spread of Christianity). Basically the Eastern tendency has been to emphasize methods of spiritual direction which attempt to overcome the anguish of the individual relative to a world which is not amenable to amelioration, and certainly not to redemption. In contrast the Western tendency, as sharply crystallized in the Christian tradition, has been to emphasize the basic goodness of this world. As Nelson puts it 'the methods of mitigating estrangements and madnesses are in the first place "a way *back*" to the primal undifferentiated ground. And then once more the new elements assert themselves strongly. The way back assumes the character of a "way forward", forward to the struggle for mastery of self and the world.'[32] Although we spoke earlier of the idea of the Christian sacraments constituting an attenuated form of initiation, we must now note strongly that growing out of Greek and then Roman circumstances there was increasing emphasis upon the spiritual direction of the individual as such, so that by the twelfth and thirteenth centuries there had emerged with considerable conspicuousness two major forms of such direction which foreshadowed the development within pre-Reformation Christianity of the division between the lay individual's functioning in a world of sin and turmoil, and the monastic life of full-time worship of God. On the one hand, especially after 1215 when all Christians were obliged to make annual confession, there was the extensive diffusion within the Christian orbit of the idea of conscience as being the basis for action in every sphere of life. On the other hand, there was the more restricted, but still very influential, contemplative tradition. In particular, in the twelfth to fourteenth centuries (as in the examples of such figures as St. Bernard of Clairvaux, St. Bonaventura and Meister Eckhart) we find elaboration of 'the image of the soul's rebirth as a result of mystical union with God, which eventually undermined the forensic institutionalizations of thought and sentiment'.[33]

Nelson's emphasis upon the conjunction of the ideas of conscience, casuistry, the cure of souls and forensic institutionalization of thought and sentiment highlights a major aspect of the individual-society connection in the Middle Ages. For within this matrix of motifs there lay the basis for an extensive form of social control that linked the innermost life of individuals to the wider sociocultural context, but at the same time laid the ground for a trajectory of individual liberation – in the sense that through the sixteenth and seventeenth centuries it was from the basis of the idea of conscience that inner-freedom gains were won.

It may be said, then, that there were two main paths of religious individualization in the Christian West. There was first the contemplative path, which owed much historically to Gnosticism and subsequently to Christian mysticism; and there was, secondly the path of conscience. That the two paths have frequently crossed and diverged in complex ways is not at all in doubt, but they do seem to be quite discernible. In arguing thus we must, however, clarify our position in relation to the earlier discussion of mysticism and asceticism. In a major sense the dominant ascetic strand within Christianity was, in the present perspective, embedded within the theme of 'the forensic institutionalization of thought and sentiment'.[34] Eventually in one form the centrality of conscience was to become confined within Lutheranism to the sphere of faith, which it was found necessary to combine with an unqualified acceptance of secular authority in the mode of inner-religious freedom and outer political bondage. In the Calvinist scheme conscience underwent a shift which involved emphasizing its rooting in the individual *vis-à-vis* his or her worldly actions. The passivity and the activism of the respective concepts of 'the calling' reflected the differences between Lutheranism and Calvinism in such respects.

Of particular relevance in the immediate context is the role of the contemplative tradition in the development of classic Protestant conceptions of conversion. Even though we often think of conversion, particularly in its mode of inner, pyschological re-birth as a cleansing, asceticism-producing process – one which through purification provides a shield against danger (or in some cases more positively addresses enticingly the joys of pure states of mind and actions) we must not ignore the fact that (in varying degrees of attenuation) the illuminist element in contemplative mysticism had a part to play in the development of certain aspects of Protestantism. The complex odyssey of illuminism is well-adumbrated by Nelson: 'Medieval illuminism provided inspiration to

Luther, the revolutionary sectarians, the English dissenters, the American Quakers, the myriad Continental Romantics whose voices sound in the philosophy and literature of the last two centuries.'[35] Nelson further states:

The illuminist philosphies which had bloomed in the meditative tradition were to attain their fullest flowering in radical Protestant cultures and their transcendental offshoots: inner light mysticism, Enlightenment rationalism, the sundry romanticisms of the 19th and 20th centuries, including Existentialism. Each step along the way was a blow on behalf of the liberation of conscience until at the end, the wholly unencumbered conscience was itself called into question by the union of utilitarianism, Darwinism, historicism, and Freudianism.[36]

The manner in which revivalist conversionism could be regarded as heavily injected with elements of the old illuminist tradition is dramatically underscored by an American polemic of the 1840s:

We have reason to stand upon our guard against the inroads of an unchurchly spirit. . . . It magnifies the inward and the spiritual, and affects to call the soul away from a religion of forms and outward show. . . . It will know nothing of a real revelation of Christ in the flesh. . . . The old Gnosticism has been long since shorn of its glory. But what is it but a more subtle phase of the same error to deny the existence of a real, historical *Church* in the world? . . . Let us beware of Gnostic, unchurchly . . . spirit. . . . Let us have no fellowship here with Antichrist.[37]

In effect what is being highlighted here is the fact that perfectionism (which is by many taken as the touchstone of the conversion experience, at the core of which lie the notions of perfect sanctification and second blessing) does appear in tandem with illuminism (involving the idea of revelation). That combination was particularly evident at various junctures of nineteenth-century American history. But its full-flowering should be dated back as far as seventeenth-century England and America. Ahlstrom draws emphatic attention to the remnants of Platonic mysticism in Puritanism, and yet shows that the distinguishing character of Puritanism, which contained both Platonic and Augustinian elements, was its emphasis upon the historical and practical consequences of Puritan inwardness. Thus the mystical aspects of Puritanism had essentially instrumental significance. It was the practical mission which was definitive. That feature of Puritanism as it relates to the general theme of conversion facilitates our suggesting, in very schematic terms, that whereas the ideal-typical mystic emphasizes the mystical state as the *raison d'être* of preparatory and supplementary asceticism, the ideal-typical ascetic, on the other hand, emphasizes the ascetic state as the *raison d'être* of preparatory and supplementary mysticism. The importance of the latter in the case of Anglo-American Puritanism is thrown into relief by Perry Miller's statement that the Puritans 'liberated men from the treadmill of indulgences and penances, but cast them on the iron couch of introspection'.[38] (That development has had much to do with American susceptibility to psychoanalysis. In an important sense the adoption of the psychoanalytic mode constituted a form of deconversion from faithful religiosity.)

These matters can again be thrown into sharp relief with Nelson's assistance. In addressing the importance of the arrival in America of dissenters from England, Holland and Germany with their inner-light ideas Nelson says:

The nonconformist illuminist sectarians effected a transvaluation of the value of conscience by subordinating the moral conscience in the medieval sense to the inner light. Neo-Platonic illuminism which had been so significant in the medieval practice of meditation trumphed over medieval rationalism, which nourished the medieval administration of the moral self and the forum of conscience. The important link between late medieval mysticism and Protestant illuminism was the concept of the spark or witness of God in the soul.[39]

The rationalism of the Enlightenment was also in some respects in cultural debt to Platonic or Neoplatonic mysticism; and in that connection Nelson draws attention to the vacillation within Protestantism between rationalism and fundamentalism. In spite of their frequent hostility to each other both have emphasized the 'sober afterglow' of a self freed from encumbrance on the basis of a fixed point of internal authority. The relationship of each to Romanticism is problematic but important to mention because of its great relevance to the development of conceptions of the changeable self.

Romanticism, particularly of the English variety, was deeply influenced by Biblical ideas, notably those emphasizing eschatology and redemption. Late eighteenth-century and early nineteenth-century Romanticism in fact shared with fundamentalism, as well as with certain strands within rationalism, some concerns with the perfection of society through the perfection of individuals. (In the case of fundamentalism – of which there have recently been some modern secular versions – there was quite frequently an injection of millennialism.) Among the writers of English Romanticism this conjunction was particularly evident. The phrase 'natural supernaturalism' has been aptly invoked by Abrams to highlight the secularization of Biblical themes in that respect.[40] And it is quite remarkable how we find parallel conceptions of conversion and self-formation in religious fundamentalism and in Romanticism. Specifically, both the Methodist model of conversion (the paradigm for many modern conceptions) and the Wordsworthian 'theodicy of the private life' (the latter being attractively rephrased by Abrams as *biodicy*) had widespread impacts in the early and mid-nineteenth century. Both drew with very different emphases upon similar Christian ideas, the Wordsworthian being of course a secularization of the latter. Abrams speaks of the Wordsworthian biodicy, which was very influential in middle class circles in nineteenth-century England, as belonging to 'the distinctive Romantic genre of the *Bildungsgeschichte*, which translates the painful process of Christian conversion and redemption into a painful process of self-formation, crisis, and self-recognition, and culminates in a stage of self-coherence, self-awareness, and assured power that is its own reward'.[41] Central to such models for the self in the romantic imagination was the notion of progress by reversion, and it is here again that we note the link between conversion at the individual level and revolution at the societal level. Progress by reversion basically involves a spiralling process, whereby reversion to a recovered unity is achieved at a higher level than the original primordial unity, because, as Abrams summarizes, 'it incorporates the intervening differentiations'.[42]

As here outlined, fundamentalism (particularly in its conjunction with either pre- or post-millennialism) and Romanticism both related closely to the idea of progress, which was such a formidable force in nineteenth-century life. However, both also became increasingly secularized along ascetic and mystical paths and in so doing became increasingly at odds with the conception of cultural-out-thereness. Thus as the twentieth century approached there began to proliferate among intellectuals a variety of new conceptions of the relationship between individuals and culture. The most significant of the crystallized conceptions was obviously the Freudian.

Culture and Individual Convertibility in the Modern World

In his attempt to sketch a theory of cultural change, Rieff argues that 'psychological man' has come to so dominate in modern societies that human autonomy from culture may be one of the most fundamental tendencies of the modern age. 'By psychologizing about themselves interminably, Western men are learning to use their internality against the primacy of any particular organization of society.'[43] The Freudian revolution signaled the shift from therapies of commitment to therapies of analysis (a shift paralleled, we may suggest, by the shift from the authoritative society to the administered society). Therapies of commitment were concerned in the traditional past with curing and healing by committing individuals to the wider communal-cultural context; whereas therapies of analysis are concerned not with curing or healing but with the imparting of ego-strength, the capacity to withstand much of the 'coerciveness' of culture. There is, then, an anti-cultural predicate to much of modern personality. Rieff's major thesis in this respect is that increasingly since Freud the therapeutic has triumphed in the form of an increasing concern with the attainment of 'a manipulable sense of well-being'. In his anti-cultural thrust modern psychological man actually runs against the grain of salient features of Freud's own thought, the focus on well-being and self-realization as ends in themselves being unFreudian extensions of Freud's own emphasis upon the mediating, non-meaning-seeking role of the ego.

The great import of Rieff's analysis for our immediate interests is the proposition that for the individual to become engaged to a widespread extent in self-therapeutic efforts 'which must either ignore or contradict the meanings by which his character was molded, suggests either that the therapy must fail or that the culture is in the process of a change as to its control mechanism'.[44] This proposition sharply demonstrates the intimate connection between long-term change at the level of individuals and cultural change. The more that individuals become concerned with their own functional autonomy then the less can culture operate in its traditional mode of authoritative informing of individual life and action. Or, phrased differently, the less that faith is empha-sized at the individual level, the less that culture is seen as a form of commitment. In the light cast by these views we may observe that the concern with intra-psychic conversion crystallized in the West in the seventeenth and eighteenth centuries in dominantly Protestant settings simultaneously, on a generalized basis, detached individual personality from culture, set-up internal protection from culture, and made it possible for there to be conversion to cultural (and in a sense social) beliefs and values. This contention in part echoes Simmel's ideas concerning the tragic relationship between culture and the individual. Put yet differently we may say that modern man has been slowly converted to the idea of being converted; that whole process having involved a 'Freudian phase' of deconversion from the 'Wesleyan model' or the Romantic 'sudden love' model. This has been a two-fold process. In very schematic terms: We are suggesting that the seventeenth and eighteenth centuries crystallized the possiblity for intra-psychic protection from intrusive cultural demands – Protestant fundamentalism and rationalism being the two major strands in this crystallization. Romanticism was a move toward utilizing the psychic freedom won thereby, while the Freudian analytic manifested a tendency to correct for losses in psychic autonomy resulting from an over-yielding tendency of Romanticism (and its successor existentialism) with respect to an increasingly pluralistic cultural circumstance.

These interpretations are not in fact very congruent with the thrust of Rieff's thesis. It was previously noted that for Rieff the Freudian phase constituted a phase of deconversion, deconversion from the traditional controls and remissions of culture. The present departure from the significance of that proposition rests in part on emphasizing the critical importance of the Romantic phase, for injection of emphasis upon the latter throws up the idea that change at the individual level proceeds in terms of 'correction steps'. If our interpretation of the Romantic phase is correct – that is, as constituting a flourishing of the recently found sense of freedom of the psychic self – then it would be reasonable to suggest that following the Freudian 'analytic revolution' there is presently occurring a new post-classical-Romantic flourishing of the further gains of the ego-self, a new kind of openness to culture but in an even less faithful, or as Habermas puts it, less auratic mode than was true in the Romantic phase of the late eighteenth and early nineteenth century.[45] Classical Romanticism was, for example, heavily in debt to, held in awe, 'high' cultural traditions, notably classical Greek culture.

Such thoughts throw doubt on Rieff's claim that modern psychological man and woman, with his or her emphasis upon a manipulable sense of well being, is appropriately seen as an extension of the ascetic mode of life. As we have remarked in the fourth chapter there is little doubt that there are many modern seemingly popular therapies and guides to living which emphasize the manipulable sense of well-being, assertiveness training, 'winning through intimidation', Est, etc., but there are many more which emphasize more consummatory aspects of self and the intrinsic virtues of changes in states of consciousness, while the apparent increase in mystic-type experiences can hardly be overlooked.[46] One of the major research programs that is needed in this area is the delineation of the new sects, cults and movements in such a way as to distinguish between intrinsic involvement in Western versions of Taoism, Sufism, Zen Buddhism, and the like, and their therapeutic spinoffs, such as transcendental meditation, biofeedback, and so on.[47]

Thus, in line with the earlier image which we explicated concerning the combination of asceticism and mysticism, we are disposed to doubt very much the generalizability of the implications of Rieff's claim that 'with Freud, individualism took a great and perhaps final step: toward that mature and calm feeling which comes from having nothing to hide. . . . To live on the surface prevents deep hurts . . . Western man has learned the technical complexity of externalizing his inwardness, and has been able at last to usher out that crowd of shadows urging him to turn inward.'[48] It is indeed tempting on some criteria to accept such comments as constituting an accurate, overall picture of the American personality in particular; but the trends of the last fifteen years or so suggest that externalization of inwardness has been overtaken by something more complex, something akin to the picture etched by Freud's contemporary, Simmel — who has been called the sociological Freud — a picture which focuses upon an increasing sense of mysterious selves; the basic idea being that the more individuals are exposed in their entitivity the more mysterious, the less understandable they become, a circumstance in part promoted by individuals seeing each other and seeing themselves from so many different angles in modern societies. It is appropriate at this point to note that for all the 'tragedy' built into their respective works both Freud and Simmel seemed to believe that the greater autonomy won by the ego created the possibility of new forms of culture being generated which would further enhance ego-freedom by making it less coerced by culture.

Indeed in some quarters the notion of identity has become closely intertwined with the subject of conversion. In attempting to elaborate a distinction between different types of identity change, Travisano maintains that alternations are 'transitions to identities which are prescribed or at least permitted within the person's established universes of discourse. Conversions are transitions to identities which are proscribed within the person's established universes of discourse, and which exist in universes of discourse that negate these formerly established ones. The ideal typical conversion can be thought of as the embracing of a negative identity'.[49] There are a number of definitional and methodological problems involved in Travisano's position (some of which are taken-up in an appendix to this chapter), but the immediately pressing question concerns the manner in which in the modern period conversion has come to be associated with identity themes. Is identity simply a new jargon word of social science, or does its modern deployment represent a signicant shift in the nature of the ways in which individuals change their 'operative Archimedean points' (to use as general a phrase as possible)? Undoubtedly, in a psychoanalytic sense, identity in the form of identification with a 'power' has been salient both within the Christian orbit of conversion as inner-psychic revolution in reference to God and in other contexts, such as the Islamic which has traditionally involved an identificatory form of submission to Allah and attachment to the Islamic sociocultural context. But, on the other hand, the way in which the term identity has been used in the modern period carries other, if not entirely exclusive connotations. Broadly speaking, as we distil these connotations from a large number of contexts, we arrive at two, interconnected aspects of the term, the first of these is primarily psychological, or social psychological, in that it refers to the organizing of the personality in diachronic and synchronic modes.[50] The second, and more sociological, has to do with the location of selves (including collective actors) in relation to other objects of orientation. In this respect identity has much to do, phenomenologically speaking, with measurement – measuring, maintaining and adjusting distances to others, and sorting-out similarities and dissimilarities in relation to alters. There are within the matrix of identity concerns some significant traces of the Freudian notion of identification, but as presented here the sociological conception of identity is more specifically social in its meaning and not exclusively concerned with identity in the mode of identification with some entity in dependent mode. In other words identity and processes of identification have sociologically to do what one might call 'lateral' as well as 'vertical' locating, and also with detachment from as well as attachment to 'authorities' in the vertical mode.

If such considerations are viable with respect to the use of the term 'identity' then we have in effect drawn attention to a mode of shift in 'Archimedean points' which is not necessarily intra-psychic and which suggests a wider frame for the use of the term 'conversion'. Thus on this view, even though it may be very appropriate to talk of a generalized deconversion at the level of personality with the triumph of the analytic mode, in a different repect conversion of the identity-transformation type becomes more, not less, likely – as the process of individuation leads to individuals having more 'room' to select from cultural options and from social reference groups.[51] Even at the intra-psychic level one can still speak in modified form of conversion in identity mode; in that such ideas as 'getting it all together', 'finding myself' – ideas which seem to be central to some of the new consciousness movements – do not necessarily entail the process of re-birth, but rather of progression to a higher state. In that connection increased self-consciousness about life-cycle liminalities expands the likelihood of relatively planned processes of conversion.

In this perspective some of the basic ideas about conversion having to do with radical change of self are retained but the term is expanded to cope with modes of self-transformation which are not duplicates of the fundamentalist conversion*ist* type.

The main thrust of the present discussion is, then, to illuminate the manner in which changes at the individual level – as pinpointed around the theme of conversion – affect the functioning of culture in modern societies. There is no doubt at all that changes in the nature of individual life are complexly bound-up with changes in other aspects of societies, but the main intention here has been to concentrate on implications for culture of change at the individual level. It would seem to follow from our discussion that in modern societies that focus is as important, if not more important, than the Weberian focus upon the social vehicles of culture maintenance and culture change.[52] What we may well be witnessing in the modern period is a freeing of the ego from culture; thus allowing for the more direct creation of culture. In a sense we are beginning to learn, as Simmel might have put it, *how culture is possible*. Or, in ways that he probably did not expect – nor would have approved – we are being tortuously released from what Marx called 'the nightmare' of cultural tradition.[53] In part this has been made possible by individuals apparently feeling freer by virtue of the 'nature-like' social system manifesting automaticity. Thus in Marxist terms social alienation has been a major determinant of decline on the hold of culture. In the perspective developed here it is doubtful whether in the foreseeable future culture will regain its old, auratic significance. The key problem in the immediate future is the degree to which individuation in relation to culture is more escapist, or more adaptive, or more constructive of new cultural forms. And that will depend to a significant degree on the manner in which these developments are recorded and interpreted.

We have suggested that Rieff's therapeutic man (and woman) is not simply a secularized, ego-resilient version of traditional Western ascetic man. Rather the new man and woman manifest both secularized, or partly secularized, ascetic and mystical tendencies, a combination which does not preclude 'culture work' to the extent implied by Rieff. Only the use of hindsight in a number of decades in the future will fully allow us to decide upon the degree of *seriousness* of the mystical component. Certainly we cannot agree with Gellner that much of the cultural flourishing of recent times has been so luxuriating as not to be really about the serious things in life.[54] A rather more attractive extreme view would be that we increasingly live in a period of a 'new Calvinism' as far as self-preoccupations are concerned – namely, there is an increasing amount of 'busy work' being done on meaning and consciousness. Increasing numbers of people preoccupy themselves with the state of 'their heads' as a way of dealing with the modern world. But interpretation in this respect depends largely on what one takes to be 'the serious things in life'.

TECHNICAL APPENDIX

Dimensions of Conversion Processes

A. *References of Conversion*

Action-system levels	Conversion categories	Effectors of conversion	Post-conversion controls
Cultural	Belief	Believing	Ideational commitment
Social	Sociation	Belonging	Social commitment
Psychological	Psychic condition	Feeling	Personal commitment
Biological[55]	Physical condition	Health	Bodily commitment

This scheme points up four major levels at which the individual may, in the broadest sense of the word, experience conversion. Clearly, it is very unlikely that there could be such an experience that was confined to one level; and much discussion of religious conversion has involved the idea that while one level, say the psychological, is of paramount importance that paramount level will serve to effect and/or subsequently control the conversion process. All that we seek to show is that one has to be clear in addressing the problem of the focal point or points of conversion. To illustrate further, there are so-called conversions, such as the oft-cited Catholicism-to-communism (or *vice versa*) examples, which very likely should not be thought of as involving the personality level to any significant degree. That case primarily involves a switch in beliefs and social involvements. On the other hand, a paradigmatic fundamentalist conversion might involve primarily a focus on the inner-psychic condition, supplemented by a concern with 'bodily cleanliness', with the ideational and social aspects being secondary.

B. *Structure of Conversion*

B.1 MAGNITUDE OF CONVERSION

Major dimensions of magnitude: Scope
Distance

Scope refers to the comprehensiveness of the change effected in conversion. Does a particular change involve a very large 'amount' of the individual's life-circumstance, or is it confined to one aspect of level (or a sub-level) of the life circumstance?

Distance has to do with 'length of space' traveled in a conversion process. This judgement may involve one or more dimensions. In principle the judgement of distance involves an averaging of distances traveled along each of the dimensions of salience. One of the problems to which the magnitude factor points is the sharp differences between those who speak of conversion as involving 'change of heart' renewal within a particular sociocultural context (such as a religious collectivity), on the one hand, and those who, on the other hand, speak of limiting the idea of conversion to switches from one sociocultural context to another. In the frame presented here the options are more various. There can be inner-renewal within and without a particular sociocultural context, as well as switches not involving much scope.

		Distance		
		Lo		
		No change	Medium change	
Scope	Lo			Hi
		Medium change	Much change	
		Hi		

B.2 SECURITY OF CONVERSION

Major dimensions of security: Speed
Purity

Speed refers to the oft-mentioned variation with respect to the suddenness or the gradualness of conversion. The extreme view is that only 'suddenly seeing the light' qualifies as genuine conversion, although many famous cases – such as that of St. Augustine – speak to the contrary.

Purity refers to the degree to which there is engendered in the conversion process the conception that the conversion is permanent. In more empirical terms, we are here concerned with debates about whether there has been entire sanctification, or whether, on the other hand there is thought to be the ever-present possibility of backsliding.

(The magnitude and the security factors together form the major basis for delineating what extent of change will count as conversion.)

C. *The Analytic Diagnosis of Conversion*

Major modes: Subjective
                        Objective

Subjective approaches involve emphasis upon what the individual seeks to obtain and/or actually does subjectively obtain through conversion.

Objective approaches emphasize objective changes in or of the individual, as well as wider background circumstances and consequences of conversion.

D. *Types of Theoretic Emphases in the Study of Conversion*

Major types: Push theories
                       Pull theories
                       Affinity theories
                       Sequence theories
                       Functional theories

Push theories focus on background conditions of convertees' conditions which make potential convertees available for conversion. Background conditions may be cast in the form of propositions about the deprived, strainful, or isolated status of the convertee, or the 'forces' which are exerted in the pre-conversion and conversion phases, or the 'set' of the convertee (in terms of disposing tendencies).

Pull theories emphasize the attractiveness of the post-conversion state, what convertees seek to get out of conversion.

Affinity theories match pre-conversion with post-conversion states as they affect particular kinds of convertees – and thus tend to be a combination of push and pull factors.

Sequence theories focus on the process of conversion. They are more directly to do with the structure of conversion itself than with its causes or consequences. They usually conform to the outline of: detachment from 'the old'; liminal phase; attachment to 'the new'.

Functional theories emphasize the wider, contextual significance of conversion – what it does for a collectivity and/or what it does for the individual in long-term perspective.

(These five main tendencies are by no means mutually exclusive.)

NOTES

1. Simmel, *The Conflict in Modern Culture* . . . , op. cit., p. 44.
2. Gellner, *The Legitimation of Belief*, op. cit.
3. Daniel Bell, *The Cultural Contradictions of Capitalism*, op. cit.; Bellah, *Beyond Belief*, op. cit., and *The Broken Covenant*, op. cit., Berger, et al., *The Homeless Mind*, op. cit.
4. Rieff, *The Triumph of the Therapeutic*, op. cit.
5. See Berger et al., op. cit., and Peter L. Berger, *Invitation to Sociology*, Garden City, New York, 1963.
6. Alvin W. Gouldner, *Enter Plato*, London, 1967; numerous works by Habermas.
7. The two books directly mentioned here: David Matza, *Becoming Deviant*, Englewood Cliffs, 1969; and Alex Inkeles and David H. Smith, *Becoming Modern*, Cambridge, Mass., 1974. The former is concerned quite a lot with the *bricolage* of 'conversion'; while the latter almost completely ignores it. *Becoming Modern* seems in both its normative implications and its empirical findings to confirm Rieff's view (*The Triumph of the Therapeutic*, op. cit., pp. 13 ff.) that 'the systematic hunting down of all settled convictions represents the anti-cultural predicate upon which modern personality is being reorganized, now not in the West only but, more slowly, in the non-West. The Orient and Africa are thus being acculturated in a

dynamism that has already grown substantial enough to torment its progenitors with nightmares of revenge for having so unsettled the world.' Our own view is that Rieff and Inkeles and Smith exaggerate, in the latter case primarily because the *bricolage* of change – which in a sense constitutes *de*conversion from traditional culture – is not dealt with; while cultural factors *per se* are not discussed. (For a remarkably insightful review of Inkeles and Smith, see Bo Anderson, 'Inkeles on Modernity', *Comparative Events*, 6, 1 (Winter, 1975), pp. 3–12.) For some very suggestive commentaries on the cultural making of modernity, see Wilson, *Magic and the Millennium*, op. cit., *passim*. On tradition in relation to modernization, see, *inter alia*, Nettl and Robertson, *International Systems . . .* , op. cit., Part II; and S. N. Eisenstadt, *Tradition, Change and Modernity*, New York, 1973.

8. For some sharp criticisms of Eriksonian views of identity and the life-cycle, see John Marx, op. cit. See also Stanley Cohen and Laurie Taylor, *Escape Attempts: The Theory and Practice of Resistance to Everyday Life*, London, 1976. Some of the more important current work on adulthood is mentioned in Gail Sheehy, *Passages: Predictable Crises of Adult Life*, New York, 1976, although substantively this is certainly not work worth scholarly recommendation.

9. The new interest in adulthood, and in death and dying, is presumably in part the result of: reaction to the 'children's crusade' of the 1960s, disillusionment with the openness-to-change messages of the 1960s (particularly among those now in their 30s who were at least marginal participants in the crusade of the late 1960s); anticipation of demographic changes, specifically the projections concerning the weighting of Western populations toward the middle-aged and old – as a consequence of the achievement of near-zero population growth.

10. Guy E. Swanson, 'A Basis of Identity and Authority in Post-Industrial Society', in Robertson and Holzner, op. cit., ch. 7.

11. See, *inter alia*, J. D. Y. Peel, 'The Religious Transformation of Africa in a Weberian Perspective', *CISR*, Acts of the 11th International Conference on the Sociology of Religions, 1973. See also various other essays by Peel. Cf. Bryan Wilson's excellent survey, *Magic and the Millennium*, op. cit., which claims also to be Weberian.

12. See numerous pieces by Robin Horton, in particular: 'African Conversion', *Africa*, XLI (1971), pp. 85–108; and Horton's contributions to Horton and Finnegan (eds.), *Modes of Thought*, op. cit.

13. Clifford Geertz, *Islam Observed*, Chicago, 1968.

14. The latter is most evident in Bellah's introduction to *Durkheim on Morality and Society*, op. cit.

15. Cf. A. D. Nock, *Conversion*, New York, 1933; Alfred C. Underwood, *Conversion: Christian and Non-Christian*, London, 1925; L. Wyatt Long, *A Study of Conversion*, London, 1931.

16. Among modern sociologists who, in our view very unwisely, wish to keep conversion out of psychological matters: Charles Y. Glock and Rodney Stark, *Religion and Society in Tension*, Chicago, 1965, esp. ch. 3; J. Milton Yinger, *The Scientific Study of Religion*, London, 1970, pp. 145 ff. See the interesting comments in David O. Moberg, *The Church as a Social Institution*, Englewood Cliffs, 1962, ch. 16.

17. Probably the most persistent in this respect has been Bryan Wilson, who has consistently maintained that it is the emphasis upon 'change of heart' that distinguishes conversion. He wisely argues that 'to convert' is not the same as 'to recruit', but almost certainly thereby makes too radical a limitation on what will count as conversion. Thus for Wilson true conversion can only take place along the lines suggested by doctrinal systems which, as he puts it, 'over-subscribe' to the change-of-heart desideratum – hence his concept of *conversionism* as a religious response to 'the world'. (Wilson, *Magic and the Millennium*, op. cit., p. 23 and *passim*.)

18. Hannah Arendt, *On Revolution*, New York, 1963, p. 21. Arendt points out (pp. 35 ff.) that the word 'revolution' was in origin an *astronomical term* indicating recurrence or cyclical movement. 'Nothing could be farther removed from the original meaning of the word "revolution" than the idea of which all revolutionary actors have been possessed and obsessed, namely, that they are agents in a process which spells the definite end of an old order and brings about the birth of a new world.' (Ibid., p. 35.) That the meanings are not so very different as Arendt suggests is indicated on p. 208 of this book. It is interesting to note that the idea of conversion has also indirect links with the inanimate world. In Taoism and Christianity, alchemy has been undertaken on the basis of initiation processes. Speaking of European alchemy Eliade says that 'in setting about this ambitious task of soteriology, the alchemists employed the classic scenario of all traditional initiation – death and resurrection of the mineral substances in order to regenerate them'. Mircea Eliade, *Rites and Symbols of Initiation* (trans. W. R. Task), New York, 1958, p. 124.

19. Ibid., p. 135. It should be emphasized that Eliade concentrates as a phenomenologist of religion on the 'real meaning' of initiation. His approach is thus not strictly sociological. A more definitely

sociological approach within the discipline of anthropology derives from the classic Arnold van Garnap, *The Rites of Passage* (trans. M. B. Vizedom and G. L. Caffee), London, 1960.

20. Eliade, op. cit., p. x. See also Mircea Eliade, *Myth and Reality* (trans. W. R. Trask), New York, 1963.

21. Eliade, *Rites and Symbols of Initiation*, op. cit., p. ix.

22. Ibid., p. xi.

23. Ibid.

24. Ibid., p. xiv.

25. William James, *Varieties of Religious Experience*, London, 1902. This has had a great influence on psychologists of religion. For a recent survey, see Geoffrey E. W. Scobie, *Psychology of Religion*, New York, 1975.

26. See the admirable discussion in Nock, op. cit.

27. Eliade, op. cit., p. 113.

28. Peel, op. cit.

29. Cf. Humphrey J. Fisher, 'Conversion Reconsidered: Some Historical Aspects of Religious Conversion in Black Africa', *Africa*, XLIII, 1 (January, 1973), pp. 27–40.

30. This is Bauman's summary. (Z. Bauman, *Culture as Praxis*, London, 1973, p. 144.)

31. Victor W. Turner, *The Ritual Process*, Chicago, 1969, p. 56.

32. Benjamin Nelson, 'Self-Images and Systems of Spiritual Direction in the History of European Civilization', in Samuel Z. Klausner (ed.), *The Quest for Self-Control*, New York, 1965, pp. 49–103. The following few pages rest *closely* on this essay. See also Vytautas Kavolis, 'Logics of Selfhood and Modes of Order', in Robertson and Holzner, op. cit., ch. 3; and 'Post-Modern Man: Psycho-Cultural Responses to Social Trends', *Social Problems* 17 (Spring, 1970), pp. 435–49.

33. Nelson, 'Self-Images . . .', op. cit.

34. Ibid.

35. Ibid.

36. Ibid.

37. Quoted in Sydney E. Ahlstrom, *A Religious History of the American People*, Vol. I (paper edn.), Garden City, New York, 1975, pp. 571–2.

38. Quoted in ibid., p. 172.

39. Nelson, 'Self-Images . . .', op. cit.

40. Abrams, *Natural Supernaturalism . . .*, op. cit.

41. Ibid., p. 96. The influence of Wordsworth in providing a model for

dealing with personal crisis has been remarkable among intellectuals, including John Stuart Mill and William James. Nothing could demonstrate the overlap between romanticism and fundamentalism better than these cases, for Mill mentions both Wordsworth and Methodism in referring to his own crisis, while in James' work on conversion one sees both influences at work.

42. Ibid., p. 184 and Parts 3 and 4, *passim*.

43. Rieff, *The Triumph of the Therapeutic*, op. cit., p. 21.

44. Ibid., p. 62.

45. Habermas' characterization being inspired by Walter Benjamin.

46. See Robert Wuthnow, *The Consciousness Reformation*, Berkeley, 1976; and articles by the same author.

47. Cf. Edwin Schur. *The Awareness Trap: Self-Absorption Instead of Social Change*, New York, 1976. In very different vein, see the influential Ralph H. Turner, 'The Theme of Contemporary Cultural Movements', *British Journal of Sociology*, 20 (December, 1969), pp. 586–99.

48. Rieff, op. cit., p. 60. See Sigmund Freud, *The Future of an Illusion* (paper edition), New York 1964, esp. p. 13.

49. Richard V. Travisano, 'Alteration and Conversion as Qualitatively Different Transformations', in G. P. Stone and H. A. Farberman (eds.), *Social Psychology Through Symbolic Interaction*, Waltham, Mass., 1970, p. 601. The general significance which we attribute here to identity is somewhat similar to the view of Rieff and Becker concerning character. The latter is a culture-related notion which in psychoanalytic terms 'restricts personality'. Identity would seem to be the more appropriate modern concept, having a more social connotation; but still fulfilling 'character functions'.

50. Talcott Parsons, 'The Position of Identity in the General Theory of Action', in Chad Gordon and Kenneth J. Gergen (eds.), *The Self in Social Interaction*, Vol. I, New York, 1968, pp. 11–24. Cf. Arthur Brittan, *Meanings and Situations*, London, 1973. The latter stands in the symbolic interactionist tradition which has since the 1950s focused continuously on the theme of identity. Connecting identity to the phenomenon of conversion has been a recent preoccupation of Hans Mol; *Identity and the Sacred*, Oxford, 1976.

51. See John Marx, op. cit. See also Richard K. Fenn, 'Religion, Identity and Authority in the Secular Society', in Robertson and Holzner, op. cit., ch. 5.

52. This is not to denigrate Weber. There is a lot to suggest that much of Weber's *œuvre* was concerned with describing, explaining and –

above all – showing the long-term implications of the development of individual and social-unit autonomy and freedom to associate. This perspective was absolutely central to many of his insights concerning the development of the Western world. On the other hand, he was very much less optimistic than Simmel, tending to believe that what had been historically wrought by processes of individuation was a form of anti-individualism. Weber seemed to believe that modern man was a bureaucratic 'order-addict' and was thus fragmented and 'dehumanized'.

53. Karl Marx, *The Eighteenth Brumaire of Louis Bonaparte*, in Karl Marx and Frederick Engels, *Selected Works*, Vol. I, Moscow, 1962, pp. 243–344. For a somewhat similar view as to modern trends, see Rieff, op. cit.

54. Gellner, *The Legitimation of Belief*, op. cit.

55. This action level is highly provisional. It might fruitfully be re-worked in terms of the ideas of Lidz and Lidz, who argue that the 'bottom' level of action should be the *behavioral system*, central to which is the medium of intelligence. Charles W. Lidz and Victor M. Lidz, 'Piaget's Psychology of Intelligence and the Theory of Action', in Loubser et al. (eds.), op. cit., ch. 8.

PART TWO

Theory, Methods and Religious Change

Chapter Seven

Religion and Everyday Life

The curious fact that the Lebenswelt, the ordinary world in which we conduct our daily life, should become problematical, is symptomatic of a very important development which could be called the Second Secularization. The notion of secularization normally suggests the elimination of transcendent religious belief, the restriction of the range of belief to *this* world. But, far more important than the amputation . . . of such additional, incremental worlds, is the transformation of *this* world itself. . . . The price of cognitive advance . . . has been its de-humanization. . . . In brief, it is of the essence of our condition that we live, not in the alleged *Lebenswelt*, the world of common sense, but in a wider world of which it is a part. . . .

Ernest Gellner

Sociotheology and Critical Sociology

Much of what appears under the rubric 'sociology of religion' is best described as sociotheology. Insofar as all theological ideas entail conceptions of the nature of man and society and insofar as all sociological ideas entail views about 'the ultimate' — even if only to deny the significance of the latter — then clearly sociotheology is no new phenomenon. What *is* new is that there now appears to be a much more conscious weaving-together of social-scientific ideas and theological or religious ideas. From the sociological side, two currently prominent examples will, we hope, suffice to make the point. In her book, *Natural Symbols*, Mary Douglas focuses upon the problem of the kind of symbol system and ritual practice which are most appropriate for the social structure of modern societies.[1]* In other words, she addresses herself to problems of a cosmological nature on a prescriptive basis. In contrast, Robert Bellah argues for an adherence among students of religion to what he calls symbolic realism.[2] For Bellah symbolic realism, as opposed to forms of symbolic reductionism, is characterized by its emphasis upon the ontological reality of all symbolic communication. Such a position has to be argued in conjunction with a commitment to the view that the major task of the contemporary sociologist of religion is to grasp the religious meanings which are expressed in such communication; and that this is best done by synthesizing sociological analysis with the work of those who tap ultimate meaningfulness in such spheres as philosophy, theology, and artistic literature. The crucial difference between the two perspectives, and it *is* a crucial difference, is that whereas Bellah argues for the autonomy of symbols – for symbols as being *the* 'ultimate' reality – Douglas quite clearly sees symbols as communicative modes which are contingent upon a prior social-structural reality. In some primitive societies the fit between social structure and symbolic structure – between, for example, the structure of kinship relations and the structure of beliefs about the cosmic significance of animals – is relatively unproblematic, in the sense that the social structure is clearly articulated and regulated.[3] In contrast, the structures of literate societies are more 'messy' and therefore less easily related (subjectively and objectively, phenomenally and analytically) to symbols and thought-categories. Hence the prescriptive nature of Douglas' analyses of modern societies. The work of Douglas may be seen more generally as part of the contemporary tendency among some social scientists to puzzle about and suggest solutions to such issues as the most appropriate or optimal relationships between man and his natural environment; the problematics of the best fit between culture and social structure, between culture and personal experience as located in social situational contexts; and so on. In brief, then, Bellah and Douglas respectively contribute to two strands of a social-scientific concern with what may best be described as cosmic meaning. Bellah talks about the ways in which religious symbols convey human anxieties, aspirations and preferences, while Douglas attempts to discover the precise nature of the social-structural features of modern societies which lead to problems at the level of symbolic communication in talking about these existential problems of meaning. It should be added that Bellah seems more concerned with religious-cultural *content*, while Douglas is more preoccupied with the *form* and *structure* of symbolic culture and associated ritual. To repeat, we describe these kinds of intellectual concern as sociotheological because they are concerned in a relatively prescriptive manner with the social dimension of cosmologies.[4] They address questions which traditionally occupied theologians, but from a sociological standpoint.

The weaving together of sociological and, in the very broadest of senses, theological modes of inquiry should be contrasted with the arguments of those sociologists of religion who have come to see an in-built tension between sociology of religion and religious-theological orientations – which frequently involves a tendency to denigrate the 'ultimate significance' of sociology itself. In turn, we can place that position against those sociologists of religion who continue to argue for the basically scientific study of religion. This involves the view, implicit or explicit (though usually the former), that religion may be seen as an object of analysis in the sense that sociology can transcend religious belief and experience.[5]

It is clear that anyone who purports to analyze X places himself in a 'superior' relationship to X. It is also clear, however, that there is a wide range of variation in the ascription of objectness to psychological, social and cultural phenomena. In its popularized meaning, positivism clearly entails an extreme form of objectification in this respect – the object of study is not permitted to 'react'. No subjectivity is allowed for in the phenomenal world – or if subjectivity is countenanced it entails a highly predetermined analytic closure. Within the sociology of religion the assignation of such closure can be traced back to the origins of the discipline, mounted as it was in contrast to the *Religionswissenschaft* of such individuals as Scheler and Otto, a school of thought which itself extends back to Schleiermacher. The sociology of religion developed from within the matrix of *Religionssoziologie*. In the latter we can include Durkheim's definition of religion as manifested collectively in societies *sui generis*; Simmel's functional orientation to the study of religion and his idea that culturally defined religious sentiments and actions are general to a large range of spheres of social behavior; and Weber's attempts to show the interconnections between religion and other social spheres.[6]

We are witnessing in the modern period a fundamental re-appraisal of the relationship between science and 'the world'. The resurrection of themes which were involved in the relationship between *Religionswissenschaft* and *Religionssoziologie* are probably best viewed in the context of this larger debate. Standing between and linking these problem areas is that of the revitalized attention which is currently being paid to the relationship between science and religion. As Barbour has succinctly stated, the dominant feature of the science/religion relationship in recent decades has been that of co-existence between, on the one hand, neo-orthodox or existentialist theology, and, on the other hand, positivistic conceptions of science:

In such a combination, the separation of the spheres of science and religion is enforced from both sides. The metaphysical disclaimers of many scientsts and philosophers today are welcomed by these men, for they help to 'clear the field' for religion by undermining rival naturalistic faiths which once claimed the support of science. Neo-orthodox writers even welcome positivistic attacks on natural theology. Moreover, if science leads only to technical knowledge of regularities in phenomena, and if in addition philosophy is confined to the analysis of language, then religious faith is outside the scope of possible scientific or philosophical attack. The independence of the two fields is guaranteed from both sides if each is restricted to its own domain.[7]

Undoubtedly, this has been a resilient 'alliance' – but in recent years it has become much less resilient. It should also be said that the *social-science/religion* relationship is much more problematic and has been less clearly established than the more traditional relationship between natural science and religion.[8]

In the earliest phase of the development of sociology – roughly the first half of the nineteenth century – religious beliefs were regarded as rivals to the scientific sociological thought-style by men such as Comte and Marx. Evolutionistically-inclined anthropologists and sociologists continued this trend until in the 1890s the conservative reaction led to a more tempered conception of religion on the part of the sociologists of the classical period (roughly 1890–1920). In their different ways, sociologists such as Simmel, Durkheim and Weber 'validated' religion, and the religious matrix came to be regarded as the core or center of sociocultural systems. It has frequently been noted that many of the standpoints, perspectives and conceptual apparati which we have inherited from the sociologists of the classical period were wrought in the process of analyzing religious phenomena. Concepts such as alienation, anomie and charisma; substantive themes such as the significance of culture as a sociological variable, personal identity, symbolism and ritual – all of these were part and parcel of the sociologies of religion of the nineteenth century and early twentieth century.

In contrast, the four decades or so following the end of the classical period witnessed a preoccupation with themes of a more *Realpolitik* nature: power, coercion, exchange, class, and so on. This same period also saw the development of 'tough minded' empiricism and associated methodological and technical concerns. To be sure, a prominent strand of sociological thought since the late 1930s has focused on the themes suggested by Durkheim et al., namely, the action theory propagated by Talcott Parsons and his pupils. Much of the latter was, however, tied to a highly self-conscious commitment to sociological professionalism, the legitimating focus of which was a version of the value-neutrality argument of Max Weber. The major effect of this commitment was an avoidance of the more thorny aspects of the relationship between scientific-sociological claims to 'know the world', and the – in principle – competing claims of systems of religious belief, ideological belief systems and so on; although in recent years Parsons and his closer followers have clearly shifted towards 'culture and meaning' questions.

It is very clear that during the past few years, sociologists have become increasingly drawn into debates about the quality of the societies in which they live and work. This drift toward a fairly comprehensive critical sociology should not be construed as being necessarily of a 'radical' nature.[9] Sociological criticism encompasses all styles of intellectual work which deploy sociological insights in the assessment or evaluation of the attributes of any sociocultural system or group of such systems. Thus, critical sociology may be either 'conservative' or 'radical', as a matter of degree. What is common to all forms of critical sociology is the use of sociology as an apparatus for analyzing and evaluating the operation of human collectivities. We deal here with some aspects of the development of a critical sociological style – chosen mainly in terms of their relevance to the sociological study of religion.

Religion and Cognition

With the benefit of hindsight it seems remarkable that such principles as value-neutrality (in its simplistic form) and the denial of the philosophical and epistemological ramifications of sociology survived so long. One of the major ways in which such resilience was maintained was undoubtedly the low degree of attention given to cognitive variables in the development of sociology during the period 1920 to the early 1960s. The somewhat paradoxical combination of an emphasis upon normative factors in substantive analysis with variations on the value-neutrality analytic maxim constituted the major prop of this neglect. The scientific *ethos* – which sociologists among all scientists have probably subscribed to most *self-consciously* – has itself heavily stressed a basic cognitive element. That is, it has stressed the utmost significance of canons of rational inquiry, of processes of knowing, of comprehending, and so on. On the other hand, there has been a great reluctance to consider and analyze the 'equivalents' of such aspects of 'everyday', phenomenal life.

Martins has brilliantly etched many of the problems involved in the relationship between, on the one hand, the internal structure of sociological knowledge and practice and, on the other hand, sociological perception of the structure of societies. He notes in particular the inconsistency in the position of those who argue in favor of a consensual methodological model of and for sociological inquiry and who yet, at the same time, are highly critical of those sociologists who hold to a consensual image of the operation of human societies and collectivities generally.[10] One of the major implications of this kind of analysis is that the boundaries between analysis and object-of-analysis become in an important, but complex, sense broken down. The process of breaking down consists in the facilitation of 'flows' from the sociological to the sociocultural spheres and *vice versa*. If one demands consistency in the relationship between intrasociological and image-of-extra-sociological structures one opens one's own criteria for sociological investigation to influence by 'the world' and conversely one's image of 'the world' is made susceptible to change and re-shaping in the light of one's investigational criteria. It should be stressed, however, that a situation of great fluidity in this respect would make sociological, or any other kind of social-scientific, inquiry impossible.[11] What is more likely to happen is that sociologists having been made aware of the problem of the degrees of synchronization between, on the one hand, sociological theory and methodology and, on the other hand, the operation of sociocultural life – i.e., the object of sociological analysis – will be more prepared to apply critically their theoretical and methodological canons to the 'real world'. In other words, the various fallacies which sociologists inflict procedurally upon themselves become equally applicable to non-sociologists. To take a very elementary example, one of the long-standing methodological tenets of sociology has been the proscription against the commission of the fallacy of misplaced concreteness (deriving from the philosophy of Whitehead). In dealing with a religious movement which is ultra-Biblical in its doctrinal stance it would behove for certain purposes the sociologist to *apply* the strictures relating to this methodological fallacy *to* the movement.[12]

The attacks mounted against schools of so-called intellectualism in the field of anthropology have been so successful that it was not until recently that a few anthropologists were able to gain some respectability for what is pejoratively known as neo-Tylorianism.[13] The reference to Tylor is established in terms of Tylor's representativeness of a school of thought which above all placed emphasis upon primitive man's religion and magic being primarily cognitive in their underpinnings. In other words, what became known in sociology, in the special and idiosyncratic senses in which Parsons used the term, as positivism was the major issue.[14] Anti-intellectualists disparaged the phenomenal-cognitive emphasis on many grounds – but the most important way in which this was done was through a rather complex exercise in Western ethno-centricism. Since the only way in which anthropologists apparently considered man could operate cognitively was in terms which are part and parcel of Western culture, it was thought to be completely wrong to impose this upon the native inhabitants of primitive societies and the cultures which those inhabitants had produced and sustained. It was, after all, in the view of the anti-intellectualists precisely this kind of thinking which had produced the, what was to them, obnoxious and invalid pre-logical mentality thesis of Lévy-Bruhl.[15] But it could be said, and indirectly this is what Lévi-Strauss has been saying for many years, that rejection of the Lévy-Bruhl argument in anti-intellectualist terms is really to go even further than Lévy-Bruhl is alleged to have done.[16] For not only does the argument deny that natives think pre-logically – it really denies that they think at all in the sense that Westerners do. It is worth saying at this juncture that Lévi-Strauss, regardless of the *minutiae* of his binary-opposition approach to the study of complexes of myth, cannot be regarded as having provided a complete restoration of the cognitive apparatus of the members of primitive societies – for his Freudian bias constrains him to talk of the cognitive processes of primitives as being sub- or pre-conscious; that is, Lévi-Strauss allows relatively little in the way of conscious explanatory and problem-solving thought processes and patterns to the primitive. In any case, Lévi-Strauss 'gives', so to speak, the problems to the primitives: their real and 'ultimate' problem is to overcome the opposition between culture and nature.[17] It is assumed that all societies accomplish this – although primitives happen to do it according to Lévi-Strauss, more elegantly – with less 'symbolic waste' – than modern Westerners. Embedded in such an approach is the view that it is only out of a Western form of culture that a comprehension of the thought processes of primitive societies is possible. Willy-nilly, the Lévi-Strauss view is only sustainable in terms of the development of Western culture having provided us with a form of a rationality which facilitates our comprehension of the thought processes of primitives.

Few, if any, social scientists would wish to deny this elementary point – that Western culture has over many hundreds of years provided an 'analytic lift' which makes possible the study of other societies and a double-leveled form of sociolcultural reflexiveness.[18] The point is that many would now claim that too much has been made of it. Probably the

first group in the modern period to make serious attempts to probe and
restore some sense of balance to this problem were those philosophers
who tackled the problem of rationality. Although beginning in large
part as an attack on the idea of a social science as such, the debate about
rationality has been most fruitfully and illuminatingly conducted with
reference to the problem of understanding 'other cultures'.[19] In turn the
debate has now coalesced with the much larger and even more crucial
problem of the psychological, social and cultural nature of analytic
inquiry itself. The upshot of this conjoining of the psychology, sociology
and philosophy of science is that 'the gap' between the nature of
scientific inquiry and the nature of phenomenal inquiry has been
substantially reduced. On the one hand, the injection into the study and
adumbration of the principles of scientific inquiry of 'non-logical'
considerations produces a diminution of the analytic stature of the
scientist in cross-cultural perspective; on the other hand, interest in
ethnoscience, the science of the concrete, ethnomethodology, and the
like, elevates the analytic stature of the 'ordinary man'. In fact, so much
has the picture changed that some can argue viably that the Western
scientist has something to learn analytically from the ways in which
primitive cosmological systems are constructed, sustained, and
modified.[20]

The sociology of religion has tended during the past few decades to
ignore the cognitive side of religious commitment – although a few
sociologists have attempted to inject cognitive factors into the sub-
discipline.[21] There has been a dominant tendency to consider symbols
and values as more relevant, at least in work of a theoretical as opposed to
descriptive nature. Where beliefs *have* been emphasized their structures
have been relatively unexplored. Even more disconcerting, the kinds of
religious belief which have been tapped have almost invariably been of
the surface, institutional kind. That is, sociologists interested in beliefs
have typically limited their analyses to the 'official' beliefs manifested in
organizationally-promoted settings. In sociological analyses of religion
there has been a tendency to assume that religion, or rather religious
belief and/or experience, is in some way phenomenally fundamental.
The stress on the cybernetic significance of religion in some of Bellah's
essays[22] and Parsons' cogent argument that Geertz's characterization of
religion-as-template is more or less a restatement of the Weberian
'grounds-of-meaning' stance point to the fact that the fundamentality of
religion has been a relatively taken-for-granted feature of the culture of
much of sociology.[23] This is not to argue – as far as some sociologists of
religion are concerned – that religion is always 'there'. In fact, among

those who adhere to the 'fundamentality-of-religion' stance there is a good deal of variation in this respect. Parsons argues, in full-blown functionalist style, that one should define religion precisely in reference to its topmost hierarchical significance in (cybernetically-conceived) systems of human action; in terms, that is, of what it does for the system. Parsons, in fact, actually now includes the supernatural or ultimate-reality realm as a boundary circumstance of the total system of action.[24] Thus, what is culturally most fundamental (whatever that may substantively mean) is by definition 'religion'. In contrast there are those for whom the degree of religiosity in a total action system is a matter of variability (which it is logically impossible for Parsons and Bellah to admit, or at least logically impermissible, given the present state of the Parsonian schema). Such 'admission' of variability has, of course, come to a head in the modern period in terms of the secularization debate.

Those who advance theses concerning the occurrence now or in the past of processes of secularization rarely, if at all, confront the problem as to whether 'something' takes the place of religion. They could argue in modified functionalist form that problems of ultimate meaning and experience have to be faced and phenomenally 'resolved' in sociocultural life and that, therefore, the 'something' does what religion did previously. Those who speak in terms of 'secularized religion' would fall into this category. They could, alternatively, argue, as Marxists almost invariably have, that the sociocultural and personal need for religion disappears as a concomitant, determinant or consequence of secularization. Weber's ideas concerning the disenchantment of industrial society are clearly relevant to this approach. Another way of considering the problem is in terms of the query which Schelsky poses concerning the possibility of institutionalizing what he calls 'continual questioning'.[25]

New Directions

Undoubtedly much of the dissatisfaction with the current state of the sociology of religion as expressed here hinges upon the very use of the term 'religion'. We would argue that many problems which lie at the heart of the sociology of 'religion' are severely limited by focusing specifically and directly on the phenomenon of religion or religiosity. This, it must be strongly emphasized, should not be seen in the present context as a plea for a particular form of definitional approach to the term 'religion', nor is it in any respect an argument against being concerned with conceptual mapping, analytic consistency, and so on. What we *are* saying is that the themes addressed by the Parsonians and neo-Parsonians are of fundamental sociological importance; but that the phenomenal significance, the 'everyday' fundamentality of these factors has hardly been tapped, let alone tested. The empiricists have operated in 'official' institutional terms and have rarely attended to the kinds of problems raised by the general theorists. It follows that what is needed is an empirical form of inquiry into the kinds of theoretic issues raised concerning phenomenal fundamentality.

What kinds of recent development are relevant in terms of achieving the kind of breakthrough at which we have been hinting? Of all recent switches in emphasis among those whose interests cluster in the sociology-of-religion domain probably the most likely and promising are those which have attempted to knit the study of religion to the sociology of knowledge − a tendency which has increasingly constrained our attentional foci in the direction of a comprehensive sociology of culture. Other relevant developments include anthropological work in the fields of cognitive anthropology, and ethnoscience. The stance known as ethnomethodology is likely to be particularly helpful − although in a form which has to be severely modified if it is to assist us in the respects which the sociology of religion needs assistance.

There are many dangers that what is described by its practitioners as ethnomethodology will disappear into a form of 'sectarian limbo' unless sociologists manage to attenuate their strong tendency to regard styles of analysis in some way as the preserve of those who adumbrate them. What we ought to be concerned with is the distillation of those elements of the ethnomethodological approach which are relevant to the problems that have here been pinpointed in the sociology of religion.

Prima facie ethnomethodology is relevant to the kinds of problem which have emerged in recent studies of religion by virtue of its commitment to comprehending systematically the ways in which individuals and groups present themselves in reference to their practical everyday concerns. In ethnomethodological terms the key concept here is that of *indexical expression*. Garfinkel's exploration of what the phenomenal term DOA (Dead on Arrival) means to those who have to cope with the problem of assigning 'deathness' is a particularly good example of this. Translated, problem-wise, to the institutional sphere of religion, one could envisage similar analyses on a sociological basis of 'religion-talk' (sociological, that is, in contrast to *philosophical* discussions of 'God-talk'). This in itself might well be an extremely illuminating and worthwhile enterprise.[26] Indeed, during the past few years some beginnings have been made – notably in the sociolinguistic study of glossalalia.) But it would not, however, quite meet the requirements which we are attempting to stipulate here.

The failure to meet the requirements stems from a major deficiency, or at least a lacuna, in the procedures of ethnomethodology. This concerns limitations arising in turn from the Schutzian underpinnings of much of ethnomethodology. Indeed both Berger-Luckmann and ethnomethodological forms of Schutzianism suffer from the major disadvantage of their being so highly relativistic. In different ways, both stances have become committed to viewing the sociocultural world in terms of finite provinces of meaning – such that that there is a built-in tendency to examine particular institutional sites or clusters of ethno-epistemic communality. This both inhibits the development of a generalized, or at least generalizable, set of concepts and/or findings, and makes it exceedingly difficult, if not impossible, to probe ethno-ontologies and ethno-epistemologies in any thoroughgoing manner. Literally interpreted, the style known as ethnomethodology probes only phenomenal methods of expression and procedure in discrete domains of sociocultural life. The tendency to stress methods sways attention from non-domain-specific fundamentalities – although some practitioners of ethnomethodology do appear to commit themselves in principle to the analysis of non-domain-specific ethno-ontology and ethno-epistemology. The Berger-Luckmann approach while addressing generally the various domains of sociocultural life – mainly of the 'everyday' kind – does not deal very much with the cultural substance of what Holzner calls epistemic communities.[27] Instead it concentrates upon the structure of phenomenality.

The common characteristics of the new forms of phenomenological sociology of knowledge and ethnomethodology center upon the thrust toward a comprehension of the deeper layers of social existence. This thrust is in some respects in alignment with the motivation to get at grounds of meaning in the Weber-to-Parsons tradition. The challenge lies in bringing them much more into alignment – such that the empirical probing of the former is constrained in the cultural-substantive directions indicated by the latter. In the dogmatic terms posed by each school this may seem a formidable enterprise. On the ethnomethodological side, in particular, the high-flown objections to sociological constructionism (which is an objection to all non-ethnomethodological sociology) can be seen as the main barrier to breakthrough and synthesis. Less problematic, but still containing difficulties, is Parsons' objection to examination of the elementary forms of social life – since he regards these evidently as forming 'merely' the substratum of sociocultural systems. But in one way or another sociology has always been plagued by controversy and cleavage along that analytic axis.

It is clear that in the terms posed here, the ethnomethodological form of probing has to be woven together with a degree of constructionism – and the probing has to be mounted in terms of constructed categories, but not necessarily carried through to completion in terms of the intially constructed categories. To take the most important example one could imagine at this stage: even though we have here spoken much about grounds of meaning, it does not follow that there really are, existentially, grounds of meaning, in the sense of individuals operating from, or on the basis of, a set of cultural premises about the working of social life (as we have seen in previous chapters). We might wish – and presumably an ultra-Parsonian would have to so wish – to label sociologically the operative premises (the fundamentalities) as grounds of meaning: but that does not mean that individuals actually in an ontological sense have grounds of meaning. All empirical inquiry has to start somewhere – but it does not mean that it has to end 'there' (although most of modern sociology operates in that manner).

How would one go about constructing a beginning set of categories? One of the very few explicated schemata is that of Loubser (who draws on the work of Bellah and Kenneth Burke).[28]

Dimension of Meaning	Existential Anxiety	Religious Action Providing Meaning
Being	Meaninglessness	Faith
Belonging	Loneliness	Worship
Doing	Guilt	Mission
Living	Survival	Therapy

There are criticisms of or doubts about this schema which could easily be presented here. However, assuming the *prima facie* attractiveness of such a schema, or a variant of it, what problems would arise in connection with its deployment?

The major problem is how one gets at the dimensions of meaning without actually assuming that they are subjectively felt or discerned. It would be easy to imagine an operationalization of the concepts in columns 1 and 2 – especially if we were to take Berger's argument that a problem of 'meaningfulness' has arisen 'not only for such institutions as the state or of the economy but for ordinary routines of everyday life. The problem has, of course, been intensely conscious to various theoreticians . . . but there is good reason to think that it is also prominent in the minds of ordinary people not normally given to theoretical speculations and interested simply in solving the crises of their own lives.'[29] In this argument, Berger echoes Weber's statement concerning 'the secret anguish of modern man'.[30]

If we knew that these and many other similar observations about 'modern man' were true then methodologically, at least, there would be little difficulty in or objection to simply going into 'the field' and questioning individuals about their sense of meaning and attendant existential anxieties (to stay with Loubser's presentation). We could then regard column 3 of the Loubser schema as manifesting testable hypotheses – although we might wish in the spirit of this essay to erase the closure imposed by Loubser's use of the term *religious* action'.

We thus arrive back at the phenomenal status of grounds of meaning. Simply in terms of Loubser's schema we need to know whether we have to take grounds of meaning as given – that is, as universal problems of sociocultural life which all individuals and/or sociocultural systems have to meet. Could it be that grounds of meaning are only 'resorted' to when an existential anxiety is felt? Or (as expressed in Homans' attempt to cope with the ritual/anxiety problem)[31] should we entertain the possibility that 'action' in Loubser's sense actually *creates* anxiety and/or the invocation of a ground of meaning?

The drift of the argument has constrained us to contend that we have to hold such queries as being open to empirical inquiry. In terms of Parsonian and neo-Parsonian sociology this means giving equal attention theoretically and methodologically to controlling and conditioning processes; individuals may be more or less control-oriented or condition-oriented. Very generally speaking, the mode of inquiry which ought to be followed, then, is set out for different purposes in Smelser's *Theory of Collective Behavior*. That is, we should envisage a hierarchy ranging from grounds of meaning through to the 'social technology of everyday life'.[32] There is clearly some (fuzzy) parallel between this standpoint and Bernstein's distinction between elaborated and restricted coding processes.[33] That is, individuals with explicable grounds of meaning are relatively elaborate – those who operate at the social-technology level are restricted. However, insofar as what has been said here can be related to the elaborated-restricted distinction the most challenging problem would be to tap the dynamics of the relationship between the two coding processes. That is, for any given individual one would wish to know whether there are occasions of switching off at one level and moving to another, or 'living' entirely at one level. One would wish to know, for example, whether relatively 'unquestioning' individuals encounter gaps which need ethno-explanatory filling – such that there is (objectively, from the standpoint of the 'constructionist' sociological observer) escalation to a higher level. What is the *nature* of the 'events which hit us'? Are they universally of the same kind and how do people cope with those hurtful (in a very broad sense) events?

It has been increasingly stressed by anthropologists in recent years that far too much attention has been paid to (anthropologically and sociologically constructed) religious belief systems or cosmic maps and far too little attention paid to what is sometimes called practical religion – the 'religion of everyday life'.[34] Both anthropology and sociology have been guilty of posing problems for the people they study. In sociology probably the best example of this is the soteriological tradition which we have inherited from the work of Max Weber. As is well known, one of the major themes – possibly *the* major theme – in Weber's sociology of religion was that of the problem of theodicy. In examining the major religious traditions, Weber almost invariably tended to raise questions about the way in which the members of a society 'solved' the theodical problem. But what evidence do we have to suggest that people always perceive that there is a theodical problem to be solved? To be sure, it is relatively easy to pinpoint aspects of belief systems which appear to relate to what we as sociologists, theologians, or whatever, discern from our standpoint to be a theodical problem. In this connection it may be useful to invoke Berger's characterization of the Buddhist 'solution'. Speaking of 'original Buddhism' Berger says:

Gods, and demons, the whole cosmos of mythology, the multitude of worlds of the Indian religious imagination – all these disappear, not by explicit denial but by being declared irrelevant. What remains is man, who, on the basis of his right understanding of the laws of being . . . rationally sets out to fashion his own salvation and ultimately to attain it in *nibbana* (or *nirvana*). There is no place here for any religious attitudes except the coolness of rational understanding. . . . (T)he problem of theodicy is solved in the most radical manner conceivable, namely by eliminating any and all intermediaries between man and the rational order of the universe. . . . (T)he problem of theodicy disappears because the anomic phenomena that gave rise to it are revealed to be but fugitive illusions. . . .[35]

Berger poses the question as to whether this form of thought constitutes an 'overreaching' of rationality – and the fact that 'magical animism' has usually co-existed with one or other of the major variants of Buddhism shows that such a system of thought is 'too rational' for everyday life.[36] Besides which, Theravada Buddhism has been adhered to by laymen in terms of a 'lower' form of Buddhist religious activity, involving merit-making – that is, the material support of temples and monks. Tambiah has elaborated the conventional wisdom in this respect by showing a number of reciprocal oppositions relating the details of religious behavior to the social structure of village life in Thailand.[37]

The religion of the everyday is clearly more easily tapped in, say, Thailand, than its equivalent in the highly differentiated societies of the industrial sector of the world. Nevertheless, it seems clear that the intellectualist tradition in its Weberian form has tended to preclude attempts to comprehend the modes and categories of thought of the 'ordinary' individual in modern societies. Through our interpretations of Weber we have come to see the modern world as consisting in: first, variants upon the Judaeo-Christian tradition in relatively full-blown, doctrinally-articulated form; second, those who have become imbued with an orientation of disenchantment to that sociocultural tradition. The fact that this dichotomized situation does little justice to the nuances of Weber's sociology of religion is in the present context not particularly important. In recent years, sociologists of religion have both widened and deepened their analyses. The deepening has consisted in an increasing concern with the protoreligious substratum – superstition, astrological interests, and so on. The broadening has consisted in an expansion of the range of religious (and irreligious) movements and cults which are being studied. But such developments do not fully meet the requirements suggested in this essay. What is now needed is an approach which probes 'below' the surfaces of specific beliefs in 'religious entities' and which yet at the same time relates these general beliefs about the operation of the world to the more culturally concrete beliefs, values and symbols which sociologists have traditionally studied.

Such a program would raise profoundly the relationship between social-scientific beliefs and the modes of cognition of the 'real world'. It would undercut the position of those who have considered religious commitments as in some way distant from social-scientific beliefs. It would demand a systematic comparison of the ways in which social scientists think and the ways in which 'ordinary mortals' think. Such a development would be in line with the broad conception of a critical sociology which was briefly sketched earlier in this essay. Moreover, the worries which some sociologists have expressed about sociology being insufficiently transcending ought to be significantly attenuated by such a program of analysis. For the prospectus which has been indicated here would allow both for analysis of religion and yet would not be guilty of explaining away the beliefs and cognitive modes of either the religious or the irreligious. Science would be preserved – but in a more open and flexible manner than has typically been the case in the last few decades.[38]

NOTES

1. Mary Douglas, *Natural Symbols*, op. cit.
2. Robert N. Bellah, *Beyond Belief*, op. cit.
3. See Mary Douglas, *Purity and Danger*, London, 1966.
4. Independently David Martin has characterized Douglas' approach in *Natural Symbols* as being sociotheological. See his review of this book in *British Journal of Sociology*, XXI, 3 (September, 1970).
5. In this connection see the debate surrounding Bellah's position: *Journal for the Scientific Study of Religion*, 9, 2 (Summer, 1970). See the arguments for conceiving of theology as a definite science in Thomas F. Torrance, *God and Rationality*, Oxford, 1970. The mixture of Durkheim *and* Kant in Bellah has been neglected.
6. See Devra Lee Davis, '*Religionswissenschaft* and *Religionssoziologie*: Two ideal types of approaches to the study of religion', Department of Sociology, University of Chicago, 1967 (mimeo).
7. Ian G. Barbour, *Issues in Science and Religion*, London, 1966, p. 124. Cf. John Dillenberger, *Protestant Thought and Natural Science*, Garden City, N.Y., 1960; Harold K. Schilling, *Science and Religion*, London, New York, 1963.
8. Cf. Roland Robertson, *The Sociological Interpretation of Religion*, op. cit., esp. ch. 7. For a philosophical discussion of scientific procedures which 'lets in' metaphysical and ultimate factors, see Romano Harre, *The Principles of Scientific Thinking*, London, 1970.
9. The quality-of-life and social indicator 'movements' have hardly been conspicuous for their radicalism.
10. Martins, 'Sociology of Knowledge and Sociology of Science', op. cit.
11. Which is the major liability of ethnomethodology.
12. See Jan Loubser, 'Calvinism, Equality and Inclusion: The Case of Afrikaaner Calvinism', in S. N. Eisenstadt (ed.), *The Protestant Ethic and Modernization*, Boston, 1968, pp. 367–83. See also Barry Barnes, *Scientific Knowledge and Sociological Theory*, London, 1974.
13. See Robin Horton, 'Neo-Tylorianism: sound sense or sinister prejudice?', *Man*, N.S. Vol. 3, No. 4 (December, 1968), pp. 625–34.
14. Talcott Parsons, *The Structure of Social Action*, Glencoe, 1937.
15. L. Lévy-Bruhl, *How Natives Think* (trans. L. Clare), London, 1926.

16. See in particular Claude Lévi-Strauss, *The Savage Mind*, London, 1965.

17. Cf. Clifford Geertz, 'Man and Ideas: The Cerebral Savage', *Encounter*, XXVIII (April, 1967), pp. 25–32.

18. Cf. Robin Horton, 'African Traditional Thought and Western Science', op. cit. See also Robin Horton, 'Lévy-Bruhl, Durkheim and the Scientific Revolution', op. cit.

19. See in particular J. D. Y. Peel, 'Understanding Alien Belief Systems', *British Journal of Sociology*, XX, 1 (March, 1969), pp. 69–84. See also, more generally, Wilson (ed.), *Rationality*, op. cit.

20. See Horton, 'African Traditional Thought and Western Science', op. cit. See also S. B. Barnes, 'Paradigms – Scientific and Social', *Man*, N.S., 4, 1 (March, 1969), pp. 94–102.

21. Notably Rodney Stark and Charles Y. Glock, *American Piety*, Berkeley, 1968.

22. See Robert N. Bellah, 'Epilogue', in Bellah (ed.), *Religion and Progress in Modern Asia*, New York, 1965, pp. 168–229.

23. Clifford Geertz, 'Religion as a Cultural System', in Michael Banton (ed.), *Anthropological Approaches to the Study of Religion*, London, 1966, pp. 1–46. Talcott Parsons, 'Commentary' (on Geertz, ibid.), in Donald R. Cutler (ed.), *The Religious Situation*, 1968, Boston, 1968, pp. 688–94.

24. Talcott Parsons, *Societies: Evolutionary and Comparative Perspectives*, Englewood Cliffs, 1966.

25. Helmut Schelsky, 'Can Continual Questioning be Institutionalized?', in Norman Birnbaum and Gertrud Lenzer (eds.), *Sociology and Religion*, Englewood Cliffs, 1969, pp. 413–23. Cf. Habermas, *Legitimation Crisis*, pp. 125 ff.

26. Harold Garfinkel, *Studies in Ethnomethodology*, Englewood Cliffs, 1967. Cf. Kenneth Burke, *The Rhetoric of Religion*, Berkeley and Los Angeles, 1970.

27. Holzner, *Reality Construction in Society*, op. cit.

28. Loubser, op. cit.

29. Berger, *The Sacred Canopy*, op. cit., p. 125.

30. Weber, *The Sociology of Religion*, op. cit., p. 206.

31. George C. Homans, *The Human Group*, New York, 1960, pp. 313–33.

32. Neil J. Smelser, *Theory of Collective Behavior*, London, 1962.

33. See, *inter alia*, Basil Bernstein, 'A Socio-Linguistic Approach to Social Learning', in Julius Gould (ed.), *Penguin Survey of the Social*

Sciences, London, 1965, pp. 144–168. Cf. the uses to which Bernstein's distinction and others associated with it are put in Douglas, *Natural Symbols*, op. cit. It would seem that the kinds of approach suggested here could be fruitfully related to the work of Piaget – in particular the latter's distinctions between thought processes of induction, transduction and deduction.

34. See, for example, E. R. Leach (ed.), *Dialectic in Practical Religion*, Cambridge, England, 1968. Such arguments have in recent years been advanced in particular reference to Buddhist societies. Cf. Melford E. Spiro, *Burmese Supernaturalism*, Englewood Cliffs, 1967.

35. Berger, *The Sacred Canopy*, op. cit., pp. 67–8.

36. Ibid., p. 68. See M. M. Ames, 'Magical-animism and Buddhism: A Structural Analysis of the Sinhalese Religious System', *Journal of Asian Studies*, vol. 23, 1964, pp. 21–52. See also Spiro, *Burmese Supernaturalism*, op. cit.

37. S. J. Tambiah, 'The Ideology of Merit and the Social Correlates of Buddhism in a Thai Village', in Leach (ed.), op. cit., pp. 41–121. See also Tambiah, 'Animals are Good to Think and Good to Prohibit', *Ethnology*, XIII, 1 (January, 1969), pp. 423–459.

38. For a somewhat similar approach to deviance and crime, see Robertson and Taylor, *Deviance, Crime and Socio-Legal Control*, op. cit.

Chapter Eight

Researching Sites of Cultural Concern: Religion in Britain*

> Instead of a serious dicussion among conflicting theories that, in their very conflict, demonstrate the intimacy with which they belong together . . . , we have a pseudo-reporting and a pseudo-criticizing. . . . This hardly attests a mutual study carried on with a consciousness of responsibility, in the spirit that characterizes serious collaboration and an intention to produce objectively valid results. 'Objectively valid results' – the phrase, after all, signifies nothing but results that have been refined by mutual criticism and that now withstand every criticism.
>
> Edmund Husserl

The study of religion in Britain has been characterized historically by a focus on official religion. Originally this was true simply in the narrow sense of a concern with established religion and it was as a consequence of the government's anxiety over the apparent failure of the Church of England to meet the challenge of industrialization and urbanization that the first official inquiries into the religious state of the nation were made in the mid-nineteenth century.[1]† These inquiries were sociographic in character, conceived as a way of estimating the 'success' of the established church and its principal rival churches and denominations through assessments of the extent of nominal adherence, formal membership and active participation. This sociographic tradition has been less explicit and visible than its flourishing counterpart in France, but it has remained a dominant strain within the sociology of religion in Britain, and its main focus is still institutional success, either examined differentially by social class, or longitudinally over time.[2]

In the past fifteen or so years this tradition has been modified in two

---

* This chapter is a slightly modified version of a paper written with Colin Campbell.

† Notes for this chapter begin on p. 256.

significant ways. First, the focus on official religion has been widened beyond its original restriction to the *de facto* plural establishment of Anglican and Roman Catholic churches and the main Protestant denominations, to include all varieties of Christian religious variance and deviance. Taking as its point of departure Bryan Wilson's study of Christian Science, Christadelphianism and the Elim Four-Square Church in 1961, a flourishing 'sect tradition' has arisen in which the case history method has successfully been employed to investigate the social morphology, life-history, explicit doctrinal stance and social context of the sect, although this perspective has also generated work of a more general theoretical significance.[3] Second, and more recently, a growing concern to probe beyond the formal structures and surface features of official religion has emerged. Although a tradition of amateur, journalistic explorations of popular religiosity had long existed, sociologists have concentrated on official religion to the neglect of the vernacular.[4] David Martin's pleas in 1967 that more attention should be given to 'superstitions and subterranean theologies' drew attention to this omission and has stimulated some preliminary studies.[5] Nevertheless, despite these two significant modifications of the dominant strain within the sociology of religion in Britain it is the case that serious deficiencies remain. The addition of the sect and 'vernacular' traditions of inquiry have not in themselves served to move the main focus of study away from official, 'surface' religious phenomena. This is well illustrated by the continued buoyancy of 'credal psephology', in which the fluctuating patterns of popular belief are plotted, with few exceptions, from the perspective of official formulations of faith; thus necessarily suffering from the disadvantages of an inherent orthodoxy bias. Such a concentration upon the surface forms of religious phenomena seems particularly inappropriate in view of the fact that there appears to have been a greater erosion of conventional modes of belief and practice in Britain than in most industrial societies. (Which is not to say that the absolute level of religious involvement in Britain is necessarily lower than that of any other industrial society, but only to point up the persistent and widespread decline in religious habits.) While it is understandable that this erosion should itself become a focus of analysis, it is clear that sociologists have to look elsewhere for an understanding of the beliefs and practices which are fundamentally articulated in everyday life. Since the sect tradition offers little promise in this respect and while the vernacular tradition remains analytically unformulated, it is necessary to explicate strategic alternatives in order to penetrate the phenomenal categories of religious meaning and experience.

Thus we seek to improve the sociological study of religion as the latter has been manifested in and with respect to British society. There are, however, two additional considerations to be stated before our suggestions can be expounded. First, it has to be emphasized that although the analytic characteristics which we have briefly indicated are intended to apply to the whole of Britain (England, Scotland and Wales), the empirical attributes which we have most definitely in mind in developing our arguments relate more specifically to England. That is to say: Whereas the study of religion in England, Scotland and Wales has established the same kind of procedural tendencies, the respective religious situations, notably in terms of dominant doctrinal traditions and relations between church and state, have been significantly different. Moreover, we do not here encompass in any sense the religious situation in Northern Ireland. This does not mean that our recommendations are in any important respect less applicable there.

This claim as to wider applicability beyond the British circumstances brings us to our second major consideration. Even though we are primarily concerned with the ways in which religion in Britain has been treated by sociologists of that society many, perhaps all, of our proposals have, we could claim, relevance to the study of religion in other societies. In most of the respects in which we advance research recommendations the study of religion in other societies, particularly those of the industrialized sector of the global scene, would be found wanting. It should not be thought, moreover, that our focus on the British – or as is more accurately the case at some points, the English – situation derives simply from a curiosity about the intrinsic characteristics of that society. An equally compelling reason for dwelling upon religion in Britain is that it can be regarded precisely as a societal phenomenon. Unlike many anthropological studies, sociological analyses of religion – as opposed to sociographic ones – have rarely attempted to probe the structure of a large-scale setting. In this respect works such as Herberg's *Protestant, Catholic, Jew* and Yang's *Religion in Chinese Society* are the exception rather than the rule.[6] In the history of the sociology of religion it has been usual to consider aspects of religion *within* a society and what little comparative study of religion there has been under the heading of 'Sociology' has hardly ever been explicitly concerned with the structures of overall societal circumstances obtaining in the societies under review.[7]

The sociological study of religion has been marked from its inception around the turn of the present century by an emphasis upon the cultural and experiential fundamentality of religion. This was a feature common to the approaches of both Weber and Durkheim, the founding fathers of the sub-discipline. As we have seen, in the modern period this view is echoed, although in different forms, most strongly and clearly in the work of theorists such as Parsons, Bellah and Geertz. As is well known, this conspicuous strand in the thinking of sociologists of religion, both classical and modern, has been heavily reinforced during the past few decades by the Tillichian conception of religion as having to do with matters of ultimate concern. It is important to stress in the present context that modern sociologists of religion have tended to substantiate this approach mainly in nominal-definitional terms – sometimes, but frequently not, backed by impressionistically-presented evidence. Thus, although there are nuances, many modern sociologists of religion take as their point of analytic departure the view that all cultural and/or experiential fundamentals – 'ultimate concerns' – are by definition religious, a point which we emphasized in the previous chapter.

Notwithstanding the strength of such views and their 'umbrella function' in the sociological study of religion, empirical work has usually been undertaken on very different lines. This dissonance is most conspicuous in the case of the society in which the ultimacy approach has had most theological and sociological impact, namely the U.S.A. But it is also evident in the study of religion in Britain. There have been a few studies in and of the U.S.A. which have attempted to combine the ultimacy theoretical approach with non-intuitive empirical investigation. One such attempt is that of Yinger, who has developed a program of research whereby individuals' conceptions of 'the ultimate' and of matters of 'ultimate concern' are tapped empirically.[9] In the main, however, a kind of dualism has pervaded the sociology of religion. General-theoretical discussions have been pivoted on the alleged templatic function and fundamental-cultural significance of religion; while empirical work has been conducted very much in terms of *ad hoc* conceptions of religious culture (deriving from lay, conventional notions of religious belief) and confining investigation to surface, institutional features of religion. In America the dualism has persisted not merely in the sense of members of the same sociological sub-profession adhering to one or the other of the two stances, but occasionally has become manifest in the same study – as in Lenski's *The Religious Factor*.[10] In Britain most of the work has been empirical, as we have noted. Judging by such indicators as textbooks used in teaching, the awarding of conversational accolades, and so on, theoretical commitment has – at least until very recently – been not dissimilar to that found in the U.S.A. Nevertheless, eclecticism at the theoretical and conceptual level has probably been the rule.

The obviously required re-alignment of theoretical speculation and empirical investigation should, we suggest, proceed in large part in terms of opening to empirical inquiry the fundamentality-of-religion (or grounds-of-meaning) approach which we have inherited from Parsons' interpretation of the classical sociologies of religion. It is important in this connexion to point out that the nearest to which modern studies have come in respect of this requirement is along the lines first initiated in any sustained way by Weber. We refer, of course, to explorations of the ways in which religious commitment relates to other types of commitment or disposition. Much has been done, notably in the U.S.A., to tap the 'face-sheet' relationships between commitment and economic disposition. In these respects there has been some examination of the degree to which the religious commitment functions as a source of meaning – as an ultimate constraint upon belief and action.

We would still contend that such inquiries do not overcome the dissonance which we have pinpointed – as valuable as they may be in enlarging our knowledge of some aspects of the significance of religion in modern societies. In any case, their impact has probably been severely mitigated in the modern period by the greater prominence in the sociology of religion of views expressed in different ways by such people as Bellah, Berger and Luckmann – each of whom has tended to perceive elements of religiosity in a very large range of modern sociocultural phenomenon. On one or more of these views 'child worship', social mobility aspirations, the 'anti-establishment' rhetoric of the young – each of these, and many more phenomena, have been characterized as religious in significance. What we propose is that the dissonance between theory and empirical inquiry which we have pointed up should be made into a central substantive problem. By this we mean that rather than seeing the disjunction as one which ought to be overcome through theorists being more sensitive to the necessities of empirical research and empirically minded investigators being more analytically conscious of master theoretical problems (although such changes are necessary), we should look at the relationship in phenomenal and historical terms. This means, first, that we should inquire into the interplay between beliefs and assumptions utilized in everyday, 'mundane' situations and the cosmic kinds of belief which fall within the conventionally accepted domain of religion. Rather than assuming that grounds of meaning actually do or phenomenologically must underlie all the situations in which individuals find themselves, we should probe the degree to which this is the case, the circumstances under which switches between the situational and the trans-situational occur. Second, on the historical side, we should investigate more closely the way in which the culture of any given society structures this relationship. This would involve such themes as the ways in which religious themes have been typically defined, the kind of public issue which evokes a widespread interpretation of cultural fundamentality, and so on.

We take up each of these modes of inquiry in more detail at a later stage. It may be helpful at this juncture, however, to spell out the full range of alternatives open to sociological investigators of religious phenomena.

Procedural Tacks

We can summarize the arguments by cross-tabulating our two methodological variables: historicity and phenomenal reactivity. In elaborated form these two variables may be defined respectively as, first, the degree of historical depth utilized in analysis of religious phenomena; and as, second, the degree to which subjective interpretation on the part of individuals and collectivities under examination is emphasized as an analytic desideratum:

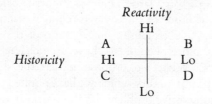

If our characterization of the study of religion in Britain is valid then it is clear that Areas A and B have been severely neglected. Area C refers to studies of the kind which have been sociographic with reference to the past, while Area D covers those studies which have been undertaken in conventional survey research terms. The two approaches which we are advocating here need a more elaborate characterization – and much of the remainder of this chapter is concerned precisely with such elaboration. In skeletal form we should say at this juncture that Area A refers to studies which are highly sensitive to historical process – how phenomena came to be structured in particular ways, the unique properties of those phenomena – *and* to the subjective responses to past situations which are bound-up with religion and analytically related matters. Area B refers to studies which are primarily concerned with subjective, phenomenal aspects of the latter in contemporary circumstances, or in ahistorical perspective. Broadly speaking, such studies take the form of probing reactions to situations in a 'deep-level' mode. Using the term very loosely, we have in mind in this respect approaches of an 'ethnomethodological' nature.[11] It should be said with particular reference to type A approaches that the attribute of high historicity does not necessarily refer to being interested in increasingly long periods of historical time, or in periods of the distant past. Rather it refers simply to an emphasis on the importance of comprehending the properties of concrete circumstances through an analysis of the forces at work over time.

In line with some persuasive recent writing on methodology in the social sciences we believe that all the tacks represented by Areas A, B, C, and D need to be pursued with respect to the same kind of substantive problem.[12] We attend here, however, to the most neglected.

Historical Analysis

There is an unfortunate absence of historically informed sociological studies of religious trends and patterns in contemporary British society. There have been numerous studies of particular religious movements, especially within the framework of the sect tradition and there is a growing concern with the interpretation of nineteenth-century statistics concerning religious commitment. There is, however, little investigation of the changing pattern of religious preoccupations, of the modes of religious expression or of the manner in which religion articulates with other elements of British life (with the exception of politics).[13] Yet there is no doubt that the study of religion would benefit from the addition of just such an historical dimension as a corrective to an apparently inherent tendency to sociological shortsightedness. Too great a stress on survey research and opinion polling can lead to exaggerations and distortions, while the discussion of secularization – the most central analytic motif in the study of religion – can be seriously deficient if conducted in a historically foreshortened perspective.

Up to this point we have stressed what are basically negative advantages of introducing more historicity into the study of religion. There are, however, more positive benefits to be gained from a greater use of historical analysis. It provides the sociologist with a major analytic perspective with which to counterbalance the contrived social and psychological circumstances of the interview and the questionnaire; while in the context of the study of religion it can add considerably to the identification of the uniqueness and the variation in sociolcultural forms that typify a given society. The uniqueness of the institutional and cultural structures of British society constitutes an important parameter of investigation and this quality requires careful specification and continual revision through historical analysis in a cross-cultural context. The historical perspective can also help guide research to the appropriate foci for analysis by revealing the dominant and recurrent societal concerns, the characteristic cultural motifs and turning points in a society's development.

The major goal of historical analysis as presented here is to comprehend as sytematically as possible the patterns and dynamics of religious cultural change as it bears upon the present condition of British society. Two orientations which seem to hold out particular promise in this respect are the classification and detailed analysis of sites of cultural concern and the search for the 'recondite'. The strategy which hopefully will help reveal the dominant presuppositions and commitments of sections of British society at certain periods is the examination of carefully chosen sites of cultural concern. These sites would be particular public debates and periods of cultural conflict in which concern was expressed that something fundamental to the character of British society was in question. Analysis of several such debates could reveal the nature of these fundamental and continuing assumptions together with the continuities and discontinuities in the associated values and beliefs, and their rationales. Such a strategy makes use of the assumption that societal concern is most prevalent and intense when the issue under debate is seen as most directly related to fundamental commonly-held values and beliefs. This may apply at the cultural level in relation to revisions in belief content, at the institutional level in relation to proposed structural reforms or even at the status-role level in matters of 'scandal'. Examples of such sites of concern might include Booth's *In Darkest England* (1890–1891); the controversy leading up to the *Education Act 1902*; the 'Have We Lost Faith?' correspondence in the *Manchester Evening News*

(1926); the report on religious belief entitled *Puzzled People* (1948); Margaret Knight's controversial broadcasts on 'Morality Without Religion' (1955); the Profumo scandal of 1963; the debate concerning the publication of *Honest to God* (1963); and the European Common Market debate. Clearly such a strategy suffers from many difficulties. There is the problem of distinguishing the considerations which are issue-specific from those which are indicative of general positions, and the no less difficult task of the initial selection of the sites. A more fundamental objection, however, is that such a strategy will still reveal a bias toward official matters if not necessarily toward the orthodox position *per se*, since only material relevant to the support or critique of established orthodoxies will be encountered. Thus, analysis of the sites of concern would reveal much about the major parties to a debate but would necessarily exclude those groups who have no interest in it. The analysis of sites of concern must therefore be complemented by a search for those groups who support a cultural position which is so heterodox or deviant as to cause them to regard the dominant debates as irrelevant.

Comprehensiveness is not a distinguishing feature of the study of religion in Britain. Overwhelmingly, analysis has been restricted to the Judaeo-Christian tradition within which the search for deviant and variant forms has largely taken place. Only in the last few years have the other world religions and irreligion become subject to sociological inquiry, while the phenomenon of the 'cultic fringe' is still largely uncharted. Research in these areas needs to be strengthened if the official bias in the study of religious culture is to be overcome.

The neglect of irreligion, conceived of as a reactive or alienative response to religion, can be accounted a serious oversight. There was a flourishing irreligious tradition in Britain in the second half of the nineteenth century and the early decades of the twentieth century, which, marked by a fierce opposition to theology and the clergy and an emphasis upon this-worldly affairs, received widespread support from the working classes.[14] This tradition is an important element in the total religious profile of British society and its neglect has thus been critical both with respect to a comprehensive view of the contemporary religious scene and for an understanding of the dynamics of religious change. A special advantage which it presents is that of studying the mirror image of a society's concrete form of phenomenally perceived religiosity. The 'cultic fringe' has a similar significance for the appreciation of the total religious profile of British society. Outside of the realm of Christian religious variance and deviance there exists a religious and quasi-religious milieu of cults and cultic movements which constitutes a small but not insignificant feature in the religious life of contemporary society. This milieu is typified by its receptiveness to new beliefs and practices, no matter where they originate, its ability to syncretize these into single systems, and its impermanent and unstable organizational forms.[15] Over the last few years this milieu has provided beliefs and practices that have been widely diffused throughout British society, such as astrology and dabbling in witchcraft; and in so doing has demonstrated its significance as a source of cultural modification. Like irreligion, cultic beliefs and practices are defined by reference to the dominant societal orthodoxy and exist in a dialectical relationship to it; but while the irreligious tradition acts principally as an abrasive, removing elements from the established religious culture, the 'cultic' acts principally as a source of diffusion of novel or rediscovered cultural items. An understanding of both must thus be accomplished alongside the existing analysis of more conventional elements of the religious profile in Britain.

In-Depth Analysis of Contemporary Religiosity

As we have noted, a kind of analysis which has rarely been undertaken is that of the in-depth kind, inquiry that probes the religiosity of individuals and groups along lines dictated by sociological, as contrasted with purely psychological, interests. Although the term means different things to different people we would consider the kind of approach which we are advocating here as being broadly *ethnomethodological* in nature. In fact, it might well be convincingly argued that some of the limitations of ethnomethodology as expressed by recent critics could be overcome through the injection of the kind of problem in which the sociologist of religion is interested. Much ethnomethodological writing suffers from its over-concentration on highly specific situations – how people interact and, above all, acquire, attribute and convey meaning in social situations. Sociologists of religion have not typically been interested in the 'religion of everyday life'; that is, the operation of transcendent meaning resources in everyday encounters. Although, it should quickly be added, that there has developed during recent years an increasing concern, particularly among anthropologists, with what is sometimes called practical religion. Interest in the latter has grown via a mounting dissatisfaction with the tendency to look at societies – or segments thereof – in terms of dominant religious-cultural traditions. Thus we now find many students of, for example, South East Asian societies analyzing the relationship between one or another of the branches of Buddhism and forms of magical animism. 'Everyday religiosity' in relation to doctrinal Christianity or Judaism has hardly been, by way of contrast, a major concern of sociological students of religion in the West.[16]

Thus we ought to be much more interested as sociologists than heretofore in the actual as opposed to the 'officially' prescribed religious behaviour of individuals and groups in British society. Recent arguments that we should focus attention upon the 'protoreligious substratum' of British society fall into line with this plea. We have for too long adopted the absolutist stance of investigating the degree to which people subscribe to beliefs and values dictated by conventional categories of Judaeo-Christian thought patterns. Or we have (much less frequently) investigated the subscription to allegedly superstitious beliefs and regarded these as departures from a particular reference point thought to be genuinely religious. These conventional procedures are not here being characterized as worthless. Such stances will continue to be an important ingredient of the sociological study of religion.

As suggested by our brief discussion of the dissonance between general theoretical approaches and typical modes of empirical inquiry, the most compelling problem is to begin to analyze the conditions of meaningfulness under which individuals operate – more specifically, circumstances that constrain individuals to invoke or revoke, as the case may be, transcendent foci of meaning. In other words we should investigate the *minutiae* of the interplay between, on the one hand, the 'social technology' of everyday life as the latter is manifested in situational contexts and, on the other hand, trans-situational points of reference for making sense of one situation in relation to another. This program of inquiry does not, of course, mean that all forms of situational transcendence should be regarded as religious. Nor, on the other hand, does it mean that all forms of situational practicality are non-religious. To deny the latter proposition would, of course, be absurd – since we as sociologists of religion have typically been interested in situational circumstances where individuals gather together for self-declared religious purposes.

In saying that analysis in terms of conventional categories of religious-doctrinal thought ought to remain part of our endeavors, we have in mind the significance of these in many societies as vocabularies of trans-situational meaning.[17] These are modes of expression which are, in a society such as Britain, easily available – even though they may not be 'adequately' known in terms of official orthodoxy. What, however, we do not know much about is the degree to which these modes of expression are 'naturally' adhered to. Traditionally, in the sociology of religion we have looked at our subject matter in almost opposite terms to those advocated here. That is, we have imposed categories of thought on the individuals and groups which we study. One major and well known example of this within the British context is provided by the Mass Observation report, *Puzzled People*.[18] The title of this survey really makes our point for us. The people surveyed were said to be puzzled because in terms of any known form of religious orthodoxy – mainstream or sectarian – they tended to manifest 'inconsistent' and 'contradictory' views when asked to respond to questions concerning such themes as belief in the divinity of Christ, existence of God, belief in miracles, and so on. The critical point is that these questions were neither asked in any definite social circumstance other than that of the social-science interview, nor were the respondents invited to interpret their own responses, nor weight them in terms of their typical array of social contexts. In other words, as in so many survey inquiries reactivity was minimal.

According to the guidelines presented here we need to probe systematically the occasions of social use of religious categories of meaning. It would be particularly satisfying to go further and learn much more about the differential degrees to which such categories are seen as instrumental ('gap filling') or consummatory. The only ways in which such sociological tasks can be satisfactorily conducted is through such vehicles as in-depth interview and, even, experimental situations.

It should be emphasized that in advocating the in-depth 'ethnomethodological' approach we have been mindful of the fact that many anthropologists are currently attempting with much success to tap actual, everyday religious practice – even though they do not typically employ the procedures suggested here. It should not, therefore, be thought that we are advocating a substantive focus of inquiry which is entirely innovative in the study of religion. Our main point is that in the study of industrial societies as carried out by sociologists we have reached an impasse. We have for too long neglected a crucial aspect of the study of religion, an aspect which is made all the more glaringly obvious by virtue of the dissonance between theory and empirical research.

The highly reactive form of inquiry advocated here, which we have characterized as being of an in-depth, 'ethnomethodological' kind, has been presented – of methodological necessity and by the terms presented in our depiction of major research tacks – in reference to highly contemporaneous, 'modern' circumstances. That is, it has primary relevance to studies which we propose in respect of the present – whether it be the 'now present' or the 'present-yet-to-come'. On the other hand, we should emphasize that the sociological perspective which animates the presentation of the highly reactive approach is not by any means confined to the ahistorical kind of circumstance. In elaborating the notion of sites of cultural concern we have attempted to inject as much reactivity as possible into the study of the past. Although it is not conventional to think in terms of historical analysis as involving degrees of reactivity, we think that it is, nevertheless, perfectly realistic to do so. Hence one of our leading concerns in advocating more historical work has been to focus in this respect upon reactions to major cultural problems. This means, for example, that we are interested not so much in the objective patterns to be discerned in a census of religious attendance undertaken in the past, but rather in the interpretations put upon these patterns by interested individuals and groups. In such respects a rough symmetry of perspectives can be maintained as between historical analysis and analysis of the present.

Conclusion

Our discussion has been directed at rectifying what we regard as the major deficiencies in the study of religion in British society. The fact that we have discussed necessary improvements in only two major respects does not mean that we consider these capable of carrying the whole analytic burden. At more than one point we have stressed the need for the simultaneous deployment of a variety of methodological approaches.[19] Thus we have in effect advocated an overall strategy of what might be called 'coordinated eclecticism', a strategy which would combine relatively reactive and relatively non-reactive techniques in both historical and contemporary (or ahistorically conceived) contexts.

Our overriding, substantive consideration has been to offset the liabilities of the official, received-doctrinal approach to the study of religion. To be sure, a number of sociologists of religion have argued in similar ways about the pitfalls of this approach – as well as anthro-pological approaches, as we have indicated. On the other hand, sociologists have not as yet pursued alternatives in terms of empirical research, as opposed to speculation. To take an example, Berger's discussion of signals of transcendence could, and should, be utilized as a basis for careful empirical study.[20] When do individuals typically invoke or revoke such signals? Are all those which Berger lists of equal significance? And so on. Thus what is now needed, and certainly not only in the case of British society, is a research stance of an open-ended kind, based on the idea that we really know very little about the inner-layers of religious belief and experience. On the latter premise a study such as Mary Douglas's *Natural Symbols* almost certainly throws more light on religion in Britain – and elsewhere – than many more conventional sociological studies in combination.[21]

A second, major concern has been to develop more interest in the study of societal religious systems. The concentration on doctrinal traditions – mainstream or sectarian – has kept our analyses within very narrow confines. We need, as a first step, to know more about the historical profile of religion in single societies. In this way, and only in this way, we can begin to comprehend the overall dynamics and 'logic' of categories of thought, symbiotic cognitive patterns, and so on. Again, some work has been done on this. But in the British (or English or Scottish or Welsh) case we do not even have such a brief sketch as that offered by Bellah in his essays on civil religion in America.[22]

NOTES

1. H. Mann, *Census of 1851: Report on Religious Worship*; C. Booth, *Life and Labour of the People of London, 3rd Series*, London, 7 vols. (1902–3); A. Hume (Rev.), *Remarks on the Census of Religious Worship, 1851* (1861); K. S. Inglis, Patterns of Religious Worship in 1851', *Journal of Ecclesiastical History* II (i) (April, 1960); P. Mudie-Smith, *The Religious Life of London*, London (1904).
2. This sociographic tradition in France is represented by, among others, the work of P. Boulard, *An Introduction to Religious Sociology* (trans. M. J. Jackson), London, 1960; and H. Carrier, *Sociology of Religious Belonging*, London, 1965.
3. B. R. Wilson, *Sects and Society*, London, 1961.
4. This popular tradition is represented by, among others, G. Gorer, *Exploring English Character*, London, 1955; B. S. Rowntree and B. R. Lavers, *English Life and Leisure*, London, 1951; and F. Zweig, *The Worker in an Affluent Society*, London, 1961.
5. D. Martin, *A Sociology of English Religion*, London, 1967, p. 74. See also Nicholas Abercrombie, John Baker, Sebastian Brett and Jane Foster, 'Superstition and Religion: The God of the Gaps', in David Martin and Michael Hill (eds.), *A Sociological Yearbook of Religion in Britain*, 3, London, 1970; and Colin Campbell, 'The Cult, the Cultic

Milieu, and Secularization', in Michael Hill (ed.), *A Sociological Yearbook of Religion in Britain*, 5, London, 1972.

6. Will Herberg, *Protestant, Catholic, Jew*, New York, 1955; C. K. Yang, *Religion in Chinese Society*, Berkeley, 1961.

7. Cf. discussion in Robertson, *The Sociological Interpretation of Religion*, op. cit., pp. 34–112.

8. See in particular Bellah, *Beyond Belief*, op. cit. (Although the Tillichianism has been attenuated during Bellah's career.)

9. J. Milton Yinger, 'Pluralism, Religion and Secularism', *Journal for the Scientific Study of Religion*, VI, 2, 1967, pp. 17–28.

10. Gerhard Lenski, *The Religious Factor*, New York, 1963 (revised edition).

11. See Jack D. Douglas (ed.), *Understanding Everyday Life*, London, 1971.

12. See in particular Eugene J. Webb et al., *Unobtrusive Measures: Nonreactive Research in the Social Sciences*, Chicago, 1966; and Norman K. Denzin, *The Research Act*, Chicago, 1970. The actual scheme presented here is grounded on a wider basis in Robertson, 'Towards Identification of the Major Axes of Sociological Analysis', op. cit.

13. For an example of the historical dimension within the sect tradition see Bryan R. Wilson (ed.), *Patterns of Sectarianism*, London, 1967, while an illustration of the increase in interest in religious statistics of the last century is found in Robert Currie and Alan Gilbert, 'Religion', in A. H. Halsey (ed.), *Social Facts on British Society*, London, 1971. Cf. Roland Robertson, 'Religion', in Paul Barker (ed.), *A Sociological Portrait*, Harmondsworth, 1972, ch. 12.

14. For an analysis of irreligion in British society see Colin Campbell, *Toward a Sociology of Irreligion*, London, 1971, especially ch. 2.

15. Cf. Roy Wallis, 'Ideology, Authority, and the Development of Cultic Movements', *Social Research*, 41, 2 (1974), pp. 299–327.

16. One of the exceptions: L. Schneider and S. M. Dornbusch, *Popular Religion*, Chicago, 1958. Cf. Martin Marty, 'The Occult Establishment', *Social Research*, 37, 2 (1970), pp. 212–30.

17. Cf. Hans Gerth and C. Wright Mills, *Character and Social Structure*, Routledge and Kegan Paul, 1954, pp. 274–305. Cf. Kenneth Burke, *The Rhetoric of Religion*, Berkeley, 1970.

18. Mass Observation *Puzzled People*, London, 1948.

19. Cf. Denzin, op. cit.

20. Berger, op. cit.

21. Douglas, *Natural Symbols*, op. cit.

22. The nearest such work is that of David Martin, op. cit.

Chapter Nine

Biases in the Analysis
of Secularization

In this secular, not to say cynical, age few tasks present greater difficulty than
that of compelling the well educated to take religious matters seriously. Yet, for
all except the most recent phases of the history of a minority of the world's
peoples, religion has been embedded in the core of human life, material as well
as spiritual. Bishop Berkeley spoke a simple truth: 'Whatever the world thinks,
he who hath not much meditated upon God, the human mind and the *summum
bonum* may possibly make a thriving earthworm, but will most indubitably
make a sorry patriot and a sorry statesman.'

Eugene Genovese

We propose here to consider the responses of 'concerned' sociologists to
the debate about secularization. We will interpret the category
'sociologist' rather loosely at some points, in order to include all those
who self-consciously invoke social and cultural factors in analyzing
religious change. A leading implication of the present discussion is, then,
that dissection of the social-scientific analysis of religion has become as
interesting, important and challenging as has the direct analysis of
religion itself. There are undoubtedly some sociologists, and even more
non-sociologists, who regret this tendency – those who would argue
that our attention is thereby diverted from the more important tasks of
analyzing changes in the 'real world', or that it is a form of unwarranted
self-indulgence, a classic example of sociologists taking themselves too
seriously. But, like many intellectual discussions, it is not simply a matter
of a few individuals choosing to study a problem which others consider
inappropriate – but rather that the problems we tackle here have become
so evident that they cannot be lightly dismissed. Sociologists have
become deeply involved in debates and disputes about secularization and
even those who have entered the arena protesting that the concept is
meaningless and/or that empirical data fail to warrant the employment

of the concept have been unable to divert much attention from the idea of secularization as a major sociological problem.

It is beyond the scope of this discussion to trace the course which has led to much of contemporary sociology to resolve around issues lying in the area conventionally known as the sociology of knowledge. To anyone who tries at least to comprehend the drift of interests in sociology generally, it must surely be striking that so many sub-disciplinary domains have in one way or another arrived at this kind of circumstance — domains which include the study of deviance; the study of the future; political sociology; of course, the study of religion; applied sociology and, not least, the study of the sociological enterprise itself. In general terms, this development represents an expansion of the self-consciousness of sociologists in respect of their work — a tendency to inquire into the purposes and consequences of their intellectual endeavors, the cultural and political relevance of sociology, and so on.

There has always been within sociology a persistent tendency to argue that sociology is the sociology of knowledge — although that tradition has been most conspicuously and continuously preserved outside of the main sphere of the development of sociology, namely the U.S.A. The fact that in one guise or another this tendency has become established in the American context during the past few years is of particular importance: reflecting, undoubtedly, the intensity and range of self-consciousness so apparent in American society at the cultural level at the present time. The notion of a sociology of sociology has become almost inexorably a key element of the sociological scene; although it is interesting to observe the respects in which particular sociologists fall short of going in for such an enterprise in a truly comprehensive manner.[1]*

The modern condition of the sociology of religion (and we include under this rubric much of the work of contemporary anthropology) has, at the most general level, a lot in common with the kinds of problem which beset the development of sociology in the nineteenth century and the early part of the twentieth century. Both Comte and Marx in the earliest part of this period saw the scientific study of society as impaired by religious culture — both, that is, saw religious belief and sociological belief as rivals. By the time that Durkheim and Weber came to write about religion the intellectual climate had undoubtedly changed in this respect. But the kinds of problem which Comte, Marx and many others had confronted before them were still clearly central to the work of both Durkheim and Weber. In their different ways, both of the latter placed

* Notes for this chapter begin on p. 274.

the study of religion in its broadest sense at the very heart of their analyses of sociocultural life. Both were concerned, analytically and 'metaphysically', about the relationship between their respective diagnoses of the significance of religion in industrial societies and the sociological perspective itself.

The present revival of interest in the sociology of knowledge; the steps taken toward establishing a serious, as opposed to half-hearted and intermittent sociology of sociology; and the revival of a healthy sociology of religion are very closely related developments. They signal two important features of modern sociology: first, that the sociological enterprise is in the process of being recast; second, and in close connexion with this, an identity crisis in the sociological community – affecting sociologsts as individuals and the sociocultural system of sociology as a (be it all fuzzily defined) collectivity. It is a central theme of the present essay that the secularization debate constitutes a particularly critical site upon which the identity crisis of the sociologist is being experienced.

None of these characteristics of the contemporary sociological situation ought to surprise us. As we have remarked, the early development of sociology was characterized by problems revolving around the relationship between the major cultural control agency in human societies – namely religion – and the scientific orientation which by its very cognitive stance and claim to comprehend sociocultural life seemed to violate the diagnosis which stressed the cultural priority and paramountcy of religion. This orientation was, of course, the developing sociological one. Of all the early and classical sociologists, it was Durkheim who certainly saw this problem most clearly. Durkheim, having supported and elaborated in detail the proposition that it was through religious practice and belief that man first came to think about society – to be cognitively reflexive – had also to confront the problem that it was sociological culture which was becoming the major locus of societal reflexiveness in modern societies.

Luckmann has cogently stated that Durkheim, Weber and their lesser contemporaries in the sociology of religion bound their inquiries into religious phenomena with such critical sociological themes as personal identity, meaingfulness, normfulness and so on.[2] Thus, Luckmann, together with Peter Berger (although they diverge on some central points), deserve much of the credit for the present re-linking of the study of sociology to religion. However, having got this far, it now seems encumbent upon us to go further sociologically in the exploration of the relationships between phenomena lying in the domain of religion in the broadest sense and sociology itself. It should quickly be added that some individuals have indeed taken steps in this direction – including, of course, Berger himself. As we saw much earlier, Berger's idea that social science could be regarded as 'a profane auxiliary to the Christian faith' is an example of this, as is his more recent and apparently contrary view that sociology suffers from relativizing worldly encapsulation. Others, such as Bellah, Glock, Stark and Martin have ventured conspicuously into this area of discussion; while Gouldner has vigorously explored some of the more general aspects of this issue, with special reference to the functionalist perspective in modern sociology. Indeed, of the many general overviews of the state of the sociology of religion published in recent years, very few have failed to give the relationship between sociology and religion some attention – if only, in some cases, to argue that the relationship ought not to be significant or troublesome.

Thus the secularization debate is a particularly interesting manifestation of some of the more general problems of contemporary sociology. It is a highly significant case of sociologists grounding their analyses in deeply held views about the *raison d'être* of human life. Notwithstanding the fact that many sociologists have used Tillich's 'ultimacy approach' ostensibly as a 'scientific' definitional base-line for their subsequent analyses of religious phenomena, it seems clear that the secularization debate touches also at the heart of those same sociologists' attitudes toward and beliefs about the 'ultimate' in a very direct sense. That is, definitions of religion – which lie at the very core of any discussion of secularization – in themselves expose metaphysical preferences. Some sociologists of religion have been explicit about this – others less so. Berger, to take a major example, has sustained an ongoing public dialogue with himself in this matter. In contrast Yinger has consistently argued in favor of a functional, 'ultimacy' definition, which in his terms makes discussion of secularization virtually impossible. Yinger can, however, through extended argument claim that even though all comprehensive belief systems are by definition religious, a 'scientific' approach to the study of religion shows Communism to be a deficient 'religion'.[3]

The dilemmas are, as we have said, old ones. But, given the current fluidity of modern sociology and the almost consensually acknowledged view that modern societies are in some kind of cultural crisis, the fact that the dilemmas are old is no reason for not exploring them. At the moment, we are witnessing some sociologists retreating from their sociological commitments because they feel that such commitments undermine what they believe (sometimes on sociological grounds!) to constitute the very pivot of personal and collective life. Others believe that sociology can help to shore-up certain key elements of the religiosity which they discern to be pivotal and essential. Still others – 'extended kin' of that group – believe, as Bellah seems to do, that sociology can assist in the development of new religious options. A less visible group believe that religion ought to be subjected to some kind of sociological critique, which does not necessarily mean attack. This latter orientation has probably been most visible among theologians lying outside the professionally demarcated domain of sociology – for example, some adherents to Death-of-God theology and the Theology-of-Hope. The fact that the position is less visible within the 'official' sociological community evidently arises in large part because 'anti-religion' sociologists have not typically thought it sufficiently interesting or challenging to be sociologists of religion. Sociologists of religion themselves have on the whole tended to be in one way or another religious, or at least sympathetic to religious belief and practice. Outside the sub-discipline the view has been widespread that the study of religion is basically a 'soft' area, concerned with phenomena which are not worthy of prestigious, or aspirantly prestigious, social scientists.[4]

The upshot of much of what has been said so far is that (in functional-definitional terms) students of religion have become increasingly 'religious about religion'. The sociology of religion is not unique in this. To take but one example, the sociological study of deviance has become increasingly 'deviant' in Britain and the U.S.A. during the past few years. Many of its younger practioners are 'deviant about deviance' – their analytic orientations have become synchronized in a major respect with the orientations to be found in the sociocultural category which they focus upon.[5] In the present context, at least, we have no wish to comment on such developments; except in one salient respect: if we are to preserve some kind of sociological, as opposed to metaphysical or 'religious', basis for discussion – if we are, that is, to continue to practice a sociology of religion – then the very least that should be undertaken is the explication of the analytic parameters of the problem of secularization, its major internal axes of dispute and, perhaps more ambitiously, the erection of some kind of logically shaped discussion framework. The intention is, then, to set out some ground rules for reflecting upon just what the secularization debate has involved during the past few years.

We suggest that there are two major axes of debate: first, whether secularization is in fact occurring at all; and, second whether the perceived direction of religious change is approved of or not. In these terms, it is in principle possible to locate all relevant participants in the debate within a property space defined by these two axes:

Secularization

Hi

Approval   Hi ┼ Lo

Lo

It might be thought that the depiction implies that diagnosis of the degree of secularization is prior to evaluation of it – that degree of approval follows such diagnosis. This is in fact not our intention. We regard the two kinds of judgement as empirically interpenetrative – although in individual cases more weight will be given to one side of the issue than in others. For example, a sociologist may not like the idea of secularization on sociological grounds (he or she judges it to be bad for the society in question, or perhaps for any society) in which case, there may be a thrust toward finding evidence of lack of secularization or invoking theoretical arguments to deny the usefulness of the concept of secularization – or, indeed, both of these.

In view of this example, we have also to propose that the grounds upon which these judgements are made will vary also. It seems empirically that in the case of both dimensions of the problem there have been two major grounds. In the case of the assessment of secularization, these are, respectively, theoretical and empirical arguments. In the case of degree of approval, they are religious/metaphysical and sociological arguments. (Here again, forms of judgement will be interpenetrative.) By dichotomizing the secularization and approval variables and introducing the grounds upon which judgements about these have been reached, we arrive at the following.

	Secularization			Approval	
	Hi	Lo		Hi	Lo
Theoretical Criteria	I	2	Religious Criteria	A	B
Empirical Criteria	3	4	Sociological Criteria	C	D

With respect to grounds for assessing secularization and/or approval any particular individual may combine, respectively, theoretical and empirical, and religious and sociological criteria; but we will here assume that one particular ground is given more emphasis than the other. The presentation indicates that there are sixteen possible orientations to the idea of contemporary secularization. It would be laborious in this (and probably any other) context to explore each of these with examples. Thus we will follow the procedure of elaborating some typical modes of reasoning with respect to the two main variables (secularization and approval) and delineating within these variable categories some salient criteria.

Secularization

Theoretical criteria: When confined to the theoretical sphere of discussion, arguments about whether secularization is or is not occurring and, indeed, whether it is a meaningful concept at all, hinge very much on problems of definition and analytic delineation. The paramount cleavage in this area of discussion has been between those advocating functional, inclusive definitions, on the one hand, and those advancing substantive, exclusive definitions, on the other hand.[6] We do not argue that functional definitions have to be inclusive, nor that substantive ones are always exclusive. We are merely generalizing that empirically this seems to be the case. We also leave largely on one side the ramifications of the point that functional definitions have to be made substantive in empirical research. For example, the functionalist use of the ultimacy definition of religion must issue in an operationalization of ultimacy if it is to be systematically applied to empirical and historical circumstance.

Some sociologists employing functional definitions try to avoid this problem by virtue of their definitions of religious phenomena being made so inclusive and general that it becomes impossible to speak of secularization in any sense having to do with a society becoming 'dereligionized'. They can only speak of different forms of religion or speak of religion as changing its relation to the sociocultural system (or systems) in question. This, broadly speaking, is the case with those who have argued that what is frequently called secularization is 'merely' a process of differentiation.

In contrast, those employing substantive, exclusive definitions are more constrained to regard secularization as a significant phenomenon of the world and to define the process itself as involving a form of dereligionization. The use of definitions which focus upon supernatural or superempirical beliefs are those which most obviously precipitate diagnoses of secularization as a major sociocultural tendency in modern societies. (But this is not always the case, as will be seen in a moment.) Supernaturalistic definitions of religion fell steadily from grace during the first half of the present century, culminating in the wide-spreadness of the 'religion-as-ultimacy' definitional tendency (or variants thereof) in the 1950s. Increasing concern with methodological and theoretical precision was undoubtedly a major factor in precipitating in turn the precariousness of the ultimacy approach – although some sociologists have managed (illogically) to interest themselves in the measurement of religiosity, while at the same time holding that all human beings are religious.[7]

In one major sense there can, of course, be no such thing as a purely technical-theoretical judgement on these issues, for all sociological work entails what Gouldner calls background and domain assumptions[8] – which in terms of the schema being employed here means that approval factors, particularly of a religious-metaphysical kind, penetrate theoretical decisions. This feature of sociological analysis is not, however, denied by the insistence that the definitional problem comprises the core of theoretical dispute about secularization.[9] On the other hand, this insistence does not mean either that the theoretical debate has been scholastic, in the pejorative sense of quibbling in the name of science over meanings of terms. The work of, *inter alia*, Stark, Glock, Berger and Fenn attests to this.[10] Among the more important of the more or less purely theoretical-procedural problems which are central to discussions of secularization we would mention: the *level-of-analysis* problem – whether one works at the level of individual religiosity or at the emergent societal, or other collectivity, level; the *dimensional* problem – which indicators of degrees of religiosity one elects to use and, not least, the basis upon which these are chosen; and the *historical-comparative* problem – a relatively neglected area of inquiry but one which clearly bears very much on the issue of the degree of significance which we attach to the idea of secularization. Each of these, about the 'soul-searching' and quest for meaning evidenced in the modern period.[14]

Empirical criteria: Empirical questions are not divorced from theoretical and conceptual issues – but there are nevertheless those who erect arguments about whether secularization is or is not occurring on primarily empirical grounds. Much depends here upon choice of data or the mode of generating data. As in other branches of sociological inquiry, different patterns of religious commitment can be obtained through relying upon different data sources. Greeley, in reference to public opinion polls and certain survey data, has demonstrated fairly convincingly – in terms of belief in the conventional appurtenances of religion – that religious commitment is not undergoing decline in contemporary America,[11] while Stark and Glock claim on the basis of their data that there are within American religious denominations patterns of changing commitment which indicate increasing detachment along what they regard as the major dimensions of religiosity.[12] Martin claims in part that secularization is not a significant process in the contemporary world by pointing at the extent to which superstitious and associated beliefs remain remarkably persistent.[13] Variants of the latter kind of empirical argument include attempts to refute the secularization thesis by producing evidence as to the vitality of supernatural beliefs in the apparent rise in popularity of 'Eastern Religion', astrology and occultic beliefs. This approach is an example of a substantive, although not very exclusive, definition being used to deny secularization – a special case which we have previously hinted at. The argument typically involved is that insofar as some form of supernaturalism and 'irrationality' persists, it is inappropriate to speak of secularization. While obviously drawing on a variety of criteria, this view must focus strongly on purely empirical evidence; and almost invariably has no theoretic underpinning. This observation applies equally to that kind of argument which denies secularization on the basis of evidence – systematically or impressionalistically collected (usually the latter) – about the 'soul-searching' and quest for meaning evidenced in the young of the modern period.[14]

A type of empirical argument which relates to the previously mentioned historical-comparative problem is one which points to evidence about the mythical distortion of the religiosity of societies in the past. By producing data, or at least empirical clues, relating to irreligiosity or areligiosity in the historical past, some sociologists claim to have thrown doubts on the viability of the secularization thesis as it applies to the modern situation.[15] A variant of this approach is to argue in empirical terms that, in spite of episodic changes in the pattern of commitment, religious adherence remains stable over long periods of time – that, in other words, if secularization is evident at this point in time, it is an ephemeral phenomenon.[16]

Whereas we were able to pinpoint a core theoretical problem – that of definition – there is no single point of departure for arguments of an empirical kind. This was to be expected, since there is inevitably a marked eclecticism and discreteness about arguments of a solely empirical nature.

Approval

Religious criteria: Use of the term 'religious criteria' raises a problem, for it implies a definition of religious phenomenon. Thus, if one tends to adhere to a relatively exclusive, supernaturalistic definition of religious phenomena, then in one sense it would only be appropriate to label as a religious criterion one which actually was premised upon belief in a supernatural realm or agency. This would, of course, severely restrict the category. Thus, for present purposes, we will rely on a subjectivist and internal definitional stance – realizing that there is a slight element of inconsistency involved, an inconsistency which is constructively attenuated by using the term 'metaphysical' in conjunction with 'religious'.

A particularly interesting point emerges from this kind of consideration. If a sociologist adheres to a diffusely functional definition of religious phenomena, then he can hardly escape being labeled 'religious'. Some, like Lenski, could not really complain of this. Lenski defines religious commitment so broadly, that all human beings are religious. Luckmann, too, in viewing religion as consisting in man's transcending of his biological givenness would have to concede even more clearly that sociologists are religious *par excellence*.[17] Gouldner has recently argued, with the backing of empirical evidence, that there is an intimate connection between favoring the functionalist perspective generally and being religiously inclined.[18] While we have severe reservations about Gouldner's treatment of functionalism, particularly with respect to its Parsonian form, it would seem that those who most strongly believe religion to be the central feature of sociocultural life – as many described as functionalists do – are most prone to become 'religious about religion'.

Arguments of a religious kind about processes of secularization tend to revolve around normative judgements as to what to be religious means – and in this sense, they are often bound in concrete instances to theoretical arguments of a definitional and conceptual kind. Just as the ultimacy definition had been theologically inspired, the move toward more circumscribed and substantive definitions was theologically facilitated.[19] In the 1960s, theological debate raised again the relevance of the substantive supernaturalistic approach to definition and, in simultaneously rejecting supernatural definitions and embracing the diagnosed processes of secularization (defined theologically as a shift away from supernaturalism) theologians brought, be it all slowly, issues to the attention of the sociological community of which the latter had either been unaware or had been too embarrassed to tackle. For some sociologists with relatively strong religious commitments of one kind or another the situation was particularly complex.

As is well known, Cox can happily approve of secularization because the process as he sees it opens up definite religious possibilities – a position which is in varying degrees rejected by those who hold to more spiritist transcendental conceptions of religious belief. In fact the issue of transcendentalism-versus-immanentism is crucial to the whole debate about secularization, but particularly in respect of religious criteria.[20] Those who adhere to an immanentalist view tend to accept the secularization thesis but not worry about it on religious grounds. Transcendentalists present a wider variety of standpoints. They may accept that secularization is occurring in the face of evidence of religious decline in the world at large and regret the 'fact'; or they may point to new forms of 'inner transcendence' as a correlate of secularization and therefore welcome it.[21] (This latter view is one which sometimes shades into a sociological value judgement concerning the merits or demerits of secularization.) They may also, as we have seen in briefly mentioning superstition, astrology and the like, base their evaluations upon highly diffuse conceptions of transcendence.

One particularly important form of religious appraisal of the secularization thesis is that which views all major cultural motifs as being historical transmissions of religiously based beliefs.[22] Thus, secular beliefs – such as political ideologies – are seen in this perspective as being in a significant sense religious. Belief systems such as ideological Marxism, existentialism, and indeed commonsense beliefs and symbols of 'everyday life' can, in this view, be regarded as manifesting cognitive, evaluate and expressive seeds sown in a more ostensibly religious past. Of course this standpoint shades into theoretical decisions about the validity of the secularization thesis; but it can be employed as a relatively independent criterion for evaluating other forms of more directly empirical evidence about secularization. Evidence of secularization will tend to be greeted ambivalently: on the one hand, this perspective will regard the secularization process as 'merely' an attenuated form of religion; but, on the other hand, it may use the evidence as a way of upholding the view that all cultural change is an emanation of religious culture, and *is* religious in a substantive respect.

Sociological criteria: We are concerned in this category with modes of evaluation of secularization which are based on primarily sociological grounds, that is, judgements about the sociocultural advantages and disadvantages of the diagnosed degree of secularization. Nisbet has succinctly traced the changing sociological views during the nineteenth century in respect of the alleged centrality or otherwise of religion in human societies – pinpointing in particular the shift from early and mid-century arguments that religion was being overcome, and that it was the role of the social scientist to assist the process, to the late nineteenth-century view that religion was a more durable and certainly more desirable feature of sociocultural life.[23] Witness the contrast between Marx's view that religion is an indicator and a manifestation of man's lack of adequate sociality and Durkheim's thesis that religion is an indicator and manifestation of precisely that sociality. Thus Durkheim was constrained to search for and advocate new modes of sacredness in modern societies which seemed to be rejecting conventionally recognized religious beliefs.

It has, of course, been the question of the functional necessity of a sacred religious 'center' which has largely dominated purely sociological discussions of secularization. Recently, however, a new turn has been taken in the form of an increasing interest in the theme of symbolization and symbolic meaning. Whereas the necessity to provide sources of ultimate meaning has for long been embedded in the functionalist concern about religion, the relatively new interest in symbolization *per se* revolves more specifically around the role of social science in assisting in the development of forms of symbolization which allow men to communicate their ultimate and sacred sentiments and cope with the exigencies of social structure and the human condition generally. Within this problem area, we can discern two main schools, to which we have had reason to refer in previous chapters. There are, first, those like

Bellah, who are most closely concerned with non-referential forms of symbolization – that is with conveying sentiments and feelings as such. Of central importance here is the idea that man cannot manage without erecting meaningful symbolizations – not symbolizations of something but expressions of autonomous sentiments, desires and so on which provide and convey meaning and experience as such. This is the position of symbolic realism.[24] In contrast, there are those like Mary Douglas, who directly relate the study of symbols and symbolic communication to social-structural patterns.[25] Here the concern is, within the Durkheim tradition, to search for relationships between social circumstances and symbolic culture. This approach is largely, but not unambiguously, of the symbolic reductionist type.

Both of these approaches – but particularly as developed in the work of Bellah and Douglas respectively – have involved giving advice about the structuring of religious belief, ritual and so on; that is, they are sociologically prescriptive. And although it is easy to say that there is a religious motivation at work the explicit point of departure is in the main sociological.

Discussion of symbolization has, of course, been important in strictly theological circles as well. The name of Tillich stands out in this connection. Robinson's *Honest to God* rested considerably upon arguments about the psychological, social and cultural viability of different forms of Christian symbolization. But it would seem that modern theologians using sociological modes of reasoning to supplement their religious theses tend to rely more directly upon the examination of trajectories of sociocultural change; as opposed to the principles governing symbolic communication. That is, they are concerned to adapt theology and religion to what they perceive to be the major sociocultural tendencies of our time and the extrapolations which one can distil from empirical trends. Variation in this respect is to be seen between those who, on the one hand, 'lock' religion into 'things as they are' – that is, they simply advocate adaptation – and those who, on the other hand, like Moltmann and the 'new' Cox, erect socioreligious aspirations on the basis of knowledge derived in a loose sense from social science.[26] The latter may constrain and limit, but it also establishes a basis for realistic choice.

The rapid upsurge of interest in the theme of secularization during the 1960s can hardly be attributed to any startling new empirical evidence. We have already noted that a relatively autonomous social-scientific interest in problems of conceptualizing and dimensionalizing religiosity and religious commitment in part facilitated the debate. It is also worth remembering that discussions of a methodological kind about the dimensions of religiosity were in some cases inspired by the desire to comprehend the degree to which there had been a religious revival in post-Second World War America. In a major respect the sociological discussion about secularization is simply a response to a culmination and popularization in the 1960s of a long-drawn out debate within the confines of theological circles. In other words, the pattern we are projecting is one of sociologists responding to a crisis in a different intellectual domain[27] and then deriving analytic tools and substantive, empirical propositions on the basis of the ensuing relationship between sociology and theology. Perceived theological change resonated in the minds of sociologists interested in religion who were themselves also in a state of confusion.

We have attempted here only to sketch some of the considerations which go into discussing the centrepiece of the contemporary analysis of religion – the concept of secularization. These considerations have in a number of respects hinged upon the problematics of the relationship between religious commitment, particularly in its theological form, and the sociological enterprise, particularly in its sociology-of-religion specialism. We wish to conclude by highlighting the structure of this complex of problems concerning the religion-sociology relationship.

The two main aspects of this controversy are: first, whether one perspective can or should – logically or metaphysically – inform the other; and second, whether empirically the two perspectives do influence each other. About the second of these there can be little doubt – one has only to open the pages of recent writings by such people as Cox, Berger, Bellah, Yinger, Greeley and Martin, to name but a very few, to see this clearly. The first dimension is more difficult, for it is there that problems arise in respect of the degree to which sociology – or social science generally – impinges on problems of cultural meaning. There is apparently some resistance – even among sections of the sociological community itself – to the idea that the social sciences constitute major cultural systems in modern societies.[28]

It was noted earlier that the secularization debate is a particularly good example of the current identity crisis which afflicts many practitioners of modern sociology, and we wish to establish that this contribution is as much a symptom of that crisis as a diagnosis of it. But unlike Bellah we see no good reason for regarding this crisis automatically as a religious one. What has here been called the identity crisis of many sociologists of religion can be expressed in terms of a number of options which are available for interpreting the contemporary religious situation, in the light of available sociological tools of analysis and substantive viewpoints.

1. *Segmentation* of sociological and religious commitments. That is, the individual may regard sociology and religious standpoint as being potentially – and, indeed, in principle – in some kind of relationship of rivalry and yet try to achieve a personal separation of each sphere. Such a task involves setting definite limits on both sociological and religious potentialities.

2. *Auxiliaration* of the sociological commitment to the religious one – as is suggested by Berger's comment about social science being a profane auxiliary of the Christian faith.[29] In this conception sociological insight and knowledge are used to supplement and perhaps suggest adjustments in religious orientation. But sociological commitment is secondary to religious commitment; and sociological praxis is predicated upon the background assumptions of the particular religious position. Historically, this stance has been maintained most consistently, continuously and visibly by Catholic *religious sociologists* – but there are many Protestant adherents to the principle involved.

3. *Auxiliaration* of religious orientation to the sociological one. Here religious beliefs and prescriptions are mounted on the basis of what are regarded from a sociological standpoint as necessary or desirable features of sociocultural life. This stance is particularly well evidenced in the structural-functional tradition.

4. *Compounding* of religious and sociological views into one generalized socio-theological role. This constitutes a *self-consciously fostered socio-theology*. The best individual examples of this perspective are some of the so-called radical theologians.

There are two further options, one of which need not detain us here. This is the case in which the religious viewpoint is regarded as paramount and sociology (or social science generally) is seen as a total rival to religion. Since sociological perspectives are not constructively involved, this stance is in no way relevant to the concerns of this chapter. In great contrast, there is the circumstance in which sociology (or social science) dissolves and supersedes theology and perhaps eventually religion itself. This of course is the view which was put strongly by Comte and was echoed on different grounds and in very difficult ways by Durkheim. There is a significant degree of overlap between this stance and that of the 'sociotheologians'.

Our major intention has been to make explicit the terms of the secularization debate and to link the latter to some more general aspects of contemporary sociology. In the main, we have eschewed concern with the correctness or persuasiveness of the stances which have been pointed-up. However, a brief outline of one major strand of the discussion as it bears prescriptively on the religion-sociology problem is warranted.

It is rather misleading for those who object to sociology setting itself critically against religious standpoints or offering radical critiques to argue that their opponents claim that sociology, or indeed any or all of the social sciences synthetically, could provide for society in the same way that religion does. For those who have offered sociological critiques of theology or, more significantly, of religious belief and practice, have rarely in the modern period made such comprehensive claims. Sociology has been criticized for being unable to provide sufficient transcendence — for indeed being anti-transcendental — by both Berger and Martin (although their worries about this are somewhat different in nature). But this appears to be a judgement on the present state of social science, as opposed to what it could be. It need not be purely technical in its social implications, nor purely therapeutic — or whatever negative characterization may be offered. Thus, some of those who have tended to opt for religious-theological superiority *vis-à-vis* sociology are open to the charge of idealizing the first and characterizing the second in terms of how it actually is.

The central point in the present context is whether a 'concerned sociology' or a 'critical sociology' can both be respectful of the historic significance of religion in human societies and at the same time be daring enough to offer considered, analytically consistent images of the viability of various sociocultural possibilities. There is much in recent sociology which suggests that a critical sociology of the possible, which subsumes the sociology of the necessary, is becoming increasingly feasible. A lot of what has been said here leads, we think, to the conclusion that the sociology of religion has in its confrontation with the secularization controversy regained for itself much of its former centrality in the discipline as a whole. This restoration is not coincidentally or fortuitously related to the tentative re-emergence of sociology as a critical discipline.

One of the major points of this chapter has been that the idea of secularization is as much, if not more, an artifact of a section of the intellegentsia, as it is a feature of the 'real world'.[30] But unlike some who have sought to rule out of court on such grounds elaborate discussion of the issues raised by the secularization controversy, we think we should embrace the problems for what they are – manifestations of a loss of confidence and direction among sociologists; a fear of repeating nineteenth-century mistakes; and a too easy characterization of social science as inevitably remaining as it has been for the past forty years or so. In a sense, what we have said here backs up what Berger and Luckmann argued some years ago about the relationship between the sociology of religion and the sociology of knowledge.[31] It is perhaps a comprehensive pursuit of the sociology of culture which will best alleviate the pains attendant upon discussion of the secularization thesis. Along these lines we might well explore again the possibility of a world without religion – although of course 'hard' functionalists will always be able to spot elements of religiosity in any such projected sociological image.

NOTES

1. The outstanding exception is Gouldner, *The Dialectic of Ideology and Technology*, op. cit.
2. Luckmann, *The Invisible Religion*, op. cit.
3. See Yinger, *The Scientific Study of Religion*, op. cit., especially ch. 22.
4. See the comments of the Sociology Panel of the (American) Behavioral Sciences Survey: Neil J. Smelser and James A. Davis (eds.), *Sociology*, op. cit., 101–4 (although the report underestimates the degree of theoretical and methodological refinement which has been recently obtained).
5. The reference point for much of this has been the work of David Matza. See his *Delinquency and Drift*, New York, 1964; and *Becoming Deviant*, op. cit., although recent years have witnessed the development of more Marxist trends.
6. For full discussion see Robertson, *The Sociological Interpretation of Religion*, loc. cit.
7. For example, Gerhard Lenski, *The Religious Factor*, op. cit. Cf. J.

Milton Yinger, 'Pluralism, Religion and Secularism', op. cit., pp. 17–28.

8. Gouldner, *The Coming Crisis . . .*, op cit.

9. Robertson, op. cit.

10. See, in particular, Peter Berger, *The Sacred Canopy*, op. cit.; Rodney Stark and Charles Y. Glock, *American Piety: The Nature of Religious Commitment*; and Richard K. Fenn, 'The Process of Secularization: A Post-Parsonian View', *Journal for the Scientific Study of Religion*, Vol. IX (Summer, 1970), pp. 117–36.

11. Andrew M. Greeley, *Religion in the Year 2000*, op. cit., and numerous other books by the same author.

12. Stark and Glock, op. cit. (But see Robert Wuthnow and Charles Y. Glock, 'God in the Gut', *Psychology Today*, November, 1974, pp. 131–6).

13. David Martin, *The Religious and the Secular*, op. cit., and *A Sociology of English Religion*, op. cit.

14. But see Wuthnow and Glock, loc. cit.

15. See Robert Nisbet's suggestions about the historical ubiquity of secularization in *The Social Bond*, New York, 1970, p. 387.

16. Which is precisely what a number of sociologists were saying in the mid-1970s about secularization in the mid-1960s.

17. Lenski, op. cit.; Luckmann, op. cit. Further light on this kind of problem is thrown by dissection of ethnomethodologists' attacks on what they call 'constructive', as opposed to 'indexical' analysis. See particularly Harold Garfinkel and Harvey Sacks, 'On Formal Structures and Practical Actions', in John C. McKinney and Edward A. Tiryakian (eds.), *Theoretical Sociology*, New York, 1970, pp. 337–66.

18. Gouldner, op. cit., ch. 7. Of course, Parsons has often been accused of *positivistic anti-religiosity*: see, for example, Thomas O'Dea, *Sociology and the Study of Religion*, New York, 1970, ch. 12.

19. The *existential-philosophic* sources of the ultimate-problems approach have been insufficiently recognized by sociologists.

20. For further discussions see Robertson, op. cit., especially pp. 93–5, 215–18 and 236–9.

21. See Herbert W. Richardson and Donald R. Cutler (eds.), *Transcendence*, 1969; Jurgen Moltmann, *Religion, Revolution and the Future*, New York, 1969; Bellah, *Beyond Belief*, op. cit., part three. (See also William A. Johnson, *The Search for Transcendence*, New York, 1974.

22. See in particular Martin, *The Religious and the Secular*, op. cit., and

Talcott Parsons, 'Christianity and Modern Industrial Society', in Edward A. Tiryakian (ed.), *Sociological Theory, Values and Sociocultural Change*, New York, 1965, pp. 33–70.

23. Robert A. Nisbet, *The Sociological Tradition*, New York, 1966, pp. 221–63.

24. See Bellah, *Beyond Belief*, op. cit., especially ch. 15. (This article was completed before Bellah's important collection of essays was made available in England.)

25. Douglas, *Natural Symbols*, op. cit. See also Douglas, *Purity and Danger*, op. cit.; Mary Douglas, 'Environments at Risk', *Times Literary Supplement*, 30 October 1970, pp. 1273–5. Cf. Roland Robertson, 'Modernisation and Overdevelopment', paper given to Ad Hoc Group on the Measurement of National Development, I.S.A., Varna, Bulgaria, 1970 (mimeo).

26. See in particular, Martin E. Mary and Dean G. Peerman (eds.), *New Theology No. 5*, New York, 1968; and Harvey Cox, Foreword to Block, op. cit.

27. See Richard K. Fenn, 'The Death of God: An Analysis of Ideological Crisis', *Review of Religious Research*, 9 (Spring, 1968), pp. 171–81.

28. We use the term cultural system here as it is employed by Talcott Parsons in Parsons et al., *Theories of Society*, New York, 1965, pp. 963–93. Frankfurt-school-inspired 'critical theory' is an exception.

29. Berger, *The Precarious Vision*, op. cit., p. 204.

30. This is a point which Martin has argued very strongly, as in *The Religious and the Secular*, op. cit.

31. Peter Berger and Thomas Luckmann, 'Sociology of Religion and Sociology of Knowledge', *Sociology and Social Research*, 47, 1963, pp. 417–27.

Subject Index

Name Index

Turner, Ralph, 221
Turner, Roy, 45
Turner, V., 204, 221
Tylor, E., 231

Underhill, E., 110, 112–13, 144
Underwood, A., 219

Van der Leeuw, G., 56
Voltaire, F. M., 174

Wach, J., 56, 92, 135
Wahl, J., 84
Wallerstein, I., 184
Wallia, C., 44
Wallis, R., 97, 258
Walzer, M., 157–8, 183
Warner, S., 94
Waskow, A., 35, 49
Watson, J., 189
Waxman, C., 42
Webb, B., 44
Webb, E., 258
Webb, S., 44

Weber, Marianne, 93
Weber, Max, 3ff., 25–6, 30, 50–101,
103ff., 114–43, 145–7, 148, 154, 166,
170, 179, 187–8, 193ff., 222, 228–30,
236, 238ff., 242, 247–8, 260
Wiener, A., 44
Weingartner, R., 47, 147
Wellmer, A., 48
Whitehead, A., 19, 31, 48, 231
Willener, A., 45
Wills, G., 43
Wilson, B. R., 96, 99, 147, 218, 219, 245,
257, 258
Wittgenstein, L., 84
Wolff, K., 47, 144, 182
Wolin, S., 43
Wordsworth, W., 221
Wuthnow, R., 221, 275

Yang, C. K., 98, 99, 246, 257
Yinger, J. M., 60, 94, 96, 219, 247, 258
261–2, 272, 274, 275

Zweig, F., 257